THE RUSSIAN MAFIA

THE RUSSIAN MAFIA

Private Protection in a
New Market Economy

Federico Varese

OXFORD

UNIVERSITY PRESS

OXFORD

UNIVERSITY PRESS

Great Clarendon Street, Oxford OX2 6DP

Oxford University Press is a department of the University of Oxford.
It furthers the University's objective of excellence in research, scholarship,
and education by publishing worldwide in

Oxford New York
Athens Auckland Bangkok Bogotá Buenos Aires Cape Town
Chennai Dar es Salaam Delhi Florence Hong Kong Istanbul Karachi
Kolkata Kuala Lumpur Madrid Melbourne Mexico City Mumbai Nairobi
Paris São Paulo Shanghai Singapore Taipei Tokyo Toronto Warsaw

with associated companies in Berlin Ibadan

Oxford is a registered trade mark of Oxford University Press
in the UK and certain other countries

Published in the United States
by Oxford University Press Inc., New York

British Library Cataloguing in Publication Data

Data available

Library of Congress Cataloging in Publication Data
Varese, Federico.
The Russian mafia: private protection in a new market economy / Federico Varese.
p. cm.
Includes bibliographical references and index.
1. Organized crime—Russia (Federation) 2. Organized crime—Russia (Federation)—Prevention.
3. Transnational crime—Russia (Federation)—Prevention. I. Title.
HV6453.R8 V37 2001 364.1'06'0947—dc21 2001016333
ISBN 0-19-829736–X

1 3 5 7 9 10 8 6 4 2

Typeset by Best-set Typesetter Ltd., Hong Kong
Printed in Great Britain by
T.J. International Ltd
Padstow, Cornwall

Acknowledgements

The reader of this book will remember the trepidation and the excitement that accompanied Gorbachev's perestroika in the late 1980s. Diego Gambetta directed my passion for the events unfolding in Russia towards the topic of this book. Diego has remained a friend and an unflagging supporter of this project, and read drafts of several chapters of this book. My intellectual debt to his work should be evident to the reader: I am also indebted to him for his encouragement and judgement that guided me from first to last.

Mark Galeotti and Roger Hood read an early incarnation of this study and suggested a number of changes, which I tried to incorporate into the final product. Dr Galeotti has also been most willing to share information and views on a topic he himself has written so much about. Avner Offer donned his various hats to offer me advice on the arguments I have been making over the years, read various papers of mine, and encouraged me at crucial moments. David Cornwell reminded me several times that I was writing a book that might be of interest to the general public, and that I should try to avoid jargon and academic niceties. I hope the final result will not displease him too much. I started to think about the topic of this book while I was a graduate student at King's College, Cambridge, and wrote it while I was doctoral student and then a Prize Research Fellow at Nuffield College. These institutions offered me an environment where the exchange of ideas is a daily routine.

Gerry Mackie and Ingrid Yngstrom read a version of the manuscript. As a result, both style and argument have improved. Karma Nabulsi also read the entire text and offered most valuable comments on what I had hoped was a final version of the book. Her comments made me change my mind. The following people have been both good friends through the years and sharp readers of portions of my work: Vittorio Bufacchi, William Fleming, Cecilia Garcia-Peñalosa, Rolf Hoijer, Erik Landis, Valeria Pizzini, George Smith, Marc Stears, and Meir Yaish. Yoram Barzel allowed me to read a version of his yet unpublished book *A Theory of the State*. I owe a great deal to the arguments advanced by Professor Barzel. Åse Grodeland, William Miller, and Tatyana Koshechkina consented to let me quote data from their now published study of corruption in Eastern Europe. Andrea Graziosi and Kathryn Hendley were kind enough to send me their comments on sections of the manuscript, although we never met. In Oxford, I discussed the contents of this project with both Laurence Whitehead and Vincent Wright. Vincent's sudden death deprived us all of a treasured friend. Dominic Byatt, Chief Editor at OUP, took an early interest in the book and has steered the production process with passion and unfailing judgement. Amanda Watkins, Assistant Editor of Politics and Sociology, has overseen the many practical issues of publication with remarkable competence. Watching Dominic and Amanda, I realized how much work lies behind the production of each book at OUP. I am most grateful to Tom Chandler who copy-edited the text. The well-known Russian maestro Oleg Tselkov allowed me to reproduce one of his paintings, *Dvoe*, on the cover of this book. Although the artist bears no responsibility for the pages that follow, his work makes this book a finer achievement.

During my stay in Russia, I greatly benefited from the help of the staff of the State Archive of the Russian Federation, the staff of the Memorial Archive in Moscow, and the staff of Perm State Archive. Andrei Suslov gave me valuable suggestions on archival research in Russia. In Moscow, I spent long periods in the house of Sergio, Marina, Anna Claudia, and Federica Rossi: their hospitality and support greatly eased my work in a large and at times inhospitable city. Cesare Martinetti shared with me material on the Russian Mafia in Italy. James Sandham was the first to suggest Perm as my fieldwork destination. At an early stage of the trip preparation, Karen Hewitt was instrumental in getting me invited by the University of Perm and did not shy away from the difficulties it created. Mary McAuley, the only western scholar to have studied this city, introduced me to the people she knew in Perm and encouraged me in many ways. Oleg Podvintsev guided me through Perm and arranged many of my interviews. His help has had a significant impact on the material I was able to collect. While in Perm, Stepan and Masha have made me feel at home.

I am deeply indebted to the individuals who spared their time to answer my questions in Perm. Most of them are mentioned in this work, at least by name. Some of them did not wish to be mentioned and, as promised, I have protected their anonymity.

The Economic and Social Research Council and Nuffield College provided me with financial support over three years. Nuffield has also been a generous employer, sponsoring various research trips to Russia. The Department of Applied Social Studies and Social Research gave me a grant that covered some of my expenses and offered me much needed assistance in the final stages of the writing of the thesis. The Director, Teresa Smith, always made me feel welcome at Barnett House.

The many years of research passed quickly and pleasantly thanks to the many friends, with whom I have shared a great deal beyond academic discussions about the Russian Mafia. I will mention only two: Roberto 'Bobo' Roversi and Vittorio Bufacchi. The debt to my parents is immense: they have supported me through many years of study, encouraged me at difficult times and have always been a source of inspiration, both moral and academic. Finally, this work would not have been finished without the help of my wife Galina. She gave me her advice on many aspects of the Russian language and culture, accompanied me to a number of interviews in Perm, worked with me in the Moscow archives and read the entire manuscript. Most importantly, she has endured my company while this work was in progress. This book is for her.

A version of chapter 8 was published in 1998 as 'The Society of the *Vory-v-Zakone*, 1930s–1950s', *Cahiers du Monde Russe*, 39/4: 515–38. I am grateful to the editors for allowing me to use this material.

F.V.

Nuffield College, Oxford
June 2000

Contents

Contents

List of Figures

List of Tables

List of Russian Abbreviations and Acronyms

AO	Joint-Stock Company
CheKa	Emergency Committee [for the Fight against Counter-Revolutionary Activities and Sabotage] (1917–22)
CBR	Central Bank of Russia
CIS	Commonwealth of Independent States
CPRF	Communist Party of the Russian Federation
CPSU	Communist Party of the Soviet Union
FNPR	Federation of Independent Trade Unions of Russia
FSB*	Federal Security Service (formerly FSK)
FSK*	Federal Service of Counter-Intelligence
GAI	State Auto Inspectorate
GAPO	State Archive of the Perm Region
GARF	State Archive of the Russian Federation
GKI	Russian Privatization Agency
Gorkom	City Committee [of the CPSU]
Goskomstat	State Statistics Committee
GRU	Main Intelligence Directorate (Military Intelligence)
GRF/RECEP	Government of the Russian Federation/Russian-European Centre for Economic Policy
GULAG	Chief Administration of Corrective Labour Camps
GUOP	Main Department for Combating Organized Crime
GUVD	Main Department of Internal Affairs
ITK	Corrective Labour Colony
ITU	Corrective Labour Institution
ITL	Corrective Labour Camp
KGB*	Committee for State Security
Komsomol	Young Communist League
KRU	Auditing and Monitoring Department
LDPR	Liberal Democratic Party of Russia
MVD	Ministry of Internal Affairs
NEP	New Economic Policy (1921–1928)
NRB	New Russia Barometer
OBEP	Department for Combating Economic Crime
Obkom	Regional Committee [of the CPSU]
OMON	Special-Purpose Militia Unit
OMRI	Open Media Research Institute
OPKh	Khrushchev Personal Files
OPO	Operative Search Department

List of Russian Abbreviations and Acronyms

RFE/RL	Radio Free Europe/Radio Liberty
RSFSR	Russian Soviet Federal Socialist Republic
RUOP	Regional Department for Combating Organized Crime
SIZO	Investigation Isolation Cell
SKF	Union of Cossack Formations
SOBR	Special Detachment of Quick Reaction
STK	Drivers' Training Organization
TOO	Limited Liability Company
TsIK	Central Electoral Commission
UPK	Criminal Procedure Code
UOP	Department for Combating Organized Crime
UVD	Department of Internal Affairs
VASRF	Supreme *Arbitrazh* Court of the Russian Federation

* The Committee for State Security (KGB) was dismantled in December 1991 into various units. The bulk of the former KGB (six units) was reorganized into the Ministry of Security (MB) in January 1992. The MB changed its name to Federal Counterintelligence Service (FSK) in December 1993 and to Federal Security Service (FSB) in April 1995.

Introduction

This is a study of the forms protection has taken during the transition from Soviet planning to the market economy in Russia. The transition to the market has often been considered solely as an economic problem. Little attention has been paid to the institutions that make a market economy work: a system of clearly defined property rights, a swift and effective court system, and a credible police force that deters crimes.

The question of property rights—their definition, diffusion, and enforcement—is crucial in the transition from a centrally planned economy to a market economy.[1] When a centrally planned economy comes to an end, the result is a dramatic increase in the number of property owners and in transactions among individuals with property rights. The transition to the market amounts to the diffusion of private property rights; such diffusion produces a whole new set of problems actors must solve.

The fear of losing property and of being cheated arises as a result of transition to the market. The increase in property and economic transactions leads to more opportunities to engage in criminal activities. The opportunities to commit crimes like theft, robbery, embezzling, the forging of wills, grow manifold. Also, new types of crimes become possible with the transition to the market, such as certain types of fraud and financial crimes.

Russia is experiencing such a transition, embarking on a path that many other countries have followed before. North and Thomas locate the time of the breakdown of feudal property rights, which did not recognize or secure private ownership, and the transition towards institutional arrangements which did, between 900 and 1700. Within this very long period, there was no smooth evolutionary passage from feudalism to capitalism, but rather a phase of 'widely divergent experiments and false starts'.[2]

The history of Western Europe supplies at least one example of a transition to the market that was, at the same time, a late transition, occurring in a relatively thriving economy, and one where property rights were poorly defined: Sicily.

The transition came much later in Sicily than elsewhere in Western Europe. Trading in land began in the South of Italy only in the early nineteenth century: vast amounts of both common and church land were auctioned for the benefit of private purchasers.[3] Moreover, in the mid-nineteenth century, trading thrived, especially prosperous commerce between interior and coastal markets, which had previously been separated.[4] However, property rights—'an unprecedented novelty' in Sicily—proved 'difficult to enforce and [were] . . . a source of constant strife'.[5]

The abolition of feudalism and the widespread introduction of private property rights greatly enhanced the fear of losing property and being cheated; as a result, the demand for protection increased. In an ideal world, where interpersonal trust is high, there would be no need for an agency to supply the protection demanded by new property owners. In such an ideal world, only a small amount of crime would occur and order would emerge spontaneously. As in most human societies, this was not the case in Sicily. In fact, distrust in Sicily and in much of Southern Italy is not only high, but also 'endemic', as pointed out by social scientists.[6]

The state—the agency that defines and protects property rights—was also unable to clearly define and protect such rights.[7] Banditry posed a threat to property owners during most of the nineteenth century. In particular, protection of agricultural produce—which must be transported, processed, and sold in urban markets—was defective.[8] Sabetti, in his study of political authority in the nineteenth century in a Sicilian village, concludes that, by the 1890s, 'it had become demonstrably most clear to most villagers that if they valued public security, it would have to come about through their own efforts'.[9]

If trust is scarce, and the state is not able or willing to protect property rights, it is sensible to expect a high demand for non-state, private protection. The existence of a demand for protection does not, however, necessarily imply that a supply of protectors will emerge. Gambetta, in his study of the Sicilian Mafia, points out that this combination of factors simply implies 'that there will be more opportunities to meet the demand [for protection], and hence that meeting it will prove more profitable than elsewhere'; but it does not necessarily follow that someone will do so.[10] In fact, demand for protection remained unmet in various parts of Southern Italy and the Mediterranean world, such as in the South Italian village studied by Banfield (1958). Elsewhere, a system of patronage developed, as in the town of Pisticci studied by J. Davis (1975).

Gambetta offers evidence of the emergence of the *supply* of private protectors in Sicily. He locates this among the field guards (the *bravi* and *campieri*) released from baronial control at the crucial historical juncture that saw the end of feudalism and the birth of a democratic society. In Sicily, noble landlords maintained private armies of field guards to protect their estates, to enforce their rights and to keep peasants in submission.[11] In addition to *bravi* and *campieri*, Sicily witnessed a long period of 'semi-private protection of public order', carried out by *compagni* and *militi* and endorsed by the Bourbons, that came to an end only in 1892.[12]

When the break-up of huge patrimonies occurred at the end of the nineteenth century, many professional protectors found themselves unemployed. *Bravi, compagni, militi,* disbanded soldiers of the Bourbon army, and bandits 'began offering their services to classes other than the aristocracy. . . . Gradually those who succeeded as protectors became autonomous suppliers. Autonomy was the key element missing in other parts of the Mediterranean'.[13]

Sicily experienced a late transition to the market economy, a poor definition of property rights on the part of the state, and a subsequent rise in the demand for private protection. At the same time, a supply of people trained in the use of violence was available. Protection did not undergo the customary process of centralization to become the monopoly of the state, but was available through autonomous suppliers. Autonomous suppliers of private protection started to offer their services to the then numerous property owners. This complex historical process gave rise to the Sicilian Mafia.

In Search of the Russian Mafia

My study of Russia is informed by the Sicilian case. The history of Sicily alerts us to the fact that, at the time of the transition to the market, property rights may be badly defined by the state and that protection may not undergo centralization and end up in the hands of the state. Other forms of protection may emerge, especially in the face of an inefficient state and in the presence of people trained in the use of violence who have, as a result of the transition, found themselves without employment.

Although the starting point of this study is Sicilian history, are we entitled to search for a 'mafia' out of its original context in a far away land such as Russia? Surely the move is controversial. For some, 'mafia' is a phenomenon typical of Sicily and such a word should be used only in reference to the Sicilian Cosa Nostra.[14] My view is that the mafia is a species of a broader *genus*, organized crime, and various criminal organizations—including the American Cosa Nostra, the Japanese Yakuza, and the Hong Kong Triads—belong to it. First a few words on the *genus*, organized crime.

Evidently, by organized crime we do not mean simply 'crime that is organized'.[15] Three burglars, who get together and plan a robbery, do not qualify as an organized criminal group (OCG). An OCG seeks 'to govern' the underworld, as argued by Thomas Schelling. Burglars may be in the underworld but do not seek to govern it. An OCG aspires to obtain a monopoly over the production and distribution of a certain commodity in the underworld. 'In the overworld', writes Schelling, 'its counterpart would not be just organised business, but monopoly.' Some kinds of crimes are organized in monopolistic fashion, and characterized by occasional gang wars and truces and market sharing arrangements. For instance, loan-sharking, gambling, and drug dealing are criminal businesses that lend themselves more than others to monopolization. We should expect to find OCGs in these specific sectors of the underworld. On the contrary, some illegal markets are difficult to monopolize and police. For instance, the sale of cigarettes to those below the legal age does not lend itself to monopoly. 'Nobody can keep a nineteen-years-old from buying a packet of cigarettes for a seventeen-year-old,' argues Schelling; 'the competition is everywhere.'[16]

A mafia group is a particular type of organized crime that specializes in one particular commodity. Gambetta has identified protection as the specific commodity the mafia 'produces, promotes, and sells'.[17] Mafia groups like drug syndicates are OCGs, but deal in different commodities: they sell and seek to monopolize the supply of *protection*, rather than drugs. In the abstract, a drug syndicate either internalizes protection or *buys* it from a mafia group. One may see this as a form of division of labour and even argue that an inevitable logic leads to a division between the production of goods and services (such as drugs and sexual favours), and the production of violent threats.

The mafia is the set of mafia groups in a given context. For instance, a number of mafia families operate in Sicily; the Sicilian Mafia is the collective entity they are part of. At different points in the history of each mafia, different arrangements regulate (or fail to regulate) the relations between mafia groups. The relations between groups are often dependent on clever institution builders and historical circumstances. In the words of Aristotelian logic, the mafia is a species of the broader *genus* organized crime.

The mafia differs from organized crime in its relation to the state. The mafia and the state are both agencies that deal in protection. While the mafia *directly* impinges on the state's jurisdiction, organized crime does not.[18] Furthermore, the mafia is willing to offer protection both to *legal* (but poorly protected by the state) and *illegal* transactions.

As far as the overworld is concerned, the mafia banks on the inefficiency of the state in supplying efficient protection to legal transactions: the more confused the legal framework of a country, the more incompetent the police, the more inefficient the courts, the more the mafia will thrive. Furthermore, the mafia offers protection the state refuses to supply and deems illegal. For instance, the mafia protects entrepreneurs against potential or real competitors and offers its muscles to collect debts in ways the state would find unacceptable.

Demand for protection is also rampant in the underworld. The greatest fear a criminal has is to be cheated by another criminal. Since he cannot rely upon the state for protection, he will search for alternative agencies. The more protection of illegal transactions is efficiently supplied, the more illegal markets will thrive. Furthermore, the greater the realm of activities *defined as* illegal by the state, the greater the demand will be for mafia services. If a state decides to prohibit not only the sale and consumption of drugs, but also alcohol and cigarettes, we should expect a higher demand for mafia services in the underworld. Gorbachev's ill-fated anti-alcohol campaign of 1985–90 gave rise to a huge new trade in moonshine, as did Prohibition for the US. The by-product of both policies was to increase the demand for dispute resolution services in the underworld.

When it offers and *promotes* its services, the mafia disregards the law: this qualifies it as a set of illegal and violent organizations. It never supplies 'protection' as a public good, in the way the modern liberal-democratic state does (or aspires to do). It does not recognize citizens' rights. For this reason, one should resist the temptation to call the mafia 'a state-within-the-state' unless one strips the state of any appeal to justice, as noted by St Augustine in his treaty *De civitate Dei*.[19] Mafia groups operate as very peculiar 'firms', in no way constrained by the legal rules that bind ordinary firms in the market economy. The mafia does not recognize customers' rights and can freely victimize its clients or impose its services on individuals who did not ask for it. In fact, mafia protection often starts as a form of extortion. Finally, the mafia penetrates politics and corrupts the police and the judiciary to enhance its interests, although these are not defining characteristics of the phenomenon. Many other groups—such as lobbies and economic conglomerates—try to influence politics and 'promote' the consumption of their goods and services.[20]

The studies by Peter Reuter, Yiu Kong Chu, and Peter Hill confirm that services of contract enforcement and more generally protection define the core operation of the American Cosa Nostra, the Hong Kong Triads, and the Yakuza respectively.[21] Thus, one can compare different 'mafias', such as the Yakuza, the Triads, the American Cosa Nostra, and the Sicilian Mafia without fear of comparing 'cats with dogs'.[22] As the Leninist vanguard party is a type of political party, the mafia is a type of organized criminal group specialized in protection. This conclusion does not imply that differences do not exist among these organizations. The most general aim of this book is to explore whether the Russian Mafia can be added to the list of the mafias and what are its particular features.

This Book

In this book I address a number of questions, some of which were inspired by Gambetta's work on Sicily, but have not all been addressed directly in either *The Sicilian Mafia* or other works on the mafia. An empirical question that springs directly from Gambetta's study of the transition to the market in Sicily is tested in the present work: has the Russian state been able to define and protect property rights and have private protectors emerged as a significant alternative to the state-managed system of protection? Chapter 1 is a study of the transition to the market. It explores the extent to which the post-Soviet Russian state emerged either as an impartial protector of rights or, on the other hand, as an erratic, predatory, and non-impartial supplier of protection.

Various authors have emphasized the fact that Russian courts are inefficient in enforcing decisions, although they overlooked the fact that many individuals do indeed apply to courts.[23] Others, upon seeing that courts are actually in use in Russia, have come to opposite conclusion, namely that the 'law works' and reports of its demise are exaggerated.[24] The extent to which individuals trust and use (legal) institutions that are supposed to supply services of protection and dispute resolution is explored in Chapter 2. Survey data are examined in order to establish whether we should expect people to use these institutions and, more generally, to know more about the levels of confidence in the legal system. In the second part of this chapter, I study one instance of state-supplied protection services: the *Arbitrazh* Court, the court where cases involving property rights and the privatization process are heard.

Chapters 1 and 2 point to the fact that the demand for protection that accompanies the spread of market transactions is met by the state only in part: a significant sector of the business world does not use state-supplied protection services. A demand for alternative sources of protection is then expected to arise. Some authors, especially economists, have been quick to conclude that, since the state does not provide a service, the market inevitably will. It cannot, however, be argued that demand will inevitably be met. A supply of people trained in the use of violence and easily available weapons must also be present. Chapter 3 focuses on the availability of people trained in the use of violence and of weapons, and the varieties of private protectors available in Russia at the time of the transition to the market, ranging from segments of the state apparatus, to private protection firms and criminal groups.

A variety of actors operate in the market for protection in Russia. In order to establish how they interact with each other and with their clients/victims, we turn to the in-depth study of a particular setting, the city of Perm, in the Ural region. Chapters 4 and 5 trace the sources of harassment small kiosk owners and businessmen are exposed to, their encounters with bogus and predatory 'roofs'—the Russian jargon word for protection—and their effort at finding effective protectors. (Chapter 4 presents a brief sketch of Perm's history and traces the impact of market reforms on the structure of the city economy; Appendix B is a study of the destination of the former Soviet elite which shows that members of the former *nomenklatura* entered the new economic elite). Although this work is mostly devoted to criminal protectors, the market for protection proved to be populated not only by criminals. Fragments of the state apparatus and private protection firms are significant players. Chapter 5 offers a glimpse of who is more likely to escape the grips of criminal protection and obtain state protection. Finally, Chapter 5 presents the services criminal protectors are able to offer. The data used in this section are mostly fieldwork interviews.

If mafia groups are present in a market, they must be organized in some form. Two questions have generated a heated and long-running debate among scholars of the mafias. First, are criminal groups organized in a hierarchical and military fashion or, on the contrary, are they loose networks of individuals, getting together to perform a specific task? Second, are these groups territorially or functionally organized? Chapter 6 addresses these two questions with reference to Perm.

The most prominent criminal of Perm belongs to a national organization of professional criminals, the society of the *vory-v-zakone* (thieves-with-a-code-of-honour), a criminal fraternity that flourished in the Soviet camps between the 1920s and the 1950s and re-emerged in the 1970s. The history of this society has yet to be written, though it is a crucial undertaking: criminal organizations do not operate in a void, the past to an extent shapes and informs their present, even if they operate under new constraints. There is a further reason why the *vory* are of particular importance: a mafia is a collection of mafia groups. In Sicily, for instance, although the various families retain their independence, they also share common 'trademarks': a ritual, norms of interaction, rules to manage the use of violence, and a shared (and entirely invented) lineage. Can the *vory* of the Soviet period provide such a baggage of rules and norms to contemporary Russian Mafiosi? Chapter 7 explores the features of the original society and offers an interpretation of its origins. (Appendix A is an empirical study of nicknames among the *vory*.) In Chapter 8, I study the features of the new society and discuss whether it is the Russian Mafia. The future of the Russian Mafia is evaluated amidst the emergence of powerful competitors, who do not subscribe to the *vory*'s ideals and norms. The chapter concludes with a discussion of the connections between politics, the church, terrorism, and today's criminal world.

There are at least two relevant aspects of the phenomenon of non-state forms of protection that I do not touch upon in this work. First, I do not study ethnic networks as a source of services of dispute settlement and protection. Though I came across some instances of non-Russian

(Tadzhik) traders in the fruit and vegetable market of Perm, a long-term immersion into this network would have been necessary in order to obtain a detailed picture. Moreover, the language barrier was for me insurmountable within the time limit set for this research. Nevertheless, the majority of the citizens of the Russian Federation, and the overwhelming majority of the citizens of Perm, are ethnic Russians. The phenomenon investigated in this work therefore retains its relevance.

Second, I am mainly concerned with legal markets, rather than with protection supplied by the mafia to sellers who operate in illegal markets. The reason for such a choice is the current lack of judicial sources. Scholars of the Russian Mafia cannot yet rely on the wealth of materials provided by trials such as, for instance, the so-called 'maxi-trial' of the Sicilian Mafia, held in Palermo in 1985–6. Trials of great significance against organized crime have not yet been held in Russia. This is not to say that the Russian mafiosi are not operating in markets for illegal goods, such as drugs, prostitution, human smuggling, and the sort. They have most certainly entered these markets and I will refer to some evidence of this throughout the book. This evidence was however insufficient to constitute the focus of this work.

Evidence and Methods of Data Collection

The Choice of Perm

I have chosen the Russian city of Perm for a combination of reasons, both theoretical and practical. Perm is an industrialized town in the rich Ural economic region, where the transition to the market has taken place at quite a sustained speed. Perm was also chosen for fieldwork since it is an area where the use of state and non-state sources of protection occurs in the absence of major ethnic networks, an important criterion for this study. The practical reasons which have also influenced the choice of this location are that: it is relatively understudied, as compared to Moscow and St Petersburg,[25] but easily accessible, especially for scholars of Oxford University;[26] and the criminal situation of the city, at the time the fieldwork began, was settled. This is not to say that Perm is a city with a low level of criminality. On the contrary, criminal activity is high, as I will show. Nevertheless, whilst the fieldwork was undertaken, there were no major conflicts among criminal groups. Researchers of crime-related questions who travel to the field are exposed to the highest risks when inter-group conflicts are underway.[27]

Dispute Settlement and the Courts

The study of the state system of commercial dispute resolution is based on data from the Perm *Arbitrazh* Court and the Russian Supreme *Arbitrazh* Court. The Supreme *Arbitrazh* Court and Perm *Arbitrazh* Court keep records of the number and types of cases disputed. Such data are only occasionally published in the official journal of the Supreme *Arbitrazh* Court, *Vestnik Vysshego Arbitrazhnogo Suda*. I obtained unpublished data on the number and types of disputes reviewed from judges in Perm and Moscow, at the Supreme Court of Arbitration.

Non-State Dispute Settlement and Organized Crime

For the study of non-state dispute settlement and organized crime, I rely on two different types of evidence: documents and published material; and interviews.

Documents and Published Material. Police reports are a source commonly used in the study of organized crime and this work also relies on classified reports and publications. Two documents in particular proved to be extremely valuable. A paper produced by the Perm Department of Internal Affairs (UVD) in 1995 is a detailed, although short, chronicle of the origins and development of the mafia in Perm (Permskoe UVD, 1995). The second document is a three-volume investigation of the 'Russian mafia' in Italy produced by the Servizio Centrale Operativo of the Italian Police (see SCO, 1997). This document had been circulated to some Italian journalists but has never been used by scholars before. It contains an extraordinary wealth of information on the operations of a Russian *vor-v-zakone* in Italy, as well as records of his activities in Russia.

I have collected about 3,000 newspaper and magazine articles related to Russian criminality published in the period 1989–2000. English and Italian sources were collected mainly in Oxford. Russian sources were collected in a variety of ways. During my field trips to Perm, I surveyed the major daily of the city, *Zvezda*, from 1985 to 2000, and collected articles relating to the criminal structure of the city, the rise of organized criminal activities, local politics and the privatization process. I also subscribed to

Zvezda, two other local newspapers (*Vechernyaya Perm'* and *Mestnoe Vremya*) and one weekly newspaper produced in conjunction with the Perm police (*Dos'e 02*) for two years (1994–6). I had an assistant in Russia who kept me up-to-date with articles on criminality, politics, and economics both in Perm and Russia. Articles on Perm were taken from *Dos'e 02*, *Mestnoe Vremya*, *Megalopolis-Express*, *Novyi Kompan'on* (weekly), *Permskie Novosti*, *Vechernyaya Perm'*, and *Zvezda*. The sources of articles relating to Russia in general were mainly *Argumenty I Fakty* (weekly), *Izvestiya*, *Kommersant-Daily*, *Komsomol'skaya Pravda*, and *Kriminal'naya Khronika* (monthly), and *Moskovskie Novosti* for the period 1994–2000. I had access to the *Sole-24 Ore* (an Italian newspaper) archive in Moscow, the *Novyi Kompan'on* and *Moscow Times* on-line archives, and to *Natsional'naya Sluzhba Novostei*, an on-line service that scans articles from the Russian local press.

Zvezda and *Dos'e 02* have produced some reports of high quality on organized crime in Perm. The *Zvezda* crime corespondent has been an important source for this research. I interviewed her several times and supplemented the information I could read in the papers.

Interview Data. I undertook two trips to the city of Perm in 1994 and 1995, and lived a total of eight months in the city. I went back to Perm in December 1997 and in the summer of 1999 for a period of two months in order to carry out further interviews. The list of the interviewees with the coding of each interview is reproduced in the List of Respondents at the end of this book.

The method that I followed during the fieldwork in Perm resembles a standard ethnographic study, though I faced the peculiar problem of researching sensitive topics, such as the use of non-state protection, tax evasion, interaction between private individuals and tax and police officers, the sources of starting capital, and the background of interviewees. Topics of a sensitive kind remain ill-suited to study by means of large and impersonal surveys, as argued by various authors.[28] In order to obtain information, I relied on the so-called 'unstructured', 'depth' or 'long' interviews.[29]

The first problem I faced at the start of my interviews was that of describing the research to interviewees. Defining the boundaries of the research topic too tightly might have precluded raising other related topics, as pointed out by Cunningham-Burley (1985). For this reason, I was attracted by Brannen's suggestion to let the topic of the research emerge

gradually over the course of the interview.[30] This strategy however raised
the issue of the subject's consent. My own solution was to provide the
interviewees with a long, detailed list of 'issues' I was planning to study
and, if they consented, the interview would begin. This list is reproduced
below, pp. 209–10.

At times, I was faced with the problem of talking about unpleasant matters or unethical behaviour on the part of the interviewee. In such situations, I followed the advice given to priests and confessors in the
sixteenth-century manuals crafted by the Roman Catholic Church, at the
time when a new doctrine of sin began to emerge in the Western Church:
'Do not show amazement; or a contorted face; do not show revulsion (no
matter what enormities are confessed); do not rebuke the penitent; or
exclaim "Oh, what vile sins!".'[31]

In order to reduce the perception of threats, questions were framed as if
referring to 'people in the same business' rather than to the interviewee in
particular. It proved to be, in fact, a successful strategy. After a few general
remarks, usually the interviewee would refer to a specific case, either his
or her own or the case of 'somebody known' to them.

In the social sciences, the method of recording data affects the data
itself. In an unstructured interview situation, answers to questions may
be recorded in the following way: filming, tape-recording, note-taking,
or memorizing. The method that is regarded as making the subject
more comfortable when dealing with sensitive topics is the latter—
memorizing[32]—the researcher has a conversation with the interviewee,
unobstructed by pens and pencils. It is however the method that assures
less reliability as memory may easily fail. Tape-recording, on the other
hand, is the most reliable method and was the method that I chose when
I began the fieldwork. I soon discovered, however, that there is a trade-off
between bad memory and evasive answers: tape-recording made subjects extremely uncomfortable, resulting in evasive answers. One interviewee, in particular, was extremely vague and, at the end of the
interview, he invited me to his house to a have a 'proper' conversation.
After this false start, I resorted to note taking. Taking notes during the
conversation reminded the interviewee of the purpose of the interaction
(namely, that of writing a public piece of research) and at the same time
reduced the threats of the misuse of the information on the part of the
interviewer (tapes can be used as evidence in a manner which notes
cannot).

At the end of each day, I typed, on a portable computer, the notes I had taken and used my memory of the encounter to supplement information I had only sketched in the notes. In a number of cases, I was accompanied to the interview by an acquaintance of the interviewee who had arranged the meeting. When this occurred, and he or she was willing, I checked the accuracy of my transcription with the interviewee's acquaintance, in order to increase its validity.

Each interview lasted approximately one hour and a half. Some (N = 6) informants were interviewed more than once. I have assured privacy and anonymity to the interviewees that asked me to do so. Some of the names are therefore fictitious.

The History of the Criminal Fraternity vory-v-zakone

Chapter 7 ('Mafia Ancestors: The Society of the *vory-v-zakone* 1920s– 1950s') is based on three types of sources: official records, published recollections of camp life, unpublished memories. Official records come from the State Archive of the Russian Federation (GARF, mainly the Gulag fund no. 9414, the MVD fund no. 9401, and the Procurator's Office fund, no. 8131 and the Khrushchev Personal Files, OPKh), and the State Archive of the Perm Region (GAPO). Unpublished memories of victims of the Gulag are housed in the Memorial Archive of the victims of [Soviet] repression (Memorial). I cite the relevant archive followed by numbers that refer, respectively, to the fund (*fond*), the list (*opis'*), the file (*delo*) and the sheet numbers (*list*).

Note on transliteration. In this work, I follow the standard transliteration system used in academic writing. Few exceptions to consistency are made for the sake of familiarity: Dostoevskii, Gor'kii, Solzhenitsin, El'tsin, Berezovskii, Lebed', and Zhirinovskii are rendered as Dostoyevsky, Gorky, Solzhenitsyn, Yeltsin, Berezovsky, Lebed, and Zhirinovsky. Perm', the city of my fieldwork, has been consistently transliterated as Perm.

Note on monetary rates. Russia has experienced severe inflation since the final years of the Soviet Union. The reader thus may be puzzled over the value of the figures quoted throughout the book. When possible, I have converted rouble sums into the prevailing US dollar rate at the time referred in the text. The following table can be used as guide to the changing value of the rouble.

Introduction

Table 1 Exchange rates against the US dollar

	Average over period
1991	67
1992	222
1993	933
1994	2,205
1995	4,562
1996	5,126
1997	5,785
1998[a]	9,965
1999[b]	24,346

Notes:
[a] On Jan. 1, 1998 the Central Bank redenominated the currency, removing three zeros from the roubles while preserving their nominal value.
[b] First three quarters only.

Source: Period 1991–92: GRF/RECEP, 1996: 139–40; Period 1993–8: GRF/RECEP, 1999: 106.

PART I

The Transition to the Market
and Protection in Russia

1
The Transition to the Market

Our journey into the world of the Russian Mafia starts with a study of the transition from a state-run to a market economy. (A crucial argument of this book is that the Mafia emerged as a consequence of an imperfect transition to the market.) Indeed, a large body of scholarship has provided ample evidence to how imperfect the transition was.[1] Even the Western scholars who advised the Russian government in the early phase of the shock therapy and mass privatization have reluctantly conceded this point.[2] The aim of this chapter is to advance an explanation of such an outcome and spell out the criminal opportunities that have arisen as a consequence of the transition. But first I present a picture of the country as it appears in the late 1990s.

According to the 1999 index of 'economic freedom' constructed by the Heritage Foundation, Russia ranks 106th in a list of 160 countries, just before Burkina Faso, Cameroon, and Guyana and is 'mostly unfree'. This index measures how well countries score on a list of ten factors, including trade policy, taxation policy, level of privatization, monetary policy, property rights, anti-trust regulations, and the extent of the black market. Not only is Russia on the bottom half of the list, but the authors caution that the index was constructed before the August 1998 crisis: 'had this information been included . . . Russia surely would receive a worse score'.[3]

This index measures how much 'market economy' (or 'capitalism') there is in a country. Other indicators show that standards of living dropped since the beginning of the transition and that economic polarization increased substantially. Mortality rates have risen alarmingly and life expectancy has fallen.[4] Russia has not yet reaped the benefits of capitalism but it has lost the safety nets of socialism.

Since the end of socialism, the legal situation has also developed in a chaotic fashion. After the Law on Co-operatives was introduced (1986), a plethora of often overlapping and conflicting laws and decrees emanate from a variety of jurisdictions. The ultimate validity of laws is difficult to establish as the same subjects are often covered by many different and mutually contradictory rulings.[5] Presidential decrees, which are often not consistent with each other, coexist with and often contradict parliamentary legislation.[6] The weakening of hierarchical links and the collapse of the Communist Party destroyed the former network of administrative co-ordination. Administrative offices have overlapping jurisdictions, each pursuing its own agenda.[7] One of the consequences of such confusion is that titles of properties—such as the ownership of a newly privatized flat—can be registered by different offices. This allows for multiple sales and frauds of perspective buyers.[8]

The tax system is similarly confused. Until January 1999, Russia did not have a tax code, and taxes were levied by decree for a total of eighteen Federal levies. Presidential Decree No. 2270 of 22 December 1993 freed regions and cities to levy taxes. According to this decree, local government may establish up to eighteen local taxes.[9] However this limit is not strictly enforced: in Yakutiya alone twenty-four regional taxes and fees are in force, while, in 1995, Moscow companies were required to submit twenty-three different quarterly tax reports.[10] Payment schedules and procedures vary by type of tax, and entrepreneurs rely heavily on bookkeepers and attorneys to maintain compliance.[11] It is the duty of the taxpayer to sort out taxes according to the budget to which they accrue, share the money between different budgets if necessary, and monitor changes in tax regulations, since many new taxes are retroactive.[12] Fines and penalties are severe: they range from 10 to 500 per cent of the amount concealed. For instance, underestimated income carries a fine of 100 per cent. On-site audits can last several months and be part of a series of audits. As noted by Morozov, a Moscow-based observer of the tax inspectorate,

A tax inspection is followed by a tax police inspection, followed by a tax inspection by a higher tax office. Moreover, the audit of the same object (e.g. the VAT tax base), for the same period of time, is made several times. Tax authorities often use on-site visits to the same taxpayer to punish him for appealing his fines in court.[13]

There is compelling evidence suggesting that, if paid in full, taxes would interfere with the efficient allocation of resources. A report prepared for the President of Russian Federation and compiled by Petr Filippov concluded that the extremely confusing tax system gives enterprises no incentives to increase profits.[14] Furthermore, perverse financial incentives lead tax collectors to extract fines. Until 1995, tax authorities were legally allowed to keep a percentage of collected fines and penalties to pay staff bonuses. (Since 1995, bonuses to the staff depend on the percentage of total tax collection.)[15] During this period Morozov noted numerous and repeated complaints on the legitimacy of the penalties inflicted by tax authorities to businesses. The suspicion is that tax authorities inflate penalties to increase their own incomes.[16]

In ten years (1985–95) registered crimes increased by 194.5 per cent. The pattern should, however, be qualified. The highest increase took place between 1988 and 1992. From 1993, crime rates stabilized.

Yet official crime statistics may be deceptive, since they include only

Table 1.1 Registered crimes in Russia 1985–1998

Year	Total no. of registered crimes (thousands)	Annual change (%)	Index (1985 = 100)
1985	1,417	1.0	100.0
1986	1,338	−5.5	94.4
1987	1,186	−11.4	83.6
1988	1,220	2.9	86.1
1989	1,619	32.7	114.2
1990	1,839	13.6	129.8
1991	2,173	18.1	153.3
1992	2,761	27.0	194.8
1993	2,800	1.4	197.6
1994	2,633	−5.9	185.8
1995	2,756	4.6	194.4
1996	2,625	−4.7	185.2
1997	2,397	−8.6	169.1
1998	2,582	7.7	182.2

Source: Data from Goskomstat, http://www.gks.ru.

reported crimes.[17] Researchers at the Ministry of Internal Affairs of the Russian Federation have observed that law enforcement agencies in Moscow returned to their old practice of avoiding registration of crimes.[18] A study carried out in 1991–3 revealed that, in general terms, the level of non-reported crimes in the Russian Federation was 40 to 70 per cent.[19] Among latent crime, the highest level was that of economic crimes and criminally significant acts of a minor character.[20] On the contrary, homicides are reasonable easily defined and well recorded in crime statistics. In Russia in 1994 there were thirty-two murders per 100,000 inhabitants. As shown by Table 1.2, this rate is three times higher than in the US and significantly higher than in several Latin American countries, such as Mexico and Brazil.[21]

Corruption is also rampant and reaches the highest echelons of power. In 1995 a Swiss company, Mabetex, owned by Kosovo-born businessman, Behgjet Pacolli, allegedly paid bribes to the head of the Kremlin property department in order to obtain contracts for renovation works in the Kremlin.[22] In June 1998, the head of the State Statistics Committee, Yuri Yurkov, was arrested on charges of helping big companies evade taxes. He was found guilty with twenty other employees of 'systematic distortion of statistical data on big companies, which allowed them to evade taxes'.[23] The recent high profile case involving the Bank of New York concerning the allegations of misuse of IMF funds and money laundering is just the tip of the iceberg. Interior Minister Anatolii Kulikov said, when appointed in July 1995, that he could not have imagined 'the level of corruption in state bodies, particularly the Ministry of Internal Affairs'.[24] An index of the perception of corruption for 54 countries was constructed by Transparency International, a non-profit organization, and the University of Götting. Based on a variety of polls, it aims 'to assess the level at which corruption is perceived by people working for multinational firms and institutions as impacting on commercial life'.[25] Scores range from zero to ten, the lower the score the higher the level of corruption. In 1996, Russia obtains a score of 2.58 points and ranks 47 (out of 54 countries) just before Venezuela (score 2.50) and Cameroon (score 2.46) and after India (2.63). New Zealand is perceived as the least corrupt country (score 9.43), while Kenya, Pakistan, and Nigeria are perceived as the most corrupt (respectively they score 2.21, 1.00, and 0.69). Over the years, Russia's position has gradually worsened, from 2.58 in 1996 to 2.4 in 1998.

The reality of the Russian transition does not match the expectations and the accounts given in the books by the (now dismissed) Western

Table 1.2 Homicides (per 100,000 inhabitants) in the Soviet Union/Russia and other countries

Country	Homicide Frequency	Year
Soviet Union/Russia	9.8	1988
Soviet Union/Russia	12.6	1989
Soviet Union/Russia	14.3	1990
Russia	15.3	1991
Russia	22.9	1992
Russia	30.4	1993
Russia	32.4	1994
Russia	30.6	1995
Russia	26.5	1996
Columbia	80.0	1994
Brazil	19.0	1992
Mexico	17.2	1995
Venezuela	15.8	1994
USA	8.6	1995
Argentina	4.4	1993
Chile	2.9	1994
Canada	1.7	1995
Ukraine	15.0	1996
Hungary	3.5	1995
Poland	2.6	1996
Czech Republic	2.1	1993
Italy	1.7	1993
Sweden	1.2	1996
France	1.1	1994
Germany	1.1	1996
U.K.	1.0	1994
Spain	0.9	1995
Japan	0.6	1994

Source: United Nations, 1995: 500; 1996: 503; 1998: 765–854; 1999: 450–70.

advisers. Rather than a virtuous 'invisible hand' bringing about a collective optimum, Russia appears to be suffering a collective failure. By pursuing individually rational goals, agents have brought about a less-than-optimal collective outcome. Why did such an outcome occur? I will offer an answer to this question first by distinguishing between the privatization process and a functioning market economy based on property rights, and then by exploring in theory what it means to have property rights in a market economy. I will show how the spread of private property almost by definition leads to a demand for protection, against other people's attempts to capture that property and the profit that it generates. However, it is not a foregone conclusion that the state is capable to meet such demand. The benefits of a generalized provision of clear property rights and state protection are often diffuse, while interest groups lobby for a distribution of property and rights that is favourable to them. By doing so, however, they reduce the credibility of the state as an impartial protector of rights.

The Russian case will be interpreted in the light of this theoretical discussion. Powerful lobbies were able to secure a profitable initial distribution of resources and property rights. They also engaged in successful lobbying to avoid paying taxes. Since the richest contributors managed to avoid paying taxes, state revenues were lower than expected. This led to a rise in state taxation and incentives for tax inspectors to collect. The remaining section of the private sector that were not obtaining major tax concessions had a strong incentive to either bribe tax officials or to conceal income.

Property Rights and the Demand for Protection

A great deal of optimism informing both newspaper reporting and early academic studies of the Russian transition sprang from the rapid privatization of assets. No doubt, extensive privatization has taken place in Russia. Data released by the Goskomstat show that a substantial portion of the Russian economy is now in private hands.[26] The virtual monopoly over property rights by the Socialist state has given way to an enormous increase in the number of people owning assets. Privatization *per se* is not, however, sufficient to produce a well-functioning market economy. As a matter of fact, giving away property is not such a difficult task. The cornerstone of a market economy is the presence of property rights. It is worth pausing a moment to consider what having a right over a property entails.

In order to explore the concept of property rights, we need to take a step back and imagine a simplified world where an individual has a 'natural control' over an asset and aspires to consume or exchange it, and keep the income flow (profit) it generates. His control over that asset is never fully secure: it is a function of others' attempts to capture that property.[27] As a consequence, he owns assets insecurely and develops a demand for protection against attempts to take his property away from him. Such attempts include theft and confiscation of the profit that derives from the asset by somebody who does not bear the costs associated with the asset's control. Profit may derive in variety of ways: the owner might exchange the asset, join forces with other agents (partners) to make that asset productive, or simply hold on to it and receive an income.

As argued above, ownership of an asset produces a demand for protection against attempts to take that asset away. The attempt to derive profit from an asset also produces a demand for protection, as I will now show. In order to obtain a profit from the ownership of an asset, the owner exchanges his asset or joins forces with a partner: when he does so, he engages in co-operative behaviour.[28] The choice of co-operating is however susceptible to the risk related to the potential defection of others.[29] Co-operation requires that people agree on a set of rules, a 'contract' which is then observed during their joint activities. As a result of this, a demand for trust in potential partners emerges.[30] However, if trust in others is low, or reputational bonds have not yet emerged to distinguish between trustworthy and non-trustworthy partners, transactors will develop a subsidiary demand for protection.

When we introduce the state into this simplified picture a tension is immediately apparent. The same agency that is supposed to protect owners against others' capture attempts must also protect owners against itself. In an ideal world, the state protects citizens against itself by a set of checks and balances and by predictable rules. A 'right' is therefore a claim or entitlement, which is normally enforceable through courts or equivalent agencies. Legally enforced ownership sanctions the 'natural control' that an owner has over an asset and as well as possession of the physical thing owned, includes rights to use it, to derive income from it, to exclude others from using it, and to exchange it.[31] A property right of a person over, say, an automobile, prevents another private person or a government official from taking that car without the owner's consent. To make this property right meaningful, it is necessary to have a registration system for automobile titles. In addition, regulations that make it possible for an owner to use his goods must be present. For instance, a taxation system making it unfeasible for an owner to pay registration and other duties, together with a lack of predictable rules on governmental confiscation, would make a title of property meaningless.[32] Finally, a criminal penalty severe enough to deter theft must also exist, as pointed out by Richard Posner.

Not just theft, robbery, embezzling, the forging of wills, certain types of frauds, and other familiar acquisitive crimes, but also bribing officials, including judges, police, and officials in charge of registering titles to real or personal property, must be prevented, or, more precisely, kept within tolerable bounds.[33]

A property right is in fact a 'bundle of nested rights', which include the clear definition of the title of property, the possibility to derive income (or pleasure) from goods owned and an apparatus for deterring crime. If and when disputes arise between individual owners, or owners and the state, courts settle them. When property rights are clearly specified, and the person who decides how to employ this asset bears full costs and enjoys full benefits of such employment, she is in the best position to put the asset to its most productive use. As Adam Smith put it in *The Wealth of Nations*, 'In all countries where there is tolerable security [of property], every man of common understanding will endeavour to employ whatever stock he can command. . . . A man must be perfectly crazy who, where there is tolerable security, does not employ all the stock which he commands . . .'.[34]

Even the ideal state I have described above, a state that clearly defines property rights and is committed to protect them, does not protect the ownership of *all* assets. First, in some cases, it chooses not to attach an owner to a property and considers the control over certain assets, such as drugs, 'illegal'. Holders of such assets must either protect them themselves, engage in exchanges with others only if they think the 'contract' does not need third-party enforcement,[35] or enter into a contract with a private protection agency that is willing to protect an illegal asset. Second, for the assets the state decides to delineate and protect, state protection is never complete, it is a function of how difficult it is both to attach an owner to a property and to protect it from theft. For instance, if a fifty-pound note is left on a street pavement, theft is very easy and tracing the legitimate owner virtually impossible. It is then more accurate to describe state protection as partial: owners do not leave the protection of their assets against theft entirely to the state and the state can protect assets only to a degree.

The ideal state committed to define and protect property rights might however not materialize. This is neither because some assets (illegal goods) will never be protected nor because the ability to define and protect assets is always limited. There is more. States differ in the degree to which they are *willing* to define and protect property rights. Since the law is ultimately upheld by the state, the state itself might disregard it. The state may behave in a *predatory* fashion and be *non-impartial* in its rulings. In the model developed by Hobbes in *The Leviathan* the ruler (the state) is not constrained by the law. He could use his power to confiscate the property of all others, as in the thirteenth century King John tried to do at the expense of the nobility after a series of defeats in France.[36] When the state is predatory, erratic and non-impartial in its ruling two consequences obtain: (1) a decrease in the demand of state-supplied protection of property rights; (2) an increase in attempts to influence the ruling of the state. Let's take them in turn.

An environment of partiality in legal rulings leads to the decrease in the demand for third-party enforcement administrated by the state. As argued convincingly by Barzel, a non-impartial ruling amounts to a form of 'legal' confiscation. Once this takes place, people will perceive that the legal system is becoming less impartial and at that point they will turn away from the state: they 'will form more of their agreements outside its jurisdiction, lowering the demand for its service'.[37] This in turn leads to a demand for non-state protection.

Second, individuals will try to influence the decisions of officials in the state apparatus to enhance the value of their assets. They can pursue this strategy through the use of bribes.[38] There are two fundamental features of the exchange between a corrupter and an official (agent of the state) who accepts a bribe: uncertainty over the delivery and uncertainty over payment. Once the corrupter has identified a public official willing to accept a bribe, how can he be sure that the official will deliver? And how can the official ensure that the corrupter will not forget or fail to pay the agreed amount?[39] The citizen who offers a bribe might meet either a corrupt but 'honest' official or a corrupt and 'dishonest' official. In the first case, the corrupt exchange takes place smoothly. In the second, the official pockets the money and does not deliver the service. The official who has delivered a service might also not receive the bribe. The corrupter and official can solve this dilemma by establishing a long-term relationship with each other. Trust would develop slowly over time. Alternatively, they might resolve the problem of delivery in illegal transactions by developing a demand for enforcement services that, as a by-product, promote corrupt exchanges.[40] The greater the variety of interactions and the number of people one has to deal with, the more likely it is that a demand for protection will emerge: it is harder to develop long-term relations of trust if one entrepreneur has dozens of officials to handle and there is a high turnover of those officials.

Individuals may be trying to influence the *choice* of new rules, rather than just the decisions of one official. In this case, the concept of corruption can hardly apply. In this case, the *corrupter* tries to influence the state itself (the so-called *principal*), rather than one of its agents. If the office that sets the rules over private property of an asset is itself 'corrupt', we are left with a state whose legal rulings are non-impartial and the concept of corruption loses its analytical clout. When a state is not impartial, state protection will—as a direct consequence—be partial, and individuals may have recourse to private sources of protection.

It is time now to summarize the argument so far. The central question we have explored is: 'How does a demand for private, non-state protection emerge in a market economy?' Even in the best possible scenario, that of a state committed to define and protect property rights, a demand for protection of goods that are defined as illegal will exist. This is the reason why, in the underworld, services of dispute settlement and protection are highly sought, even in the presence of an effective state and a functioning market economy. By definition, the state will never protect drug dealers, only the mafia might do. Second, even in such an ideal scenario, the state will be able effectively to protect assets only to a degree, and it is most likely that individual owners will not leave it entirely to the state to protect their assets, but to some extent will engage in efforts at self-protection. Ideal scenarios do not always materialize: not all states are the same, some are not committed to the protection of property rights, they are predatory, erratic, and non-impartial in their legal rulings. We might call them 'less-than-ideal states'. Demand for private protection in these states is then much wider. First, individuals will not be willing to accept the state as an impartial third-party enforcer of contracts. Second, they might try to influence in their favour the state's rulings, for example by engaging in corruption. I have argued that corruption, being an illegal activity, produces a demand for protection because the actors in this exchange do not know for sure if the other party will deliver what was promised (the money of the bribe or the favourable official decision). Besides corrupting officials supposed to implement certain rules, individuals might engage in attempts to influence the content of those very same rules. In this case the concept of corruption no longer applies, rather we are faced with a partial state that legalizes theft. All the same, the protection dilemma still applies: one may try to influence state rulings and consume resources in the process but still have no certainty that another party will not pay more and obtain his own preferred rule. Competition among agents may well include the use of violent threats. Even if one actor establishes a long-term relationship with a segment of the political elite, violence may be used to keep competitors at bay and politicians in line.

The question I will turn to next is the following: under which conditions might a 'less-than-ideal' outcome emerge?

First, we should be clear that the process that leads to the emergence of an 'ideal' outcome is not without cost and does not occur in a void. The protection of property rights implies the provision of a wide range of services. For both tort and criminal law to be meaningful, a public machinery must be in place, providing police, prosecutors, judges, and even lawyers free of charge for those who cannot afford to hire their own defence.[41] Also, while some crimes, such as 'speculation', disappear with the transition to the market, new ones emerge, such as crimes that pertain to financial misdeeds (e.g. 'insider trading'). A further cost—which is usually underestimated—is the cost of learning. The Soviet Union had a highly educated population. Lawyers, judges, and state officials had gone through many years of formal training in order to qualify for their positions. The transition to the market led to the introduction of new concepts, such as 'shares', and entirely new legal phenomena. Not just a process of learning, but also a change in attitude would be necessary. Legal education did not reward jurists for 'independent thinking' and it still does not.[42] Ideally, a massive retraining programme for the state employees would have been necessary or, alternatively, a significant influx of young officials into the state apparatus. Although the effects of either policy may differ, they both imply substantial investments in education (or, in the jargon of economists, in 'intangible' commodities). The suggestion put forward for instance by Rudiger Dornbush, a prominent

MIT economist, to simply 'copy' the civil code of another country would not suffice.[43]

The transition to an effective system of property rights is therefore a costly undertaking. It is not only costly. Since the law is ultimately upheld by the state, constraints on the ability to confiscate property can only come from the *collective actions* of individuals within a polity. Those same individuals, however, might engage in actions to induce partiality in state rulings and thereby encourage both corruption and state predatory behaviour. Russia faced the challenge of transferring rights from the nominal collective owner, the Soviet State, to citizens. The adoption of one or another system to allocate property rights has distributional consequences: some benefit at the expense of others. Was there in Russia a group of individuals powerful enough to engage in effective collective action which in turn would have produced a functioning state, committed to the impartial definition and protection of property rights? The answer that will follow below is in the negative.

The benefits of both the clear definition and effective enforcement of property rights, as well as the proper functioning of a market economy more generally, are often diffuse. At the time of the transition, there was no lobby of ordinary property owners able to pressure the government into providing general and simple rules. There was no lobby of shareholders, no lobby of estate developers, and so forth. The reason why such a lobby was not there is twofold: *size* and *time*. Size must be taken into account in order to assess the likelihood that a broad-based lobby of private owners will emerge—a lobby that favours an efficient system of property rights. Larger groups are more difficult to organize and therefore, if they emerge at all, it takes more effort.[44]

Time is also a crucial factor: before privatization, when the relevant rules and regulations were framed, private owners could not have exercised any pressure, because no property owner existed. Political pressure on such rules can occur only *after* privatization. For Hay, Shleifer, and Vishny, 'legal reforms [that foster the optimal functioning of the economy] often are not introduced by benevolent dictators or Parliaments, but are rather an outcome of political pressure from property owners'.[45] They then argue that a lobby of owners, who have a private interest in the functioning of the market and the establishment of a secure system of property rights, will emerge in due course. They quote the repeal of the 1720s Bubbles Act in Britain, which came about after vigorous pressure from the British business community.[46] Similarly, Raeff documents how the legal system developed in Germany in the seventeenth and eighteenth centuries, and how participants in an emergent market economy shaped it.[47]

The case of the repeal of the 1720s Bubbles Act in Britain refers to a century-long struggle. The German case refers to a process that took over two centuries. It might therefore take a long time before we see anything resembling a functioning institutional setting in Russia. But there is more than a time lag. Both Mancur Olson and Yoram Barzel recognize that it is very hard to bring about collective action, which could restrain a predatory state, if the state itself does not endorse and promote it. This explains—they argue convincingly—why dictatorships and predatory rulers are the most common form of rule in history. The transition from a dictatorship to a rule-of-law state is, typically, 'exceedingly slow'.[48] In the meantime, organized groups of actors with a strong interest in the final distribution of property rights may lobby for an outcome that is less than the rule of law. Early privatization in the absence of laws and regulations creates vested interests to block subsequent attempts at regulating markets. This outcome would be an instance of what economists and political scientists refer to as 'path dependency': once a path has been entered, suboptimal outcomes may persist for a long time.

The Russian Transition

This section is devoted to a presentation of the main actors involved in the transition—enterprise managers, industrial ministers, workers, and local governments and Yeltsin's reform team. We shall try to see which of these lobbies were best positioned to engage in collective action to determine some aspects of the transition, and the final outcome.

The Lobbies

Enterprise managers were, at the time of the transition, a small and resourceful group. In Soviet times, enterprise managers had acquired the 'natural control' over the enterprises they were managing. Top managers were appointed by the Industrial Ministries, which guaranteed inputs to enterprises and fixed production quotas. As the regime grew more and more inefficient, the ministries were less able to supply inputs and a decentralized network of exchanges of favours—which had always been in place—flourished, in effect replacing the centralized system.[49] The law of 1 January 1988 on State Enterprises formalized the end of the Industrial Ministries' control over enterprises by giving enterprises the right to make production decisions, choose customers, retain profit, and set wages.[50] The same law allowed enterprises to engage in foreign trade. From 1988, enterprise managers could create private co-operatives and arbitrage with their government-owned businesses.[51] For instance, managers of state oil companies were able to buy oil from their enterprises privately at the fixed price and to sell it abroad at the market price through the newly established co-operatives. The margins for profit were immense: in 1992 the Russian price of oil was still only 1 per cent of the world market.[52] In order to do so, oil companies managers extracted export licences and quotas from officials. And so did managers of state agricultural monopolies: Roskhleboprodukt and other state companies in charge of the distribution of goods to shops during the Soviet period were the recipients of Western 'humanitarian' export credit, later added to Russia's state deficit. Thanks to these credits, the traders who operated through Roskhleboprodukt and other state agricultural monopolies paid only 1 per cent of the going exchange rate while purchasing essential foods from abroad, but could resell them freely on the domestic market and pocket the subsidy.[53]

Enterprise managers assumed control over the operation and use of enterprises, supplemented their individual wealth by hiding profits and skimming extra production,[54] and relied on officials to secure favourable regulations. These people were well placed to engage in covert, though highly effective, collective action in order to acquire resources and property rights when the transition came. Olson put it as follows:

There will normally be only a small number of factory managers in a given industry or locality. Because the numbers involved are small, the managers in a given industry can collude in much less time than would be required for a large group. The restrains on independent organisation in a communist society . . . requires inconspicuous, informal, and secret collusion, and the need to proceed covertly makes collective action emerge much more slowly than it otherwise would. But small groups can typically collude secretly.[55]

Other lobbies included the industrial ministers, workers, and local governments. Ministries had lost considerable power since the Gorbachev reforms, while workers, although they saw a relative increase in their lobbying power with the end of regime, were weakly organized. The Federation of Independent Trade Unions of Russia—the successor of the communist trade unions—did not have a history of strong lobbying for workers' interests and suffered from weak sectorial co-ordination and inability to organize mass actions.[56] Local governments emerged as a significant political actor. They had increased their political power *vis-à-vis* the central government and the enterprises: they started to exercise control over and retain some of the taxes collected locally and could affect significantly the operations of local enterprises by adopting new regulations and carrying out inspections.[57] Finally, the reform team of Egor Gaidar and Anatolii Chubais should also be counted as a player in the process. We might assume that they wanted to establish a form of capitalism that reached as many people as possible, at a time when it was far from clear that the market economy would not be reversed in Russia. In conclusion, enterprise managers were the interest group with the strongest lobbying power.

The Outcome

We now turn to the outcome of the transition. Enterprise managers, represented by Arkadii Vol'skii, chairman of the Russian Union of Industrialists and Entrepreneurs, obtained the most favourable initial distribution of property rights. The first voucher-based privatization project, devised by Gaidar, David Lipton, and Jeffrey Sachs, was meant to produce a separation of management from ownership. Although this plan—Option One of the 1992 Privatization Programme—granted various benefits to enterprise managers,[58] it was greatly resisted. Eventually enterprise managers were able to have the programme altered and were offered a second option, Option Two, allowing directors and workers to purchase 51 per cent of all shares, at a discount and even using the enterprise's own funds. Not surprisingly, more than 80 per cent of enterprises chose Option Two.[59] Some directors were content to have ownership dispersed among workers of the company: in most cases workers' collectives agreed not to interfere with the management of the enterprise in exchange for job security.[60] Others acquired a controlling block of shares through a variety of manipulative schemes against their own workers. As described by McFaul, the most direct method was simply to buy out workers' shares before they had any market value. Alternatively they outbid workers either directly or through proxies, and often in collaboration with director-friendly commercial banks, during the closed subscription for shares that took place under Option Two.[61] Some other directors contrived that their companies or entire sectors of the economy would be subject to special regulations, outside the provision of the privatization scheme. Others still were allowed to adopt special corporate statutes. For instance, Yeltsin issued special decrees on the privatization rules that applied only to AvtoVaz and GAZ. The regulations for the privatization of Gazprom excluded participation by outsiders. Surgutneftegaz was granted the right to adopt a special statute that also limited the rights of outside shareholders.[62]

Other lobbies were either defeated or obtained very little. Industrial Ministries failed to secure any major concession,[63] while local governments were granted control over small-scale privatization. They sold most of the existing small shops and some of the small firms for cash.[64] If the privatization team had wanted ordinary Russians to benefit from the privatization, it failed. Most of the savings of ordinary Russians evaporated as a consequence of the 2 January 1992 decision of Gaidar to free most prices, and the ensuing 2,500 per cent inflation.[65] Ordinary Russians had no money to invest in the voucher-based privatization scheme.

A December 1994 survey of sixty-one privatized firms in nineteen regions found that managers and workers owed on average 59 per cent of the shares. The average ownership of top managers was 9 per cent.[66] A survey conducted by the Russian Privatization Agency (GKI), found that workers owned on average 53 per cent of the enterprise, managers 17 per cent, outsiders 14 per cent and the state 16 per cent. Yet Frye notes that these figures understate managerial control rights: 'Managers often find friendly outside investors who retain them in exchange for preferential treatment, gain voting rights of workers' shares, dominate shareholders' meetings, and use their informational advantage to frustrate outsiders.'[67] Company boards are under the firm control of company insiders who hold the majority of voting shares in roughly 70 per cent of privatized companies; a majority of 75 per cent of shareholders is necessary to change company charters, which are most often favourable to insiders; and voting rules are rarely based on the 'one-share-one vote' principle.[68]

Furthermore, managers try to block the registration of shares and to hold auctions in remote regions inaccessible to outsider investors.[69] In Russia, evidence of shares' ownership is a name in a registrar's book. For a share transaction to take place, an agent has to go physically to the company's registrar and reregister ownership. According to Russian law, any enterprise with more than 500 shareholders is obliged to entrust its register to a separate organization. Yet, in practice, many of the registers of

Russia's largest factories are controlled directly by the company and are located in the company headquarters. Moreover, these companies control many of the broker or financial houses conducting shareholder registers on behalf of companies, and their independence is pure formality.[70] The fear is that shares will disappear from the record, as has already happened in the case of Krasnoyarsk Aluminium Smelter, and the oil companies Sidanko and Sibneft'.[71]

There is a clear asymmetry in the protection of property rights, and such an asymmetry derives from a difference in resources held by different lobbies at the time of the transition. Some actors were able to influence state agencies and to obtain control of valued assets. Others have seen their rights (over shares, for instance) weakly protected. The state did not emerge as an impartial and credible protector of property rights, even in the eyes of those who benefited from the transfer of resources. The absence of clearly defined property rights and an open and effective corporate structure leads even the beneficiaries of the transition to engage in strategies that maximize short-term parasitic profits, rather than long-term productive investments: even they do not know who will be in power next and cannot afford to see their rights being overruled.[72] This situation led to both asset stripping and capital flight.

Some of the so-called Russian 'oligarchs' emerged as a by-product of the parasitic economic activities of enterprise managers. For instance, Boris Berezovskii, the 96th richest man in 1998 and a close ally of Yeltsin, made his fortune as the chairman of a society connected to Avtovaz, the enterprise that produces Lada cars. He bought Ladas at artificially low export prices from Avtovaz, reselling them at market prices within Russia. Although the public paid him in cash, he delayed the transfer of profits to Avtovaz and this at the time of high inflation. Accordingly, Avtovaz went almost bankrupt. Asset stripping continued in the mid-1990s. In new, controversial privatization auctions, the 'loan-for-shares' scheme, Uneksimbank (headed by another 'oligarch' close to Yeltsin, Vladimir Potanin)[73] was allowed to buy Noril'sk Nickel, the largest producer of nickel in the world, the oil company Sidanko and Novolipetsk Metal factory at a non-competitive price in a closed auction managed by the bank itself. Once the bank acquired a majority share, it did not behave like a self-interested proprietor but just continued the management theft, primarily selling the products below market prices to their own trading companies, letting the old state companies deteriorate. As noted by Åslund, shortly afterwards the company's value fell even below the low purchase price. Two other oil companies sold at this round of auctions, Yukos and Sibneft', shared the same fate.[74] Enterprise directors maximize their personal profits, but do not divide it with other shareowners. Instead they create parasitic, subsidiary companies attached to the parent enterprise. Directors channel revenues into these small, close joint-stock companies, where profits are divided among a handful of directors, rather than thousands of small shareholders.[75] Given the uncertainty described above and in the full knowledge of having obtained their profit in dubious ways, the new Russian magnates have been quick to take their wealth out of the country, to make any attempt to expropriate them difficult.[76]

The events that led to the loan-for-share scheme point to the non-impartiality of the Russian state. Indeed, they show that individuals could succeed in influencing the state in framing the rules rather than simply corrupting officials in order to be able to break the rules. In 1997, several individuals in charge of drafting the regulations for the loan-for-shares auctions allegedly obtained 'veiled bribes' in the form of a $US100,000 advance to write a chapter in a book by a Swiss company. Vladimir Potanin, the Russian magnate who was allowed to supervise, take part in, and eventually win several auctions in the loan-for-shares scheme, controlled the company.[77]

Widespread corruption and the non-impartiality of the state undermine the security of private property and encourage the view that state officials are not impartial defenders of rights. Officials in charge of registering titles might want a bribe either to fulfil their duties or might be prepared to enhance the rights of bribe-paying property owners at the expense of those who do not pay. Pervasive corruption, non-impartiality and wrongdoing also reduce the cost of identifying dishonest officials. Where corruption is pervasive, uncertainty over who will accept a bribe is greatly reduced and the citizen's dominant strategy will always be to offer a bribe. This behaviour, of course, leads to even further corruption, since the officials' opportunities to accept bribes inevitably increase.[78]

The bundle of nested rights, which forms the property right over an asset, include the right to derive income from the object owned. The Russian tax system appears to infringe upon such a right. Both the enterprise managers and the new 'oligarchs' successfully managed to secure not only preferential treatment in the transfer of property, but also tax concessions. Oil and gas companies, such as Yuganskneftegaz, Nizhnevartovskneftegaz, and Noyabr'skneftegaz, the automobile giant Avtovaz, and the gas monopoly Gazprom have paid hardly any taxes in recent years.[79] Large enterprises are not alone in lobbying for tax breaks. Sporting organizations for instance have received import tax breaks worth as much as 1.3 trillion roubles ($300 million) since a presidential decree (signed on 1 March 1992) relieved them from paying import duties, value-added and excise taxes. Entire regions also try and often succeed in reducing the transfer of resources to the central government.[80] Since major contributors to state coffers have successfully avoided paying taxes, the entire burden switches on to taxpayers with weaker lobbying power. As a consequence, the tax burden becomes excessive and the private sector has strong incentive to avoid taxes and offer bribes to tax officials.[81] As Olson noted, 'essentially all of the private sector incentives are on the side of undermining the rule of law, either by bribing enforcement officers or lobbying politicians'.[82] The collective outcome is a tremendous amount of tax evasion, as testified by data on tax collection.[83]

In conclusion, a property transfer that was in the interest of the most powerful lobby of the Soviet Union took place at the time of the transition, as shown above. Insider ownership led to a number of negative economic consequences, such as employment restrictions, excessive wages, and difficulties with raising capital.[84] It also reduced managerial discipline. Since owners and managers to a large extent coincide, it is hard to imagine owners firing incompetent or plundering managers.[85] What is most important for our purposes is that the state did not emerge as an impartial and credible protector of property rights. First and foremost, the titles of property were poorly defined and protected, while a basic function of the state is to register titles of ownership and protect them against misappropriation. Furthermore, the privatization process has been characterized by many exceptions, undermining the perception of the state as an impartial distributor of rights and resources. Some enterprises were subject to special regulations, others were granted tax exemptions. This in turn overburdened the private sector that had not been granted tax exemptions. Collective action on the part of Soviet-era lobbies promoted predatory and non-impartial behaviour on the part of the state, rather than the birth of a society based on the rule of law.

Ten years after the start of the transition productivity is down, inequality is up, laws contradict each other, corruption is widespread, and crime (as measured by homicide rates) puts Russia below Mexico and Brazil in terms of safety. In this chapter I have offered an interpretation of this out-come. The powerful lobbies that Russia had inherited from the collapse of the Soviet economic system were successful in obtaining a privileged dis-tribution of assets and tax concessions. A generalized provision of protec-tion and clearly defined property rights was lacking. Such an outcome generated criminal opportunities: high incentives to strip assets, corrupt officials, evade taxes, illegally export capitals and launder money. As I have indicated above, these criminal activities generate a specific demand for criminal protection.

2

The State as Supplier of Protection

Various authors have suggested that courts are inefficient in enforcing decisions, although they base their view on anecdotal evidence.[1] Recent empirical research on the functioning of the legal system in Russia points to a different conclusion. Kathryn Hendley, Peter Murrell, and Randi Ryterman argue that 'the law works in Russia'.[2] Contrary to the perception that the legal system lacks a structure to enforce contracts or uphold property rights, Hendley *et al.* find that entrepreneurs have 'confidence' in the legal system: 'It would certainly be erroneous to claim that Russian businessmen view their legal system negatively and one might even claim that the businessmen have confidence in the legal system.'[3] Furthermore, confidence in the system leads businessmen to use the courts when they have to settle a dispute between themselves. The fear of being brought to court is so great that it operates as a deterrent against opportunistic behaviour. In fact, businessmen consider going to court 'a more serious problem' than the activity of criminal groups: 'Table 4 shows that litigation is perceived as a more serious problem for Russian enterprises than is the activity of criminal groups.'[4] They conclude that, despite many obstacles, the law and legal institutions might constitute a 'bright light' in what is often regarded as a dismal picture.[5]

Where do Hendley *et al.* see 'the law working'? They focus their attention on the *Arbitrazh* court system. The *Arbitrazh* transformed itself from an administrative body in charge of settling disputes between enterprises within the planned economy to a court system regulated by a procedural code. It hears cases that range from simple disputes over delivery of shampoos to complex issues of commercial law, bankruptcy, and governance. On paper, judges are supposed to take decisions based solely on the law and not consider the political or economic consequences of their resolutions.

In the following we shall take a similar look, although wider than the one chosen by Hendley *et al.*, at the state as a supplier of protection. We shall first explore how Russian citizens perceive the institutions of authority, such as the juridical system, state officials and the police. We then turn to the court of arbitration. We are interested in exploring whether Russian businessmen use the court to settle their disputes and how effective the court is.

Expectation of Fair Treatment from Institutions of Authority

Sofiya Bogatyreva, a Moscow writer, described the Soviet Union as a society where 'everyone looked at everyone else with distrust, they avoided meeting another person's gaze, and everyone—acquaintance or stranger—was seen as a secret enemy'.[6] Bogatyreva's impressions could not be tested through mass surveys of the Soviet population. The regime did not allow it. Surveys were none the less conducted on the émigré population. Low levels of trust in the Soviet system and the use of alternative, non-legal methods to obtain private gains, were reported in a survey of 1,161 Soviet émigrés living in Israel, and published in 1984.[7] These émigrés considered *protektsiya* (patronage) and *svyazi* (connections) crucial to change an unwelcome assignment or to get an untalented son into a good university department. It would be improper to generalize the result of this survey to all population of the Soviet Union at the time: the interviewees had already rejected life under the Soviet system, managed to escape from it and start life in a different country.[8] They did not qualify as a random sample, because of an in-built mechanism of self-selection.

Only with the end of the Soviet Union, could mass surveys be carried out in Russia and the former Soviet republics. The *New Russia Barometer* (*NRB*), for instance, is a series of surveys that monitors mass response to the transformation of post-communist societies.[9] The 1994 *NRB* survey showed that distrust was rife in the case of institutions of authority—such

Table 2.1 Expectation of fair treatment (%)

	Yes	No	Difference
Post Office	78	22	56
Doctor	67	33	34
Bank	67	33	34
Grocery Shop	55	45	10
Social Security Office	49	51	−2
Municipal Office	30	70	−40
Police	30	70	−40

Note: Responding to the question 'if you had a grievance, would you expect fair treatment from . . .'

Source: Rose (1995).

as the police, courts, and civil servants—and political institutions, such as Parliament and political parties. These institutions obtained an average distrust value of 71 per cent. The highest level of trust (though still very low) was enjoyed by the church (51 per cent) and, before the Chechnya war, the army (41 per cent).[10]

The authors of this survey then inquired into the level of trust of local institutions, as opposed to national ones. It is plausible that the closer the institution is to the citizen, the greater the confidence he has in it. Table 2.1 reports the results. The majority of Russians, in 1994, expected to be treated fairly by some institutions, such as the post office, the bank, and the grocery store. Moreover, doctors, a traditionally helping profession, were believed to treat people fairly. The picture that emerges from the 1994 *NRB* mitigates the impression of generalized distrust offered by Sofiya Bogatyreva. Only some institutions of authority proved to be scarcely trusted by the public at the local level, namely the municipal office and the police. Officials and the police are precisely those authorities more directly concerned with the protection of citizens. In order to have a more detailed picture of attitudes towards officials and the police, we now turn to a survey that focuses directly on them.

A survey administered in 1993–4 by a team at the University of Glasgow to respondents in five countries in the Former Soviet Union (FSU) and East Central Europe (ECE), tapped expectation of fair (or unfair) treatment from government officials, what the authors call 'sub-jective competence'.[11] The question asked was:

Suppose there were some problems you had to take to a government office—for example, a problem about tax or housing. Do you think you would be treated fairly by officials in that office?

In the Ukraine and Russia, two-thirds of the general public and three-quarters of Members of Parliament interviewed did not expect fair treat-ment in their day-to-day dealings with government officials. The picture that obtains in the former Czechoslovakia is substantially different: only one-third of the public and one-sixth of the MPs expected to be treated unfairly by officials. The authors also found that more than half of those who thought that they could get fair treatment in the Ukraine and Russia, spontaneously added the view that they would have to use bribes or influence to get it. In effect, they were saying that without bribes or con-nections they would not be treated fairly.

Those who expected unfair treatment from officials were not opposing the government. Quite the contrary. In the Czech or Slovak cases, those who 'completely distrusted' their government still expected fairer treat-ment than those who 'completely trusted' their government in Russia or the Ukraine. Respondents were also asked whether they 'supported' or

Table 2.2   Public's expectation of fair treatment by officials (%)

	Ukraine	Russia	Hungary	Slovakia	Czech.Rep.
Amongst the public					
Yes	12	16	43	53	61
Only with connections or bribes	20	17	7	14	5
No	67	67	50	33	34
Amongst MPs					
Yes	21	19	79	n.a.	79
Only with connections or bribes	5	8	4	n.a.	5
No	74	73	17	n.a.	16

Source: Miller, Grodeland, and Koshechkina (1999). Based on 5,769 (hour long) interviews with representative samples of the public, Nov.–Dec. 1993, and 504 interviews with MPs, Oct.–Dec. 1994.

'opposed' the government of their country. The same patterns obtained: 'supporters' of their government in Russia and the Ukraine expected worse treatment than 'opponents' of the government of Slovakia or the Czech Republic. This check helps to establish that negative expectations of fair treatment were not expressing general political dissatisfaction.[12]

The above data refer to expectations of fair treatment from state officials. Legal institutions do not fare better. In a survey conducted by the Centre for Sociological Research of Moscow University, Russians were asked whether they 'think that legal institutions protect the interest of all the citizens equally'. In 1993, 5.1 per cent answered in the positive while in 1994 those in agreement fell to 4.4 per cent. The majority replied that only those who possess 'power' have their interests protected by legal institutions (79.0 and 82.6 per cent for the years 1993 and 1994 respectively).[13] People seem to avoid the police as well: Sergei, who in August 1993 was hiding in his mother's flat in order to avoid racketeers, told *The Independent*: 'I can't go to the police. They take an interest only if someone has actually been shot . . . Anyway, you can't trust the Moscow police.'[14] Surveys do reflect this perception: the 1994 *NRB* reported that 70 per cent of Russians do not expect fair treatment from the police, the legitimate supplier of protection.[15] A poll conducted in Nizhnii Novgorod found

Table 2.3 Public's expectation of fair treatment (without bribes etc.) correlated to attitudes to government

From people who	All	Ukraine	Russia	Hungary	Slovakia	Czech Rep.
completely trust the govt.	55	n.a.	28	n.a.	76	87
mostly trust the govt.	48	28	25	61	64	74
neither	42	17	18	5	64	65
mostly distrust govt.	26	9	13	42	46	50
completely distrust the govt.	17	8	1	3	34	32
'support' govt.	48	30	22	60	65	71
neither	32	12	15	45	52	65
'oppose' govt.	22	8	13	34	45	42

Source: Miller, Grodeland, and Koshechkina, 1999: ch. 1.

that 46 per cent of crime victims felt they could not turn to the police for help.[16] Many Russians are more afraid of the police than they are of the mafia, claimed a similar report published in *Izvestiya*.[17]

Certainly Russians do not have much confidence in some crucial institutions of authority. Distrust in the Soviet legal system—as it emerges from interviews with émigrés in the 1980s—appears justified. The Soviet legal system was far from being sheltered from political influences, nor were officials in charge of the Soviet state sufficiently bound by their own laws. This is most clearly demonstrated by the judicial system's surrender to the KGB's efforts to fight Soviet dissidents. Rather than the impartial application of the law, the preservation and the running of the system guided judges.

Do perceptions translate in practice? In other words, do Russians actually try to avoid legal institutions and the police because of the perceptions they have of these institutions? A detailed exposé of the militia appeared in the Perm's daily *Mestnoe Vremya* with the title: 'My militia will not kill me—I am grateful for this', by journalist Boris Stashevskii (9 Dec. 1994). He reports a dozen cases of abuse of power and harassment from the local police: car drivers are stopped and fined by the traffic police on various pretexts and receipts are rarely given; people brought to the police offices are routinely beaten up; calls for help to the militia are not answered or, if answered, patrols often do not show up.[18] He concludes as follows:

It is no secret that in the last few years, people very rarely go to the militia to report stolen cars, minor fraud, burglaries, and pick-pocketing. The probability of revealing such crimes and receiving recompense for damage is practically equal to zero. More and more often you hear that owners of stolen cars get their cars back with the help of friends. It is safer, quicker and more profitable—and I am not referring to the pocket, but rather to one's own health.

These anecdotes suggest that people avoid turning to the police for help. To what extent Russian businessmen also settle dispute outside the provision of the law? In order to elucidate this question, we turn to data on the use of the court of arbitration.

Arbitrazh[19]

Arbitration courts are special courts. Considerations related to them should not be taken as an indication of the use of courts in general in the

Russian Federation. These courts have broad jurisdiction over commercial disputes, including claims arising out of contractual breaches and property claims, and over disputes arising out of government activities. They are the place where a businessman having a dispute with another businessman would turn in order to settle the issue. The study of these courts could shed light on a more general question, namely on whether the state is a credible supplier of protection.

Any Russian legal business entity can bring disputes to the Arbitration courts. Ordinary civil courts handle all other cases. The adoption of the new Law on *Arbitrazh* Courts in July 1991 and the subsequent enactment of the *Arbitrazh* Procedural Code in April 1992 mark the birthday of The *Arbitrazh* court system, which exists in addition to the already functioning system of civil courts.[20] The jurisdiction of the different systems depends on the status of the parties involved: claims involving legal entities are filed with the *Arbitrazh* courts. *Arbitrazh* courts exist at the regional and republican levels within the Russian Federation.[21] In 1995 a new procedural code was adopted. The main innovation consists in the creation of an appellate system and the requirement that petitioners bear responsibility for proving their case to the court.[22]

Two departments operate within each court, the 'civil' department and the 'administrative' department.[23] The latter deals with claims arising out of government activities and decisions (such as taxation and privatization procedures), while the 'civil' department deals with contractual breaches and property claims. Each court, up to the Supreme Court of Arbitration of Russia, passes sentences.[24] Every judge is independent in his or her application of the code. Prior to 1995, a three-judge panel conducted trials. With the introduction of the new 1995 code, a single judge now hears cases at the trial level.[25]

The *Arbitrazh* system was not created *ex novo* to meet the new demand for services of dispute settlement and protection created by the collapse of the planning system and the legalization of market transactions. It is the direct successor of the former *Gosarbitrazh* system, a part of the management of the planned economy. The Soviet definition of the term *Arbitrazh* reads, 'in the USSR, *Arbitrazh* is a state organ which settles disputes concerning property between state, communal, and co-operative institutions, enterprises, and organizations'.[26] *Gosarbitrazh* decided an enormous number of cases. By 1938, 330,000 cases were litigated in this system.[27] In the 1980s, 800,000 cases were litigated on average a year in the

Table 2.4 Number of decisions at the Russian *Arbitrazh* courts by year, percentage of cases delayed at trial level, real GDP and inflation

Year	Court decisions					Real GDP (growth rates over same period of the prev. year)	Inflation Rate
	Civil	Change on the previous year (%)	Administrative	Change on the previous year (%)	Cases delayed at trial level (%)		
1991	358,000	—	N/A	—	—	−12.8	100.3
1992	330,000	−8.4	5,446	—	N/A	−19.2	1,468.0
1993	264,447	−30.0	10,857	+99.3	3.4	−12.0	911.3[a]
1994	190,471	−27.9	17,610	+62.1	1.5	−15.0	214.8
1995	213,662	+12.1	23,629	+34.1	1.6	−4.2	131.4
1996	244,467	+14.4	44,272	+87.3	3.6	−6.0	21.8
1997	258,999	+5.9	80,043	+80.7	4.1	0.9	11.0
1998	280,583	+8.3	115,108	+43.8	3.3	−4.6	84.5

[a] January over December.

Sources: Civil disputes: Official data from the Supreme Court of Arbitration, quoted in Pistor (1996: 71) for 1991–4; in Hendley (1998a: 381) for 1995–6; collected by the author at the Supreme Court of Arbitration (Moscow) for 1997–98. Administrative disputes: Official data from the Supreme Court of Arbitration, quoted in Hendley (1998a: 381) for 1992–1996; collected by the author at the Supreme Court of Arbitration (Moscow) for 1997–8. Data on GDP compiled from: UN/ECE: 1995: 70; UN/ECE: 1997: 61; UN/ECE: 1999: 16. Data on inflation compiled from: UN/ECE, 1994: 75; UN/ECE: 1996: 96; UN/ECE: 1997: 120; UN/ECE: 1998: 17; UN/ECE: 1999: 23.

Soviet Union. In Russia alone, 358,191 cases were decided in 1990, and 190,220 in the first half of 1991.[28]

Post-Soviet *Arbitrazh* courts are not idle. As Table 2.1 shows, the number of civil and administrative disputes settled by the *Arbitrazh* court system amounted to almost 400,000 in 1998.[29]

The number of civil disputes decided decreased significantly from 1992 and 1994 and then began to recover (Table 2.4). The number of administrative cases has increased constantly, to the extent that in 1998 it amounts to almost 30 per cent of all cases decided.[30] The court administration keeps a record of how long it takes to process a case. The number of cases delayed ranged from 1.5 to 4.1 of the total cases decided in the period 1993–98. Among the civil cases, cases of non-payment dominate the courts from 1993 onwards, when they account roughly for 50 per cent of all civil cases disputes. Disputes involving bank services (credit contracts and bank accounts) account for roughly 5 per cent of all cases in *Arbitrazh* courts up to 1996, when the cases started to drop in number.[31]

Clearly, the courts of arbitration are operating. Should we conclude that they are quick, cheap, and effective? In order to answer these questions, we explore the length of decision, cost of applying, and the effectiveness of their enforcement mechanisms.

The time limit for taking a decision is strict and Russian *Arbitrazh* outperforms most of their counterparts in developed market economies. The results are quite stunning: judges do manage to decide cases rather speedily, as testified by the data on delays at trial level.[32] There are internal provisions that help maintain such efficiency. Decisions on civil disputes should take no more than two months,'while decisions related to non-property matters must be taken within a month.[33] The Supreme Court of Arbitration is putting pressure on lower courts to decide cases relating to the civil sphere (i.e. the cases dealt by the 'civil' department) in one month.[34] According to Judge Tat'yana Aleksandrovna Trapeznikova of Perm *Arbitrazh* Court, the average time this takes is 2–3 weeks, if the documents are well-presented. If the documents are unclear, supplementary evidence may be requested and the decision time will be longer.[35] Judges interviewed by Hendley also tended to blame the parties for delays.[36] Moreover, the Supreme *Arbitrazh* Court keeps track of the performance of the lower-level courts, and in fact, for each individual judge, data are kept on their performance, including the ability to meet deadlines as well as the number of their decisions appealed against.[37] It is not clear whether violation of the two-month rule has an effect on pay-raises and promotions within the system. Judges at the Saratov *Arbitrazh* court believed it did. At any rate, information about the compliance level of each judge was known within the court and would affect an individual's reputation.[38]

The original fee structure for claims to be filed with the *Arbitrazh* courts depended both on the nature of the claim and on its value.[39] Claims related to property were charged with 10 per cent of the value of the claim, which had to be paid up front by the plaintiff. For disputes concerning the conclusion, change or cancellation of contracts, a fixed 1,000 rubles was charged. From 1996, the 10 per cent fee (*gosposhlina*) was lowered, and a new scale now applies. The scale is based on the amount sought in the case and slides downwards as the amount involved increases.[40] If the plaintiff wins the case the defendant will reimburse him, while, if he loses, the money goes to the state. The courts do not keep the money 'in house'. Rather they are paid into the federal budget and only a fraction is then reallocated to the *Arbitrazh* courts.[41] A ruling of the Supreme *Arbitrazh* Court sought to mitigate the impact of the *gosposhlina* by urging judges to make more frequent use of a provision in the *Arbitrazh* Procedural Code allowing them to postpone fee payment until a court decision was reached.[42] If the plaintiff can demonstrate that he has no cash,[43] he can ask for a delay on the payment of the fee, although every judge is free to require different evidence. For the period 1996–7, petitions were, when filed, generally successful, as documented by Hendley.[44]

We turn to the last and thornier issue concerning the ability of the court to enforce decisions. The enforcement of a sentence (*reshenie*) imposed by the court is a rather complex matter.[45] Attached to the sentence, there is an order. With the order, the decision can be executed and the law obliges the losing party to comply with the decision.[46] The sentence does not become legally enforceable until one month after it has been made.[47] In cases where the losing party does not comply with the court order, the court can stop all financial and banking operations of the non-complying party until the order is completed. The court is empowered to issue an order to a bank or any other institution holding the funds of the award debtor, to seize and pay an appropriate amount to the petitioner of the award.[48] To obtain such a ruling, the petitioner must file a motion in the arbitration court with an attached certificate of non-compliance with the award signed by the bailiff.[49] In other words, it is the petitioner who must ensure that the decision is enforced.[50] If the liquid assets of the debtor are not sufficient to satisfy the award, the court may issue an order to execute the award on physical property of the debtor through the bailiff (*sudebnyi ispolnitel'*) of the civil court.[51]

How effective and reliable is the banking system? Entrepreneurs interviewed in 1992 in St Petersburg reported that banking delays in payment between different cities of the Russian Federation were as long as four or five months. In several cases, payments initiated in the first quarter of 1992 were not cleared by November 1992. Problems with inter-republic transfers were even more severe. Some entrepreneurs reported that they routinely travelled to collect payments directly from their customers in other republics.[52]

The national average for inter-regional transfers used to be two months until 1994 and only recently have efforts been made to reduce it.[53] According to Johnson, it took between 14 to 17 days on average to clear transactions between banks, but this period could easily stretch to over three weeks.[54] In the period 1992–4, a delay of even a few weeks could lead to a significant loss of income due to the high level of inflation.[55] Despite Boffito's drastic characterization of the Russian banking system as 'chaotic and primitive',[56] technological innovations are reducing payment delays. For instance, a new, non-state transfer system called SWIFT that rapidly clears transactions among its members has been recently set up, and over forty commercial banks now participate in it.[57] Boffito's words however do not appear to apply to provincial Russia. For instance, innovations such as SWIFT had not reached the city of Perm in 1994 and 1995. Rather, banks relied on the postal system, as it emerged from a case heard at Perm *Arbitrazh* Court in 1994. This case dealt with what appeared as a non-payment on the part of Permagropromsnab—a kolkhoz turned private agricultural enterprise—to Rybinskie Motory, a producer of agricultural equipment based in the city of Rybinsk. Permagropromsnab had in fact asked its bank to pay the 194,544,640 roubles into the account of Rybinskie Motory. After some months, Rybinskie Motory filed a suit against Permagropromsnab for failing to pay. A further inquiry established that six different branches of various banks had dealt with the payment notice, which never reached its final destination. The lack of an electronic clearance system meant that the various branches relied on the postal system. From a legal point of view, the payment responsibility laid with Permagropromsnab who had to pay a penalty for the delayed payment. Permagropromsnab then filed a suit against all six bank branches to recover the penalty paid to Rybinskie Motory. Deficiencies in the banking system gave rise to further delays and litigation.[58]

Inefficiencies in the banking system are not the only factor affecting enforcement of decisions. In the Soviet period, enterprises had only one bank account, while, in the early 1990s, the rules changed and allowed banks to open several accounts. These accounts could be used to hide money. When this loophole was closed, new ones opened. Since many enterprises operate in cash, it is harder to establish their financial situation.[59]

If the debtor does not hold sufficient liquid assets to satisfy the award, the court may issue an order to execute the award on physical property of the debtor through the bailiff of the civil court. The bailiff is then obliged to find the defendant and locate assets equal to the amount of the damage within twenty days of the order. This process includes enumerating the assets, seizing them, and auctioning them off. Auctioning assets may take months. In Saratov, of the twenty-five enforcement actions pending in July 1996, only five stood reasonable chance of collection, according to the local *sudebnyi ispolnitel'*.[60]

The *sudebnyi ispolnitel'* is not part of an enforcement arm within the court, but rather works for courts of general jurisdiction and most of his time is spent enforcing orders by other courts.[61] The resources available at the Perm bailiff office are insubstantial: the office consists of three women and a man, all over the age of 40. According to a judge, they are 'all easily frightened by whoever raises his voice'.[62] They do not have at their disposal the use of a truck or a car, and either use public transport or their own cars to locate the assets. Once they have found the assets, they cannot store them in a warehouse and often leave them in their office. A similar situation obtains in Saratov. Also, in Saratov and Ekaterinburg the majority of *sudebnye ispolniteli* are women and—writes Hendley—'often call on their husbands to help them haul heavy machinery'.[63]

The bailiffs were under the spotlight for events concerning the case of the financial firm Nashe Delo,[64] which was responsible for a case of fraud in Perm. Nashe Delo promised windfall interest rates and convinced roughly 150,000 Permians to deposit a total of nearly 40 billion roubles. Overnight, the executive director disappeared and reports emerged that the money had been transferred to Switzerland through Chase Manhattan Bank. Eventually, a civil suit was filed against Nashe Delo and, according to the prosecution magistrate's order, all items of furniture, office equipment and files were to be confiscated. The night after the order was issued, unknown people entered the office and emptied it. The next day a picket of citizens formed outside the office to prevent others from stealing more from the office. The bailiffs did not appear until three days after the order had been issued, even though the case had aroused a great deal of attention in the public and the local papers. Claimants have reason to distrust the enforcement system as they have no assurance that valuable and marketable assets will actually be confiscated, at least not without a considerable time lag.[65] Hendley recounts a simliar case of diverted assets, in the case of a stock pyramid scheme in Saratov in 1995.

A Saratov *sudebnyi ispolnitel'* recounted her unsuccessful efforts to help the victims of stock pyramid schemes over the past few years. At one point in 1995, as many as twenty victims would come to her every day with court judgements. According to their bank statements and other records, the defendants had no money. Yet to this *sudebnyi ispolnitel'*, it was absolutely clear that the bank funds had been dispersed in illegal ways, such as overpaying for worthless assets. She is sure that she could have unravelled these illegals transactions if she had had the time, authority, and resources.[66]

The above stories point to the difficulties of finding diverted assets. It is rather common for the losing defendant to transfer assets to family members or other trusted colleagues. Court officials are limited to seizing assets that are owned by the defendant, and, differently from the USA, have no means to investigate beyond one company.[67]

Complaints on the ability of the court to enforce its decisions have been voiced through the years. The Chairman of the Higher *Arbitrazh* Court has strongly criticized the courts capacity to enforce decisions.[68] Hendley concludes her 1998 study of the court pointing out that 'for the most part, present-day Russian economic actors neither fear nor respect *arbitrazh* courts'.[69] Even Hendley *et al.* find that the 328 enterprise managers they interviewed in 1997 identified the enforcement of judgements as the most serious obstacle to using *Arbitrazh* courts.[70]

The puzzle is then the following: why would people apply to the court even if the system is so inefficient in enforcing its decisions? First, let us examine the rise in administrative cases. These cases involve alleged state administration improprieties, such as confiscation of property by tax inspectors. If one has a grievance with the state, he could turn *only* to a court. The use of this court to redress state decisions is not an indication that entrepreneurs consider the state as a credible supplier of protection when they have disputes among themselves. If a tax has been unfairly applied to a firm, such firm can recover the money only through a court. The high number of administrative cases points to the fact that entrepreneurs perceive the state as predatory and unfair, but do not fear to challenge its decisions. Obviously, the fact that an applicant goes to court indicates that the relationship with the official 'failed', either they did not find a 'common language' or the official was not prepared to accommodate the needs of the business-person. Still, the high number of applications also points to the fact that applicants believe they can reverse the decision of the officials.[71] The 1995 decision to abolish the three-judge panel and have the cases decided at trial level by one judge surely improved efficiency and met the demand expressed by judges themselves.[72] A single judge may however be more easily influenced (or bribed) than a panel of three. If judges are not guided, for the most, by the application of the law, and there is nobody to lobby in favour of the state, the applicant has indeed a chance to win the case and reverse the decision taken by the official. Enforcing a decision that affects the state is not as difficult as in the case of non-state legal entities. State administrations have official bank accounts or can be ordered to reverse a decision. In case of taxes, the applicant can deduct some of the money he paid in excess from the subsequent year tax payment. Problems with enforcement appear limited. As discussed above, the cost of applying has been consistently lowered since 1994, and increasingly applicants are allowed to pay after the case has been heard.[73] The extensive use of courts produces an overly bureaucratized and legalistic society, where everybody has a grievance with the system but has also a chance to reverse the decision of an official at some different level of the system.

Civil cases decline sharply from 1992 to 1994 and then start to rise again. This initial decline could be attributed to the systemic change the court was going through in the period 1991–2. In the Soviet period, *Gosarbitrazh* provided an administrative procedure to harmonize enterprise relations before and during the implementation of the economic plan. The incentives to file a suit under the old system were different from the incentive to litigate a commercial dispute in the present system. In the past, it mainly served the purpose of allocating responsibilities in order to avoid future sanctions.[74] Furthermore, the cost of litigating was negligible and not incurred by the individuals filing a suit. On the contrary, from 1992 onwards the cost of litigation—which includes both court fees, fees for attorneys, and investment in time—was significant and was borne by the private litigant. Restructuring was complete by 1995, and from this date also courts were encouraged to delay the payment of fees. As the cost of applying went down, the number of cases increased. This trend took place while both GDP was decreasing and inflation rising.

Given that the costs of applying may have become relatively inexpensive and that delays may no longer consume the value of the resources recovered, nevertheless, why would a firm apply to the court for the recovery of a debt when it knows that the chances of recovering it are slim? An interesting finding of Hendley is that some entrepreneurs use complementary means to settle disputes. These individuals would first obtain an *Arbitrazh* court ruling and *then* use private means to enforce it. Private enforcers themselves review legal decisions before taking (illegal) action.[75] Private enforcers must perceive that it is less risky to enforce a legal decision. This indicates a tendency towards the privatization of enforcement. Although the complementary use of state and private enforcement explains a number of applications, there might be more. A significant sector of the economy is prepared to use courts to settle disputes with partners without much hope of recovering their assets. In order to find out 'why' they apply we might need to know 'who' they are.

The most comprehensive survey of business-people has been conducted by Vadim Radaev of the Russian Academy of Science in collaboration with the Moscow-based *Tsentr politicheskikh tekhnologii*. The respondents were 227 directors of state, non-state, and privatized (formerly state-owned) enterprises from twenty-one regions of Russia.[76] Who would turn to *Arbitrazh* as opposed to the other methods? Using factor and cluster analysis, the author groups the respondents of the survey into three groups, 'large and middle-sized businesses', 'small businesses who operate in a risky environment', and 'small businesses who operate in a "quiet" market segment'.[77]

All the large and middle-sized enterprises cluster in one group. Sixty-three per cent of respondents think that business breaches are common, while 50 per cent have themselves come across breaches of contracts 'often'. When they come across cheating behaviour, the majority of them (71 per cent) applies to the local *Arbitrazh* court. Only 25 per cent prefer to use informal ways to persuade unreliable partners, and none is in favour of using violent ways to recover assets. This group spends relatively little resources for protection and information gathering. Four-fifths of the enterprises the respondents belong to existed before 1994 and were state-owned, having been privatized in the 1990s. These enterprises are also large, employing an average of 2,226 people. They are mainly concentrated in industry, building, transport, retail trade, public catering, and consumer service. The business-people and managers in this group never started an enterprise themselves or, if they started one, did not leave their former job: in other words, the businesses they started were connected to the main enterprise.

The second group of respondents identified by the factor analysis consists of entrepreneurs operating only in small businesses. Almost all of them (98 per cent) consider breaches of obligations a 'frequent' phenomenon, and 70 per cent encounter such breaches constantly. Nor do they expect the situation to improve in the future. What is most significant for our purposes is that only 13 per cent are inclined to apply to the *Arbitrazh*

Table 2.5 Types of business

Type of business	Breaches of contracts	Remedies	Features
Large and middle-sized businesses	For 63% are 'common', 50% have themselves come across breaches 'often'	71%: Court of Arbitration; 25%: informal ways; 0%: violence	4/5 of the respondents work in enterprises that existed before 1994 and were state-owned, having been privatized in the 1990s. These enterprises are also large, employing an average of 2,226 people. Sectors: industry, building and transport, retail trade, public catering, and consumer service.
Small businesses who operate in a risky environment	98% consider breaches 'frequent'; 70% come across it themselves 'often'	57% informal negotiations; 20% violence ; 13% Court of Arbitration; 7% 'let it go'	94% are new and have no connection to the state; 69% were formed after 1992 Sectors: wholesale and retail trade, public catering, consumer and market services, and financial sector.
Small businesses who operate in a 'quiet' market segment	10% consider breaches 'frequent'; 0% came across it themselves 'often'	56% informal negotiations; 21% Court of Arbitration; 11% violence	High number of managers with little education; 32% of women-managers; 65% started their own business. Highest number of repeated, long-term trade relationships.

Source: Adapted from Radaev, 1998: 141–54.

court if cheated. The percentage of those willing to settle a dispute with the use of force is the highest of the three groups (20 per cent) while those willing to 'let it go' is 7 per cent. The majority will try to solve the problem by informal negotiations (57 per cent). This group also contains the smallest number of those prone to apply to militia in case of violent extortion and threats, and the highest number of those inclined to enlist the help of private protection agencies and criminal groups. Almost all of these enterprises (94 per cent) are new and have no connection to the state, 69 per cent were formed after 1992; they operate in the wholesale and retail trade, catering, consumer and market services, and financial sectors.

The third group of respondents also belongs to small business but differs quite sharply from the second. Only one in ten of the respondents in this group indicates breaches of obligations as a frequent feature of the Russian market environment, and nobody reported frequent encounters with such breaches. If a breach occurs, only 11 per cent is inclined to use force, while 21 per cent would turn to *Arbitrazh*, the majority (56 per cent) still preferring informal means of persuasion. This is the group where business-people have the closest connection to their partners and suppliers. The general picture that emerges is that of business-people operating in segments of the market that are predictable, quiet, and less profitable. An indication of this is that managers in this group have the lowest level of formal education and additional skills of the three groups.[78]

This survey is enlightening in a number of ways. It suggests that large enterprises, which were formerly state-owned and were privatized in the 1990s, form the majority of the customers of the *Arbitrazh* courts. There are at least three possible explanations for this. First, that they are simply inefficient managers. Although these enterprises have been privatized, no real change in the style and effectiveness of the management has occurred. The prediction would be that these enterprises can survive in the market economy as long as the state supports them in one form or another, otherwise they are destined to succumb to their competitors. The second possible explanation invokes a rational strategy: the managers of these enterprises are themselves involved in asset stripping and other predatory strategies described in Chapter 1. They are not deeply concerned with recovering assets. Indeed, it is more likely that they are themselves connected with companies that breach contracts, fail to pay for resources obtained, or do not deliver goods after being paid. They routinely apply to *Arbitrazh* and are therefore perceived as trying to recover assets in a legal way, but in effect squander resources they are not accountable for. Finally, in order to obtain certain loans and state subsidies, the firm must prove to have tried to recover bad debts.[79] This interpretation is compatible both with their propensity to use the court and the knowledge that the court itself is inefficient in enforcing its decisions.

Let us consider the possibility that some large enterprises are committed to production and efficient economic performance. They might want to use the court in order to send a signal. The cost of non-compliance would be loss of reputation for the guilty party while the victim of the breach would find it less costly to apply since it can postpone payment.[80] Further data must be collected in order to evaluate the likelihood of this scenario. Hendley wrote in 1998 that 'non-compliance with *arbitrazh* court decisions has no adverse reputational effect. It has become so commonplace that few pay any heed'.[81]

Smaller businesses in the private sector inhabit a world that is less stable than the one populated by the large and middle-sized enterprises. In this world, the time-scale is also likely to be shorter and therefore cheating more frequent. One takes more risks and faces more cheating. When cheating occurs, the entrepreneur is less likely to believe that fear of a bad reputation will be sufficient to induce payment by negligent partners. Moreover, small firms cannot afford to wait and forego assets as much as larger ones. This leads them to search for effective enforcement outside the scope of the law (incidentally, such a strategy increases the reputation of the cheated partner for not turning a blind eye to cheating behaviour).

In conclusion, courts are used, yet it is not an indication that 'law matters'. Rather it might be the case that a segment of the business world lawfully predates the resources they had acquired as a result of a less than perfect transition. Another segment engaging in trading and profitable business activities distrusts courts, does not use them, but cannot afford to be cheated.[82] The data we have do not entirely rule out the hypothesis that a good reputation matters and that large firms have an incentive to behave in a virtuous way. Some institutional developments are indeed facilitating such behaviour, such as the reduction in the cost of the application fee.[83] One should however evaluate any hope for change in a context where private protectors abound. These actors have an interest in 'promoting' the use of their services and hampering the development of interpersonal trust. In the next chapter, we consider the wide varieties of protectors available in Russia.

3

Varieties of Protectors

If the demand for protection that accompanies the spread of market trans-actions is not met by the state, a demand for *alternative* sources of protec-tion is then expected to arise. It cannot, however, be argued that demand will inevitably be met, otherwise we will yield to functionalist reasoning.[1] Lack of protection implies that there will be more opportunities to meet that demand, and hence that meeting it will be more profitable than else-where. However, *demand* for alternative sources of protection alone is not sufficient to explain the emergence of protection agencies. A *supply* of people trained in the use of violence must also be present on the market.[2] If the laws of a country do not pose enough constraints on the activities of such a supply, individuals trained in the use of violence not only meet the demand for protection, they can also force it on reluctant customers through the use of violence.

Was such a supply present in Russia at the time of the transition to the market? In order to answer this question, we first need to focus on two resources needed in this trade, violence and weapons.

The ability to make credible threats is crucial to the role of a protector. He must be able to inflict punishment. The violent resources available to him to inflict punishment must be greater than the combined violent resources of those parties he protects. Both parties must know that in case of 'misbehaviour', punishment is feasible and, for the protector, not too costly.[3] People trained in the use of violence are therefore in great demand in this market. They usually come from a few specific quarters. Vigilantes, ex-soldiers, private guards, prison inmates, bandits, individ-uals who enjoy violent activities provide a pool of potential suppliers.[4]

To organize an efficient firm providing protection, it is also necessary to have a minimal level of equipment, most importantly weapons. Below, I review the evidence for Russia that points to the presence of both people trained in the use of violence who became suddenly unemployed at the time of the transition, and a vast amount of weapons easily available.

The greater the amount of unemployed, the higher the chance of finding among the newly unemployed people trained in or accustomed to using violence. It has been estimated that over the three-year period 1987–9 economic reform was responsible for 3 million people losing their jobs in industry, only 20 per cent of whom were offered suitable alternative employment.[5] Prime Minister V. Chernomyrdin stated that unemployment in Russia stood at 4.5 million at the end of 1991.[6]

A number of servicemen were made 'redundant' in the early 1990s. At the end of January 1992, Viktor Barannikov, chief of Russia's security service, announced a cut in staff from 36,000 to 2,800, a reduction unprecedented in KGB history. Those retired include chauffeurs, medical personnel, highly skilled specialists (in particular 'code crackers' and experts in computer security).[7] Twenty-five thousand officers of the former Soviet Army were dismissed on political grounds in 1991. The Russian Defence Ministry's press officer announced on 2 February 1993 that between 40,000 and 50,000 officers would be discharged every year.[8] The Army newspaper *Krasnaya Zvezda* published data on cadre officers' discharges for 1992–4, as shown in Table 3.1. In November 1996, President Yeltsin ordered 15 per cent of Russian army personnel to be cut during 1997.[9] A series of dismissals affected the police as well. For example, in the period 1987–8, 25,000 policemen were discharged on various grounds, and a further 32,000 were dismissed in 1989.[10] This led the force to be understaffed. Moscow's Main Department for Internal Affairs was short of about 4,000 agents in 1989. Officers were also underpaid and left of their own will. The best-trained and equipped forces of the MVD were offered a three-year contract and a miserable 200 roubles a month in 1989.[11] In the first six months of 1990, over 100 skilled law enforcement experts in the Khabarovsk Territory left their jobs because of low salaries.[12] An Interior Ministry spokesman voiced the concern that the Ministry lacked 60 per cent of skilled experts considered necessary to effectively fight organized crime, and that the equipment available to officers was 'just nothing to talk about'.[13] According to figures revealed at a closed conference on organized crime by Russian Interior Minister Viktor

Table 3.1 Reasons for discharge of officers from Russian Military, 1992–4

Reason for discharge	1992 (since 1 May)	1993	1994 (first six months)
Completion of service obligation	13,530	13,823	6,341
Personnel organization measures	23,182	15,005	5,263
Not meeting the established requirements for service members	10,358	10,974	2,680
Actions besmirching the honour of the service	2,603	4,040	1,282
Other reasons	9,490	25,191	10,925
Total number of cadre officers discharged	59,163	69,033	26,491

Source: Krasnaya Zvezda, 2 Aug. 1994.

Erin, 63,000 professionals left the militia in 1992 and one in every five of them 'went over to the enemy'.[14]

The collapse of the Soviet Union also led to the collapse of the network of sports clubs supported by the regime. Some sportsmen—such as wrestlers, weightlifters, bodybuilders, and boxers—were in a position to sell their services on the market for protection.

Sport was greatly valued by the Soviet Union. It was regarded as 'the active relaxation of the workers' and 'the way to develop the individual harmoniously'.[15] In 1978, 52 million (one-third of the total population in the 10–60 age group) were taking part in sports and 209 educational establishments provided instruction for would-be sports teachers and coaches. Each major economic and social concern had its own sporting facilities and employed instructors. In 1972 'sports clubs' existed at 282 factories, 326 specialized secondary schools, and 22 collective and state farms. 'Sports clubs' formed the elite of the network of sporting associations, and often supplied athletes to national and international competitions (some 218,000 'physical culture groups' also existed, but rarely provided athletes at national level). In 1976, 56,326 professional athletes were employed by state structures.[16] Sporting instructors were the first to be laid off by firms. 'Sportsmen were the Regime's gems, well fed, cuddled, allowed to travel abroad, all acquainted with each other,' declared Lev

Brekhman, a sports doctor. 'When the regime collapsed, they found themselves without the money to buy decent food and no skills to find an honest job.'[17]

Russia is a world leader in the production of arms, which can be bought without difficulty, both legally and illegally. Lack of morale and pressing economic problems pushed many members of the security services and the army to sell a considerable number of weapons on the black market. According to Gennadii Deinega, of the St Petersburg police investigation department, the local firearms black market offers, for the most part, weapons stolen from the army, KGB, and police units. Another significant source is the so-called 'conversion business'. Warrant officers at military warehouses often sell stolen weapons on the black market that are later listed as 'written off and destroyed'.[18] In 1993, the Defence Ministry reported 6,430 instances of weapons theft from military depots, a 75 per cent increase over the previous year.[19]

The Russian military remains 'the major and stable source' of arms used by criminals and those fighting in regions plagued by ethnic conflict, according to the Russian Ministry of Internal Affairs.[20] Aleksandr Dement'ev, the deputy head of the Ministry's Department for Combating Organised Crime, told *Interfax* that the bulk of illegally held arms came from warehouses of the Defence Ministry. He added that arms were also stolen directly from manufacturing enterprises. In 1994, the Ministry investigated a group who tried to deliver 4,350 hand guns from an Izhevsk arms plant to Grozny in Chechnya. Dement'ev said 1,247 thefts of arms and ammunition were reported in 1994, while nearly 17,000 crimes were committed involving firearms.[21] In the Ural city of Nizhnii Tagil, gangsters broke into an army tank training ground, overpowered security guards and seized a T-90 army tank. Subsequently, they used it in a battle with Muslim market traders, one of whom was killed and two seriously wounded, according to a Reuter report (3 Apr. 1993). Similarly, Konstantin Tsyganov, a Ekaterinburg crime boss, and his men 'hijacked a tank from a military testing ground and parked it in the central square' in order to scare off a band of Chechens.[22]

Economically pressed army soldiers and officers are not the only suppliers of arms. A steady flow of weapons also comes from 'amateur manufactories': 'Any turner who has the basic skills can make hand-guns,' says Deinega. Prices are not high: at the St Petersburg Sennoi market in 1991, hand-guns were priced between 3,000 and 10,000 roubles, while a submachine gun cost 100,000 roubles.[23]

Poorly paid militia members, discharged army officers and soldiers, and sportsmen who found themselves suddenly unemployed were ready to take up the new opportunities offered by the private market for protection.

The *Krysha*

In Russian slang, the word for protection is *krysha* (lit. 'roof'). It was used during the Soviet period to refer to front activities for Committee of State Security (KGB), Military Intelligence (GRU), and Ministry of Internal Affairs (MVD) agents both in the country and abroad. Cultural institutions, publishing houses, embassies, and ministries all supplied a cover to people engaged in intelligence gathering. Since the Soviet Union collapsed, *krysha* refers to protection against ordinary criminals and 'unprofessional' racketeers, unruly business partners, and competitors. A *krysha* may ensure tax evasion and help in finding investment and credit opportunities. A Russian businessman, in his testimony to a US Senate committee, maintains that to operate a successful business in Moscow one must 'pay the right government officials' and 'purchase a *krysha*, . . . which has come to mean protection. The more important you are, the higher the roof must be.'[24] Reputable newspapers advise Russians to obtain a sound protection before starting any business. The search for a safe 'roof' is considered by *Komsomol'skaya Pravda* as the 'the most important element in the modern business world'.[25] Very practical suggestions on the pros and cons of various 'roofs' were given to entrepreneurs by *Argumenty i Fakty*.[26] Sportsmen and security personnel started to offer private protection in a variety of ways. Below, we review them.

Privately Sold State Protection

In an effort to raise money and reduce the outflow of quality personnel to private security agencies, the state itself started to sell private protection. In 1989, the Interior Ministry (MVD) issued an order allowing local Soviet policemen to enter into contracts with the co-operatives to provide security services for commercial establishments.[27] In 1989, contracts for such services totalling 600,000 roubles were signed by the Moscow militia (in 1989 a rouble was approximately one dollar). The Union of Veterans of

Afghanistan and Moscow police formed a joint venture in 1991.[28] The head of the MVD suggested that policemen might form private co-operatives, which would be supervised by their own department.[29] A law passed in August 1992 allowed units within the MVD to offer 'extrade-partmental protection'. Mark Galeotti, an expert on policing and security in the former Soviet Union, writes,

Most police commands include a department known as the Extra-Depart-mental Guard (*Vnevedomstvennaya okhrana*) which is precisely there to offer [private protection] services. In some cases this is provided by regular police attached to the unit (and thus not available for 'proper' police work), in others by officers in effect moonlighting on their own time, but on behalf of their employer. Other agencies often provide such services, from army garrisons to Border Troops.[30]

The police ensure that potential customers are informed of the available services. In 1994, foreign companies in Moscow received by fax an adver-tisement from the city police offering a variety of protection services. Seven thousand roubles (then a little more than $US3) was quoted as the price to employ a policeman for one hour to protect one's business.[31] Where cash is short, the police accept payment in kind. In faraway Siberia, a Tadzhik fruit and vegetable import company pays for police protection in radio equipment and cars imported from the Far East.[32] A Russian–German joint venture called Malkom was obtaining extra pro-tection from a very heavily armed police unit specially formed for the purpose. Subsequently, the special protection was taken over by the Extra-Departmental Guard. In this way, Malkom obtains protection from what is in effect a private protection agency, which has a market advan-tage over other agencies because it can ignore the restrictions on weapons (since it is a police unit) even though it is full-time attached to Malkom. Malkom first was paying for these services by subsidizing a local school and allegedly providing generous gifts to police officers, including the region's police chief. Afterwards, it simply paid a fee.[33]

Extra police protection is also available to criminals. Vasilii Naumov, the head of a Moscow gang, the Koptevskaya criminal group, was assas-sinated in January 1997. It later emerged that his bodyguards were mem-bers of Saturn, an elite police commando unit. He had simply hired them through the *Vnevedomstvennaya okhrana* in order to protect his company, Miranda.[34] This instance may be interpreted in two different ways: either Naumov was paying off the local police by signing a lucrative contract

with the Extra-Departmental Guard, or he was in real need of extra protection, being unable to protect himself and his business. The police are
either taking bribes or protecting (rather badly) criminals.[35]

Since criminal protectors offer protection services beyond the limits set
by the law, some policemen compete directly with criminals and double
as racketeers or private protectors unconstrained by the law. For instance,
in the city of Tol'yatti a *militseiskaya krysha* [militia-provided protection]
appears to be operating according to the rules of criminality. Officers as
high-ranking as a lieutenant colonel are involved in racketeering and
rumoured to be behind the murder of colleagues that threatened to
expose their activities.[36] *Kriminal'naya Khronika* reported in 1995 of a band
called 'white cross', formed by militia officers and headed by a man called
Makeev.[37]

It may be the case that the Ministry of Internal Affairs has not pondered
a perverse by-product of providing protection only to some commercial
outlets: assuming that selective police protection is effective, thieves will
be deterred from stealing from premises that enjoy extra police protection. Once these protected outlets become known to thieves, unprotected
agents will easily be identified and crime will tend to be more concentrated in those places. Since protection is selective, it will be easier to spot
the unprotected enterprises and target them.[38] The choice for entrepreneurs is between paying for extra police protection or being exposed to
greater danger. The effect of such a policy is to shift the burden of crime
onto the segment of the public, which does not pay the extra fee to the
police officers. This in turn gives unprotected entrepreneurs a strong
incentive to hire extra protection.

The use of privately sold state protection is not an indication that the
state is fulfilling its role, just as the use of the Court of Arbitration is not an
indication that the law works in Russia. On the contrary, it indicates that
state protection is available to those who pay.

Private Security Firms

Private Security Firms (PSFs), a feature of post-Soviet Russia, are another
possible 'roof'. Reportedly 500 such firms sprang up in Russia around
1989 and at least fifteen licensed training camps existed outside Moscow.
By the end of 1999, 6,775 private security firms and 4,612 armed security
services (attached to a specific parent firm) were registered in Russia.
Licensed security personnel stood at 196,266 people,[39] while estimates of

the State Duma Security Committee (reported in *Moscow Times*, 31 Oct. 1995) suggest a total figure of 800,000 employees. Unregistered firms are also operating. The KGB claimed to have checked 6,000 such firms during one operation directed against them.[40] Unlicensed firms, according to *Argumenty i Fakty* (22/1997), employ no less than 200,000 people.[41]

A law passed in April 1992 allowed security firms and detective agencies to buy arms, including rifles. A new law 'on Private Detectives and Security' was passed in 1995. This law, as Galeotti writes, grants firms 'considerable powers of surveillance, search and even arrest, giving them far more latitude than envisaged in the 1992 law'. A firm must still obtain a licence to operate from the local police (cost was the equivalent of $US500 in 1997) and cannot employ individuals with a criminal record, although this requirement can be bypassed by registering one as a 'probationer' attached to a registered investigator.[42]

PSFs are staffed mainly by former officers of the KGB, the MVD, the GRU, and veterans of the Afghan and Chechen wars.[43] According to a study of the Russian Ministry of Internal Affairs (MVD), 17,000 former employees of the MVD and 12,000 from the KGB worked for registered and non-registered security and detective firms in 1995.[44] Prominent Soviet-era security officers have formed their own companies.[45] Close links between the PSFs and state securities and the police remain. Valerii Velichko, formerly chief of staff of the KGB's Ninth Directorate (in charge of VIP protection) and now head of Commercial Structures' Protection Bureau, says that his firm maintains 'good relations with the anti-mafiya [*sic*] unit RUOP'. 'That is', he adds, 'when we are not in a position to protect someone with our forces, we go to our [RUOP] colleagues, who can quickly render assistance.'[46] Private security companies may even be housed within military compounds. One security firm has been established at the paratroop school at Ryazan', 200 miles south of Moscow, according to *InterSec*, a newsletter specializing in private security.[47] The company employs 300 of the school's best ex-pupils, recently released from the army. They are available for hire by private commercial concerns or individual businessmen. The commandant of the school has given permission to the company to use its weapons, in return for a percentage of the profit the firm makes. The firm also makes use of the school's military transport. As reported by *InterSec*, '40,000 video-cassette players have already been transported across Russia on behalf of a Canadian firm'.[48]

These firms offer private security and investigation services (such as

legal advice, security audits, and vetting of employees and possible partners and investors) to individual and corporate clients.[49] Among the first
to be established was Alex, founded in Moscow in 1989 by former members of the KGB and promising four main services: 'Guarding objects,
engineering security, information-analytical security, counter-terrorist
activity.'[50] On the Alex internet home page one can find a brief history of
the company, including a reference to its services to the Russian government: 'In August of 1991 at government of Russia request our departments defended the building of Russian White House. And in the October
of 1993 we protected the building of Russian TV centre from the thugs.' [51]
Sherif is the largest firm currently operating in Russia, uniting four
detective agencies, eight security firms, and a variety of other consultan-
cies, with a total staff of nearly 1,000 and a branch office in Kiev.[52]

At least two constraints should be analysed in regard to legal
PSFs: costs and the range of services. The first constraint is imposed on
their clients by the firms themselves. Substantial sums of money are
required in order to purchase the services of PSFs. The average price for
posting a guard at a firm's office was $US1,000 a month in 1994.[53] Small
businesses and even kiosk owners can afford them only if they join forces.
One such case was reported in *Izvestiya* (12 Mar. 1997): 'Kiosk owners pool
resources and hire a security firm with the stipulation that if a criminal
gets away, the guys in uniform will pay compensation for all losses.'

The second constraint is imposed by the state on both supplier and
client and limits the range of services that can be offered and demanded.
PSF are supposed to provide *legal* protection against violent attacks. They
are not supposed to engage in activities such as twisting the arms of
unwelcome competitors or settling disputes outside the scope of the law.
Certain businesses only require security services: the nature of their interactions with the Russian business environment is quite limited or they
are safely protected by other arrangements, such as foreign government
sponsorship. Foreign consulting companies, who come to Russia on
fairly detailed contracts with the Russian state, may qualify as businesses
who do not require illegal protection services. We should therefore expect
them to opt more readily for PSF protection. This seems to be the case of a
US consultancy working in Russia on a contract with the Russian government. When it was visited by four men in long, black leather jackets
proposing a protection deal, the firm refused and turned for help to a
British security concern allied with a squad of retired Russian special
forces troops. The Russians tracked down the four gangsters and warned

them off.[54] A further incentive for US-based firms to employ legitimate security firms is the existence of a law that forbids American businesses to engage in 'corrupt practices' abroad.[55]

Still, this does not always prevent PSFs from offering a wider range of services, both legal and illegal, depending on the alternatives available to the customer. The chairperson of a PSF called Bastion, a woman, told *Moscow Times*: 'To the bandits we say we are a *krysha*, to the tax inspector we say we are consultants, and to the police we say we are private guards.'[56] Most likely she is telling (part of) the truth to all of them. A company was reported to offer protection and escort services to its clients.[57] In the city of Krasnokamsk, in the Perm Region, the body of a man who had been stabbed to death emerged from the waters of the river Las'va. The man had been put into a metal container and cement was poured over him, a clear reference to an 'Italian-style' mafia murder. It later emerged that the man was killed for failing to return a debt. The employees of a private security firm based in the Kirovskii district of Perm confessed the murder.[58]

In a similar although not equally brutal case, the Stavropol' Saving Bank hired the services of the firm MBK, which specializes in 'protection'. MBK signed a formal contract for the recovery of debts outside of ordinary legal procedures. The Bank, in turn, pledged to provide MBK with a percentage of the value of all assets they recovered.[59] The contract provided for the supply of an illegal service: the violent recovery of assets outside the provision of the law contravenes article 200 of the Criminal Code of the Russian Federation, which can lead to a maximum six-month term of imprisonment.[60] Either the company MBK is a private security firm, which has started to compete with criminal firms offering illegal services, or it was criminal from the start. These examples point to the difficulty of distinguishing the two.

Some PSFs are closely connected to established criminal groups.[61] Skorpion, a St Petersburg-based protection firm established in 1993 and with over a hundred staff, reportedly was a front for the city's dominant Tambov gang. The police accused its director, Aleksandr Efimov (nicknamed Fima) of being a criminal *avtoritet*. The raid proved that several Skorpion staff had criminal records and the police revoked the firm's license in March 1997. Efimov was arrested a year later in the Ukraine.[62] Ruslan Kolyak, nicknamed Pucheglazyi, also a member of the Tambov criminal group and accused of extortion, is the president of the Kuguar and Krechet security agencies.[63] Igor' Rimer, with a long criminal record, and Vladimir Podatev, nicknamed Pudel', the most respected and feared criminal 'authority' of Khabarovsk, are the founders of Svoboda (freedom), a private protection firm. The firm has been involved in instances of extortion and kidnapping and is considered as a front for the criminal activities of Pudel'.[64]

PSFs are ready to offer services that go beyond those legally provided by their Western counterparts, thereby indicating that the state is only partially able to constrain them.

Internalization of Protection

Major economic conglomerates have internalized protection, hiring a host of bodyguards, which constitute in effect little private armies. The gas monopoly Gazprom has a 20,000-strong security service under Vladimir Marushchenko, a KGB veteran who also served as senior officer within the state tax service. The financial group Most can resort to more than 2,500 armed officers in Moscow alone, while Lukoil has an army of a similar size in its Novorossiisk oil terminal. These economic giants also employ commercial intelligence officers and a system of secure communications.[65] Economic conglomerates have benefited from the initial distribution of resources because of their connections with the political elite. Internalization of protection in these cases goes hand-in-hand with a privileged relationship with the state. Russian newspapers have pointed out that 'sizeable economic concerns ... are quite often forced to "go under the roof", although in this instance we are referring to organs of state power, which are often law-enforcing agencies'.[66] Table 3.2 summarizes the most well-known connections for the mid-1990s.

The individuals listed under the heading 'political affiliation' offer a variety of favours, such as company tax concessions, protectionist measures against competitors, and exemptions from duties. These politicians are also able to mobilize violent resources and sometimes face confrontations of a military nature. *Izvestiya* reported that 'competition among different "legal roof-builders" in relation to the affairs of their "clients" often leads to quite violent confrontations [*razborki*]'.[67] On 2 December 1994 the offices of Mostbank—protected by the Moscow mayor who was at that point in competition with the Kremlin—were raided by a group of masked men armed with automatic weapons. The men, who initially refused to identify themselves, turned out to be a detachment of President Boris Yeltsin's security staff. In order to protect their client, the troops of

Table 3.2 Russian conglomerates and their political affiliations, 1994–2000

Group/Head	Industrial holdings	Political affiliation
Oneksimbank/ Vladimir Potanin	Owns 38% of Noril'sk Nickel, 26% of jet-engine maker Perm Motors, 26% of auto maker ZiL, Sidanko, plus oil, metallurgy and real estate interests.	(then) President of Russian Federation, Boris Yeltsin and Anatolii Chubais
Menatep[a]/ Mikhail Khodorkovskii	Most diversified conglomerate, with 78% of oil giant Yukos, plus controlling interests in plastics, metallurgy, textiles, chemicals, and food-processing companies. 10th largest bank in Russia.	Former Communist apparatus
Rossiiskaya Metallurgiya	Links 14 institutes and troubled plants producing steel, alloys, and other metals.	(then) Deputy Prime Minister, Oleg Soskovets
Most Group/ Vladimir Gussinskii	Active in Moscow, its interests are spread across banking, real estate, government, construction, independent TV network NTV, and the paper *Segodnya*.	Moscow Mayor, Yurii Luzhkov
Gazprom/ Rem Vyakhirev Lukoil/ Vagit Alegperov	This group links Russia's gas monopoly, its largest oil company and their jointly owned bank. Gazprom supplies gas to Europe and Lukoil deals with Libya and the Persian Gulf.	(then) Prime Minister, Viktor Chernomyrdin
Boris Berezovsky	LogoVaz, Aeroflot, Sibneft', Russia's fifth-largest aluminum producer Novokuznetsk, the Krasnoyarsk and Bratsk aluminum plants, *Kommersant-daily* newspaper, ORT TV Station, and SBS-Agro bank.	(then) President of Russian Federation, Boris Yeltsin and his family

[a] Menatep ceased to exist in 1998, although Menatep St Petersburg and Yukos are said to be its inheritors.

Source: Various newspapers including *Business Week Magazine*, 1 Apr. 1996, *The Economist*, 21 Jan. 1995 and 8 Apr. 1995.

the city guard, led by Mr Sevost'yanov, intervened. At least two people were hospitalized.[68] Another incident of a similar nature occurred in March 1995. The headquarters of LogoVaz, an automobile consortium owned by Boris Berezovsky, were visited by a detachment of Moscow anti-organized crime unit (RUOP) in connection with the murder of television journalist Vladislav List'ev. Such an intrusion was quickly and successfully 'repelled' by FSK agents (the successor to the KGB). Different branches of the state apparatus protect different clients. *Izvestiya* concludes that, 'as a rule, the side whose "roof" is higher in the state hierarchy, wins'.[69]

Those who oppose major conglomerates may suffer severe consequences. Vladimir Petukhov, mayor of Nefteyugansk in western Siberia, was involved in a bitter fight against Yukos, the company headed by Mikhail Khodorkovskii. Petukhov opposed the sale of the local gas producer, Yuganskneftegaz, to Yukos and supported various actions against the company, including a demonstration protesting against delayed wage payments to workers. Allegedly, Yukos had a direct link with the President's administration and the General Procurator's office and, as a consequence, a probe into the way the city administration handled financial affairs was started.[70]

Criminals refrain from entering into conflict with political protectors. A deputy of Egor, one of the leaders of the Moscow's Izmailovskaya gang, granted an interview to Italian investigative journalist Cesare Martinetti. When asked whether the gang dealt in gas, he replied: 'No. We do not deal in gas because the government, or rather PM Chernomyrdin, controls it. We cannot reach those echelons, although recently we started to deal in gasoline.'[71] Similarly, Yurii Esin, a prominent member of the Solntsevo crime group with a fifteen-year prison background, started to deal in oil and gas between Italy and Moscow. Esin had set up a sophisticated network of high-profile connections in Rome, which included the former Deputy President of ENI, the Italian oil and gas agency. Esin's operation in Italy attracted the interest of the Italian police. In a telephone conversation recorded by the police, Esin warns his interlocutor to keep away from deals that might conflict with the interest of Lukoil: 'I do not want to have anything to do with Lukoil. Sure, they kill. And what do you want from me? Whoever gets hold of their oil becomes an obstacle on their path and is finished. You have no idea what sort of bitches they are!'[72]

Only sizeable firms can afford the high costs of internalizing protection. These firms also nurture connections with prominent political leaders. Politicians should act as 'agents' of the Russian people, uphold the law, and fulfil their election promises. Instead, they favour a corrupter who pays them a bribe in return for the use of the state resources. Economic conglomerates are not alone in engaging in corruption.[73] Their links are simply more high profile and more widely reported. Politicians depend on their tenure of office for supplying favours: access to state means of violence ends whenever a different president or city mayor is elected. For this reason, these conglomerates are both internalizing protection and are actively involved in sponsoring their own candidates.

Banditskaya Krysha

A report by the United Nations placed the number of individuals involved in organized crime in Russia at 3 million, employed in about 5,700 gangs.[74] These people come from a variety of backgrounds, including the police and sports. Russian Interior Minister Viktor Erin revealed in 1993 that 20 per cent of the professionals who left the police in 1992 'went over to the enemy', for a total of 12,600 individuals.[75] Criminal figures were quick to realize the importance of sportsmen and organized associations and charities in order to attract them. The most well-known patron of sports among Russian criminals was Otari Kvantrishvili.[76] He headed the Sportsmen's Social Protection Fund named after the Russian goalkeeper Lev Yashin and became one of the founders and the director of a Sports Academy, devoted to encouraging sports in Russia. In 1993, he even founded a party supposedly devoted to the interests of sportsmen— Sportsmen of Russia. Valentina Yashina, the widow of Lev, acknowledged Otari's role in the promotion of sports and the protection of retired sportsmen in a speech at Otari's grave. Among other things, she said, '[Kvantrishvili] was a man of great spiritual purity . . . Wherever his money came from, even if it may have come by coercion, this money went to the poor.'[77]

Criminal protectors are involved in a variety of sectors and, contrary to widespread belief, offer genuine services, at least in some cases. The owner of an Italian restaurant in Moscow described how he was initially forced into a contract with a criminal group but then the relationship evolved into one of genuine protection.

After I rented these premises, restoration works started. One day, young lad comes in, looks around and says: 'You will need protection.' I hesitate and shortly afterwards my car is burned. At that point, a refined gentleman comes forward and tells me: 'Those young lads who offered you protection are just naughty boys. Let us handle the matter.' I am afraid so I pay. The gentleman visits me again. 'I see that restoration works are going rather slowly. If you wish, I could send in my crew.' I agree. The fee (*tangente*) increases, but the restoration works actually improve. After a month, the gentleman comes again: 'Don't you need credit?' To tell you the truth, I did. He recommends a bank, and so we became partners, so to speak. Better to make some profit, rather than none at all.[78]

The Filippov Report—a special report on organized crime in Russia prepared for the President of the Russian Federation and published in January 1994—confirms that credit is accessed through criminal links. It is usually in the area of 'specific-purpose credit'. As stated by this report, 'In the banking sphere, the economic foundation of organized crime is centralized credits allocated outside the regular credit auctions. Such credits are provided in exchange for a 10–20 per cent commission paid in cash.'[79]

The collection of debts or delayed payments is one of the genuine services they offer. 'Bad bank credit, refusals to pay for goods delivered, non-delivery or partial delivery of goods, swindling and roguery: in order to seek justice in these spheres', writes Ladyzhenskii, 'it is useless to go to the court of arbitration.' In these cases, it is the 'roof' that 'steps in and helps'.[80] A correspondent for *Komsomol'skaya Pravda* from the city of Samara writes: 'In principle, all financial-ownership quarrels in our country should be decided by such an institution called the Court of Arbitration. However, as already noted, all attempts to use this method are condemned to failure. At present, the only effective way of settling a situation of conflict between businessmen is known as *strelka*.'[81] Strelka (lit. arrow) is slang referring to disputes settled with the help of violence.

One criminal *brigada* in the city of Samara is involved in recovering bad debts for established banks. In principle, banks should apply to the *Arbitrazh* court, however they are afraid that the debtor may declare himself bankrupt.

That is why banks operate in an unofficial way. They assign the task of recovering debt to an especially reliable and competent *brigadir*, who adjusts his tactics depending on the situation. For example, in one case, he simply scares the person; in another, he physically 'strains' him. The debtor is taken out of town (to the cemetery, to the forest, or by the river), beaten, threatened, and beaten again. In another case, the debtor is forced to apply for credit to another bank, in order to return money to the bank who hired the *brigadir*. This debtor is doomed to receive soon the visit of the brigade of the other bank.[82]

The article adds that an experienced *brigadir* might indeed cheat the bank, obtain from the debtor a sum, which ranges from 10 to 50 per cent of the debt, and report to the bank that the person in question turned to the department for the fight against organized crime and now he is under their protection.

Criminal groups, with the reputation for using violence, are called in to supply effective muscle against actual or potential competitors. As General Gennadii Chebotarev, Deputy Chief of Police for combating organized crime, declared to *Literaturnaya Gazeta*:

Quite often, we hear that a businessman fell victim of criminals and when the police start investigating who issued the 'contract' for 'the hit', it appears that it was another businessman. So it transpires that businessmen are 'feeding' the bandits, extortionists and racketeers.[83]

Similarly, the police discovered that fifteen assassinations were ordered by one prominent industrialist caught up in a fight over the control of some natural resources in the Siberian city of Krasnoyarsk. In the same city, a businessman preferred to have his partner killed instead of buying him out. The reporter was told that it turned to be cheaper to order a hit rather than to pay what the partner was entitled to.[84] A Moscow businessman, Sergei N., had been cheated by his partner and forced to give up his share of a jointly owned business. By chance he met a new protector: a surgeon friend had just operated on a powerful criminal, who said he was willing to look after Sergei's new business. The weekly *Stolitsa* reports: 'The wounded mafioso had guaranteed a good *krysha* . . . : for 25 per cent of profits, his boys were not only sheltering him from other bandits, but they also solved the many problems he was facing with local authorities, militia, and customs.' Sergei had also asked his 'roof' to kill his former partner, who was found dead some time later.[85]

The Filippov Report mentions the city of Tver', where criminals offer a competitive advantage to certain entrepreneurs, at the expense of others.

In Tver', entrepreneurs who want to set up a booth or open a store have to get permission from the unit leaders of gangsters' groupings. Local authorities will issue licenses only with the gangsters' consent. The activity of independent entrepreneurs has been completely squeezed out of some provinces, since organized crime provides financing on very easy terms (for example, very large interest-free loans) to young people who are prepared to co-operate and who, as a result, have a significant advantage over their competitors (needless to say, when they achieve a certain degree of success, they turn over a sizeable portion of their profits as payment for the loan).[86]

The report adds that the additional 'tax' paid to gangsters, as well as the restrictions put on business activity with the aim of obtaining monopoly profit, 'leads to price increases of 20 to 30 per cent'. The losers are both the consumers, who pay higher prices for goods and services, and unprotected competitors.

There is at least one instance where a gang intervened to stop a workers' strike. It occurred in Vorkuta, a city of about 90,000 people located 160 kilometres north of the Arctic Circle. The strike leader, Konstantin Pimonov, was threatened at gunpoint in order to end a month-long strike against the company that owns the Vorgashurskaya coalmine.[87] This episode reminds one of American, Japanese, and Sicilian mafias intervention in labour disputes.[88]

Coal mining is riddled with criminality in Russia.[89] Although most of the press refers to the mines as 'having been taken over' by the mafia, the picture is more complex. Vladimir Kudeshkin, head of the Barzasskaya mine in the Kemerovo region (western Siberia) since August 1999, complained about the criminals' interference with the operation of his mine. However, he added, they not only used violence to persuade him: 'They also have ready cash to pay the high railroad tariffs and the means to ship the coal through the crime-ridden ports.'[90]

Criminal protectors operate in a crowded market, competing with state protectors and legal security firms (PSFs). In turn, the latter two compete with each other over price and services for clients. As far as prices, police protectors can charge the same price as PSFs, although they can also free ride on existing state structures for equipment. They do have to pass on to the administration a portion of their earnings, but can keep most of them 'in-house'. Police protectors have less expenses and greater income than PSFs. They also have access to police files, can bypass restrictions on armament and carry a greater weight when dealing with the public. Police protectors are also supposed to supervise their own competitors and grant them permission to operate. Given that PSFs are at a disadvantage with police protectors, they expand the range of services by offering customers semi-legal enforcement and protection. This might lead the Extra-Departmental Guard to evolve in the same direction, competing with both criminals and PSFs over services.

Only severe intra-police competition might lead to police protectors being exposed by colleagues for providing illegal protection services. Still, potential for conflicts among different arms of the state is high.

When different fragments of the state apparatus protect different clients, the state administration is drawn into the clients' conflicts. Military confrontation between the Presidential guard and Moscow city guard (as in a case involving Mostbank), or the Interior Ministry anti-mafia unit and the new FSB (as in the case involving LogoVaz) are a by-product of the privatization of state protection. Business disputes are adjudicated not by independent tribunals, but by the use of compromising material, confidential police information, secret services reports, and ultimately the use of state violence.

Legal protectors operate in the same market as criminals and might even be prepared to use similar methods, although we should not conclude that they inevitably fight criminals, even for the wrong reasons (such as reducing competition). Instead they can eschew conflict in favour of tacit co-operation and agreements to share clients or segments of the market. We now turn to a specific setting, the city of Perm, and explore the interaction between criminal protectors, legal protectors, and businesspeople.

PART II

Private Protection in Perm

4

Searching for Protection

The Kama is a wonderful river. We ought somehow to rent a little steamer for the whole family and journey unhurriedly to Perm and back again, and that would be a summer vacation in earnest, of a sort we have never even dreamed of.

*(Anton Chekhov, from a letter to his wife,
dated Perm, 22 June 1802)*

Perm and its Environment

Many things revolve around the Kama River in the city of Perm, the easternmost city of the European continent. The name of the river has been given to nearby villages, factories, art galleries, cinema halls, and trains. When approaching the city on the *Kama Express*, a fast train service which covers the 1,500 miles between Moscow and Perm with few stops in between, the traveller's first sight of the city is a view from the bridge over the Kama River.

The city is relatively young; it was established two centuries ago. A small copper-smelting factory was founded in May 1723. The settlement stood at the intersection of both water and land routes. On the border between Europe and Asia, Perm was a stopping place where travellers could replenish their food supplies and trade their cargoes. In 1735 the first school opened, with one teacher and thirty-three pupils. Perm's surrounding forests provided shelter for peasants fleeing from the cruelty of their masters along the only road to Siberia, which passed through Perm. Robbers' bands plundered vessels on the Kama. Sable, squirrel, and marten pelts, honey, candles, and salt were the most widely traded goods.

In November 1780, Empress Catherine the Great signed a decree that gave the name *Perm* to the settlement that housed the labour force of the copper-smelting factory, and made it the capital of the province. In six years' time the first state school opened and in another six a printing press had begun operating. By the end of the eighteenth century, there were over 150 metallurgical plants. In the nineteenth century, the river ports on the Kama became an important transport route of Eastern Europe and the Trans-Siberian main line was built, making Perm a major railway junction in Russia. Also, between 1807 and 1830, Perm housed the headquarters for the administration of the mining enterprises of the Ural region. From the middle of the nineteenth century, shipbuilding enterprises were started, testifying to Perm's increased importance as a river port.

The fame of Perm among students of Russian literature and thought comes about because Aleksander Herzen, the great writer and political thinker, was forced to begin a term of banishment there in 1835. In 1880–91 Chekhov's friend, the author V. G. Korolenko (1853–1921), also was sent into exile to the city which, around that time (1897), numbered about 45,000 people. Perm can also boast a mildly revolutionary past, heavily emphasized in the city museum, where the achievements of Perm revolutionaries still monopolize the museum's space.[1] During the Bolshevik Revolution of 1917, Socialist Revolutionaries, Mensheviks, and other non-Bolshevik elements controlled the Perm City Soviet.[2] This might explain Perm's slow acceptance of Lenin's regime. During the Russian Civil War, Perm was in the hands of the White Army until 1 July 1919.[3]

By 1923 the Soviet authorities had decided to make Perm a major centre of what was later to be called 'the Soviet military-industrial complex', and this trend deepened after the German invasion of 1940 (in 1940, Perm was renamed *Molotov*, which continued until 1957). By the end of the 1980s, twenty-three enterprises of the defence complex employed one-third of the working population of the entire Perm region and characterized the region's economic profile. Given the sensitivity of military-industrial production, Perm was, until 1989, a city closed to foreign visitors.

Fig. 4.1 The Perm region

The population of the city grew from about 68,000 people in the 1920s to just over 1,200,000 in 1997, the region having an additional 2 million inhabitants. The majority are Russians.[4] There are six institutions of higher learning, including the university and the teacher training and polytechnic institutes. In the late 1970s and 1980s, a number of housing programmes were initiated, in order to reduce the acute housing shortage and the lack of a comprehensive water, sewer, and gas supply system.[5] Mary McAuley, a political scientist who studied the city, describes Soviet Perm as a moderate city where the regional party leadership was accustomed for years to following instructions from above: 'if *arenda* was the new policy, a little *arenda* campaign followed; if alcoholism was the target, so be it.'[6]

Post-Soviet Perm

The transition to the market started in the final years of perestroika and proceeded at a fairly rapid speed: by 1994 most enterprises had became joint-stock companies.[7] Perm ranks fourteenth in terms of industrial output among Russian regions—heavy industry, primarily metallurgy and machine building, still being the largest sector of the economy. Perm produces 30 per cent of Russia's paper and 98 per cent of its potassium-based fertilizers. The military-industrial complex survived post-Soviet restructuring rather well and still produces aircraft engines, Proton rockets, and space control systems. Perm has over 100 known deposits of oil and gas and two oil refineries.[8] It exports refined oil, petrochemical products, fertilizers, and metals.

As in the rest of Russia, most of the former Soviet elite moved into business (See Appendix B) and a class of 'oligarchs' has emerged around the main industries. Dmitrii Rybolovlev, the president of the commercial bank Kredit FD, controls most of the region's potassium production (Ural-Kalii and Sil'vinit). In 1996, he was arrested for the murder of the director general of Neftekhimik Evgenii Panteleimonov, although the accusation did not stand at the trial. The press reports that the regional governor, Gennadii Igumnov, is his strong political ally.

Andrei Kuzyaev is the chairman of Perm financial-industrial group (PFP-group), and director general of Lukoil-Perm, the local branch of Lukoil. He also struck a deal with the governor over taxes: Lukoil promises a steady flow of taxes to the administration in exchange for a monopoly control over oil fields in the region. Reportedly, the deal was easened by the fact that Kuzyaev is chairman of the committee on economic policy and taxes of the region's Duma.

Yurii Trutnev and Oleg Chirkunov, both of EKS Ltd. and formerly of Perm's Komsomol, control wholesale and to a great extent retail trade in the city. A member of the local duma since March 1994, Trutnev handed over to Chirkunov the day-to-day running of the company after he was elected major of Perm in 1996. EKS Ltd. has more than 6,000 employees and fourteen subsidiaries, including a department store chain, a trucking company, an armed escort service, a pharmaceutical business, real estate, shares in local banks, and investment in food production. In 1997, Oleg Chirkunov was elected to the Regional Duma. Pavel Anokhin and Mikhail Demenev end the list of the most prominent local 'oligarchs'. Their company, FPK DAN deals in oil (in competition with Kuzyaev),

Table 4.1   Perm's business leaders

Name (age in brackets)	Estimated value of assets they control	Companies under control
Dmitrii Rybolovlev (32)	$1 bn.	AKB 'Kredit FD', AKB 'Permstroibank', AO 'Uralkalii', AO 'Sil'vinit', AO 'Kama', AO 'Metafrax', investment company 'Finansovyi dom', 'Audit FD'
Andrei Kuzyaev (33)	$600 m.	OAO 'Permskaya finansovo-proizvodstvennaya gruppa', ZAO 'Lukoil', ZAO 'Permskaya fondovaya kompaniya', ZAO 'Permskaya torgovaya kompaniya', OOO 'Yaivinskii lesopil'nyi zavod', ZAO 'Permzernoprodukt', ZAO 'SF Adonis', ZAO 'Permskoe agentstvo nedvizhimosti', ZAO 'Ural'skaya korporatsiya vzaimnykh raschetov', ZAO 'Reklamnaya gruppa 'Ozon', ZAO 'Perm-Asko', AKB 'Permkredit', AKB 'Permskii bank razvitiya'
Oleg Chirkunov	$250 m.	group of enterprises EKS, OOO 'EKS-opt', OOO 'Doktor EKS'
Pavel Anokhin (36) Mikhail Demenev	$200 m.	FPK DAN

Source: *Profil'*, 20 June 1999.

metallurgical products, wood, industrial and civil construction, and motor cars. Anokhin is a deputy of the Regional Legislative Board and is very successful at keeping tax authorities at bay: once the company was visited by tax authorities and threatened with huge fines. The tax inspectors were later charged with extortion and went behind bars.[9]

Since the presidential elections of 1991, the Ural regions, including Perm, have been strong supporters of the 'democratic', pro-Yeltsin parties (they include Russia's Choice, Yabloko, Russian Unity and Accord, and the Russian Movement for Democratic Reform).[10] In the 1993 elections for the State Duma, the 'democratic' camp won with 50.1 per cent against a national average of 34.18. The Liberal Democratic Party of Zhirinovsky obtained only 14.8 per cent of the vote, against a national average of 22.92 per cent, while the Communists and Agrarians obtained only 11.8 per cent (against a national average of 20.39 per cent).[11] In the 1995 State Duma elections, known for a massive victory of the Communist Party nationwide, the 'democratic' parties maintained a 34.5 per cent of the vote (compared to the national average of 30.3 per cent), although the LDPR obtained more votes (15.1 per cent) than its national average (11.40 per cent). In the 1996 presidential elections, Perm supported Yeltsin in both rounds (56.1 and 71.6 per cent respectively), well above the national average (35.79 and 54.39 per cent).[12] Gennadii Igumnov, a centrist, pro-central government politician (and former Soviet administrator), was re-elected Governor of the region in December 1996 with 64 per cent of the vote in the second round.

Crime Rates

Perm experienced a rise in crime rates rather higher than the rest of Russia. Between 1989 to 1995, total recorded crime rose from 37,505 to 80,057, a 113.4 per cent increase on the 1989 figure (Russia's increased by 70.2 per cent). With an overall figure of 71,855 crimes committed in 1994, the Perm region was ranked ninth in Russia as the place with most criminal activity per 100,000 population, while it is the eleventh most populated region. In 1995, the Perm region moved from the ninth to the fourth most 'criminal' region of the country and the second most criminal region of the Ural area, after Sverdlovsk region.[13] From 1995 to 1998, crime rates reduced at a lower speed in the Perm region (−2.2 per cent) than in Russia as a whole (−6.3 per cent).

Post-1988 data on arson and hooliganism provide confirmation of the growth in aggressive behaviour leading to criminal acts.[14] The deliberate

Table 4.2 Number of registered crimes (per year) in the Perm region, annual change, and annual change in registered crimes in the Russian Federation

Year	Total no. of registered crimes	Annual change (%)	Russian Federation Annual change (%)
1989	37,505	=	=
1990	42,572	+13.5	+13.6
1991	38,245	−10.1	+18.1
1992	51,632	+35.0	+27.0
1993	74,307	+43.9	+1.4
1994	71,855	−3.2	−5.9
1995	80,057	+11.4	+4.6
1996	80,476	+0.5	−4.7
1997	72,285	−10.1	−8.6
1998	78,269	+8.3	+7.7

Source: *Megalopolis-Kontinent*, no. 27 (7 Aug. 1992); *Mestnoe Vremya*, 9 Dec. 1994; *Dos'e 02*, 21 Mar. 1996; *Dos'e 02*, 26 Jan. 1996; *Dos'e 02*, 14 Feb. 1997; *Dos'e 02*, 22 Jan. 1999.

destruction of property by means of arson was quite rare in 1988 (N = 68); 167 cases were recorded in 1989 and 462 in 1993. Acts of arson against private property (which include commercial enterprises) increased between 1988 and 1993 more dramatically than arson against state property. In the same period, acts of hooliganism increased noticeably: from 1,840 in 1988 to 4,008 in 1993. Whereas before the period of economic transformation arson was mostly committed by hooligans or teenagers and was considered a form of vandalism, in recent years the local police believe that this type of crime is of a different nature, namely, a form of pressure or intimidation for settling economic problems.[15]

Table 4.3 lists the businessmen who have been victims of severe assaults on their life in 1994 and 1995. Nail' Salakhov, head of the city department of the militia, commented on this long list of murders and attempted murders in Perm. According to him, 'anarchy and extremes of behaviour (*bespredel*) rule in the sphere of small and middle-sized enterprises—financial obligations are broken with impunity.' He linked these criminal acts with the inefficiency of the law, in particular of the courts: 'The State has not worked out effective measures to protect contracts in civil courts and in courts of arbitration. Under such conditions, criminal

Table 4.3 Attempts on the lives of prominent Perm businessmen, 1994–5, and states of the investigation

Name	Position	Date of attempt on life/murder	Status
Suslov	General Director AO 'Initsiator'	1994, killed	solved
V. Khlyzov	President of AO 'Kompaniya ITR'	5 Apr. 94, killed	unsolved
O. Kul'beda	Director General of the Ural military-insurance association 'Egida'	June 94, killed	unsolved
I. Malinin	Commercial Director of Berezniki' chemical factory, head of TOO 'Kul'tura'	29 Aug. 94, killed	unsolved
A. Kuzhma	Head of the Union of Businessmen of Prikam'e, President of Western-Ural Outer Economic Association	28 June 93, attempt on life; July 95, killed	unsolved
B. Koshkin	Head of firm 'Western Ural'	11 Aug. 95, killed	unsolved
E. Panteleimonov	Director General of AO 'Neftekhimik'	4 Sept. 95, killed	under investigation
K. Bulgakov	Director-General of Scientific-Industrial Association 'Stankoinkom'	4 Sept. 95, killed	under investigation
A. Aratunyan	Director General of Firm 'Karen'	17 Aug. 95 attempt on life; 12 Sept. 95, killed	under investigation

Source: *Megalopolis-Express*, 6 July 1994; *Zvezda*, 27 May 1995; *Zvezda*, 13 Sept. 1995; *Zvezda*, 28 Nov. 1995.

groups provide the most real and effective protection, and this leads to new crimes.'[16]

Data on revealed crime, which are supposed to be an indicator of local police efficacy, grew by 9 per cent between 1993 and 1994, but Perm's figure of 55.7 is still lower than the national average of 59.6 per cent.[17] The police are understaffed and find it hard to attract quality personnel. Despite the militia increasing its ranks by 2,000 in 1994, 4,000 service people are urgently required. Two districts of the region—which have not been named for reasons of security—do not have a patrol-post service.[18] The Chief of the city Department of Internal Affairs (UVD), Col. Salakhov, lamented that the qualifications of the newly hired militia officers are insufficient: only 42 per cent of those hired in 1994 had the required legal qualifications.[19] Moreover, 692 militiamen were dismissed in 1994 on grounds of incompetence or corruption.[20]

Protection in Practice

The evidence used in the rest of this and in the following chapter is mostly based upon interviews I carried out in Perm over a period of two years (1994–5). Additional interviews were done between 1996 to 1999. The coding of each interview and a brief sketch of each interviewee are reported in the List of Respondents at the back of this book.

Most of the interviewees are entrepreneurs who deal in legal commodities and are involved in some aspect of commerce. The majority own a fixed establishment, such as a small kiosk or a shop. Some of the interviewees (Inna, Petr, Andrei, Aleksandr, and Anvar) own one kiosk each in the Visim sub-district of Perm, that is part of Motovilikha, one of the seven districts into which the city is divided. The five kiosks are all located in the proximity of the same cross-roads.[21] Others manage large business concerns, such as Konstantin (B11), the director of the biggest retail chain in the city with the greatest variety of activities, and Leonid (B1). Most businesses employ few people, with, again, the exception of Uralbis (B11) and Uralkom (B1). Only two interviewees have a criminal record, although a number of them had been fined for breaking trade laws and regulations. Age and professional backgrounds differ. Three had been members of the so-called Soviet *nomenklatura*. For instance, Leonid was in charge of a factory which used forced labour in the 1970s, operating in the Perm region; Nikolai (B13) was an official of the Communist Party; and Konstantin was the head of a Young Communist League (Komsomol) department.[22] I have also interviewed sales persons, police officers, journalists, politicians, criminals involved in protection rackets, and an ordinary citizen who used criminal protection.

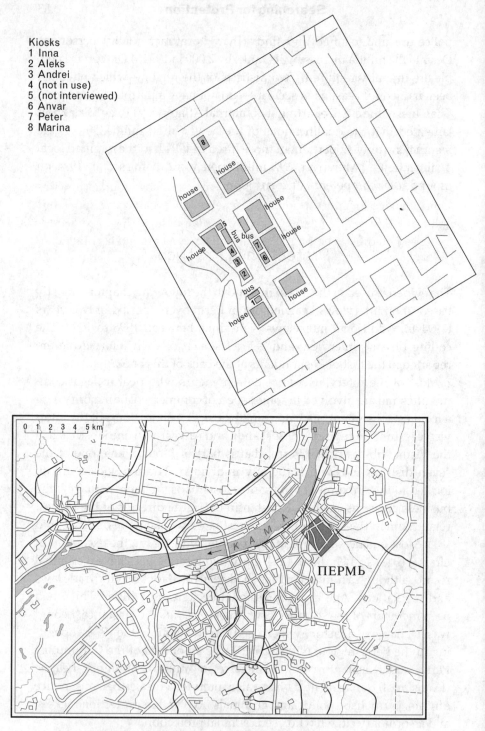

Fig. 4.2 Location of kiosks in the Visim sub-district, Perm

Sources of Harassment

Certain types of legitimate businesses are more vulnerable than others to harassment by officials, fraudsters, robbers, and gangs. A study of the penetration of legitimate businesses by organized crime in New York State (USA) concludes that 'the vulnerability of business firms to predation . . . is greatest where the enterprise is relatively small, so that the decision-making authority is centred in one or few individuals'.[23] The small scale of an operation is associated with 'limited resources to withstand damage or interruption; few or relatively weak commercial and political allies; relatively low visibility to the public at large'.[24] Furthermore, as noted by Schelling, fixed establishments are more vulnerable, since they cannot move easily to another part of town and rely on reputation to attract customers.[25]

The majority of kiosk owners in Perm owns 1 to 3 establishments: the size of their operation and the resources available to them are limited. Kiosk owners have not yet formed a trade union, nor can they count on powerful political allies. Public visibility is in fact high *but* negative, which increases the risk of harassment. Andrei remarked that they are surrounded by a lot of 'envy': 'People think that all we know is counting money, and that we do not really work. Nobody thinks that there could be an engineer sitting behind the counter' (K3). Some Russian politicians have tried to make a career out of clamping down on kiosks, though this has not been the case in Perm.[26] Shop owners are also vulnerable to harassment, although there are not strong feelings against them. Owners of bigger retail chains, such as Konstantin, can count on political allies and have more resources to withstand damage. Other businesses, such as the import–export firm managed by Leonid (B1), can go into hiding more easily and move. In the following, I focus on four sources of aggravation, *khuligany* (drunken customers and petty thieves), militia and tax inspectors, competitors, and employees.

Khuligany

In January 1994, Inna opened her kiosk in the Visim sub-district where the cost of renting land was lower than in the centre of the city.[27] The location was nevertheless convenient for her, since she lived nearby. She raised the starting capital by drawing on her previous earnings as a street seller. Her own family and former university friends also lent money to her.

The kiosk gave her husband Volodya employment, which at the time he did not have. A sportsman, with a qualification as cross-country skier ('master of sport'), he was employed by a large factory in Perm when his active sporting career ended. In 1992, the factory underwent a conversion programme and, as a result, Volodya was laid off. He now helps his wife in the running of her business. She still spends most of her working day selling goods from the truck, while he goes to the market or the warehouses to buy goods for the kiosk and keeps an eye on it during the day. Inna hired a salesperson who can ring Volodya at home in case he is needed. Usually, the salesperson calls Volodya if tax inspectors come, if dissatisfied customers complain about the quality of the goods, or in case more goods of a certain sort are needed to replenish stocks during opening hours.

Inna took two very important business decisions when she opened her kiosk: she did not buy a licence to sell alcohol nor one to open at night. Her husband pressed her to do otherwise since their prospective income would have been considerably higher. She argued, to the contrary, that the resulting problems would not have been offset by the financial gains. She was especially afraid of being attacked by drunken customers (*khuligany*) at night and what she called more generally people 'not in control of themselves' (*nekontroliruemye lyudi*). To offset such dangers, they would have had to enter into some kind of protection arrangement: either hiring another person, a man able to protect the kiosk at night, or Volodya himself would have to spend many nights sleeping in the kiosk. She considered that this would have been dangerous for her husband and would have altered their family life too much. 'Old women or kids buying chewing gum in the middle of the day are easier to manage than wild gangs of uncontrolled people who raid the city at night' (K1).

Fear of the *khuligany* was a common concern among all kiosk owners, even more so among those who open at night and sell alcohol. Olga, whose kiosk is in a central street of the city, was the least worried: 'The pavilion works also in the evening and there the sellers are paid more. We never really had any problems with *khuligany*. We did suffer, however, from a major theft of merchandise in our warehouse' (K9). Shop owners did not express huge concerns over this issue. Konstantin claimed that his shops had never been the object of criminal harassment (B11).

Militia and Tax Inspectors

According to a national survey, '[in Russia] private businessmen and managers of enterprises are twice as afraid as ordinary people of the authorities' arbitrary acts'.[28] The following is Inna's own account of an episode of abuse of power.

Q: What can you tell me about the militia, the KRU (tax collectors) and their interactions with sellers in Visim?
A: I was recently fined 150,000 roubles. It was a case of ordinary abuse of power.
Q: Why?
A: I had not done anything wrong but anyway two officials came up to my kiosk and demanded a million roubles. One was dressed up in militia uniform. I could not tell his rank but he had a rubber stick with him. The other was supposed to be a civil financial inspector (a female), but neither of them showed their identity card. I told them that I did not have this kind of money. After some discussion we settled for 150,000. I asked for a receipt, which they gave me. But the signature on it is just an incomprehensible scribble, which does not enable anybody to identify the name of the official (K1).

This was the first and only instance of this sort happening to her since the kiosk opened.

Anvar said that he was 'constantly harassed by militia men. They come up, look at the window and start saying: "this is wrong, that is wrong" and then "give me this, give me that". All I can do is to give them what they want' (K5).[29] Olga had a similar experience: 'the police and sanitary inspectors came around regularly and ask openly for gifts. One female inspector said she preferred Champagne to vodka' (K9). Andrei and Aleks recollected similar episodes to those related by Anvar, while Petr said that so far he had no problem with the militia.

Fines are the nightmare of all kiosk owners I met, and can bring about their ruin. A fine for selling goods without a quality certificate could amount to 5 million roubles in 1995. Andrei was fined 50,000 roubles for having filled in the account-books incorrectly. He complained that nobody had told him how to fill them in and therefore he was unjustly fined. Of course, the possibility that he was fiddling the books cannot be ruled out. Nevertheless, it was a proper fine: he was taken to an office and a receipt was issued. The clerk did not appear to be pocketing the money. Anvar had a rather paranoid aversion to KRU officers. According to him, they would wait by his kiosk to see whether or not his customers were given the obligatory receipt.

They are trying to fine me for not giving the receipt to the customers. So they stand outside and wait until they see a customer buying a product without getting a receipt. But I cannot run after the customer if he takes the stuff, turns around and runs away. Tax-inspectors can even order the closure of a kiosk until the fine is paid (K5).

Sasha owns a kiosk of his own and also supplies goods to pavement sellers, and he himself (with Inna) sells from a truck. Sasha's salespeople were also the objects of what he regarded as unjustified militia harassment. During a highly publicized anti-mafia operation named Signal (March 1994, see below p. 110), two of his salespersons were brought to the militia station and fined. According to the militia, they were selling in the wrong place and therefore fined a total 270,000 roubles. According to Sasha, operation Signal was for the most part an exercise in window-dressing. The operation consisted mostly of stopping cars and checking all documents, as well as sellers' documents. Its starting date was announced in advance on television, 'so that the real mafia bosses could escape'. Sasha nevertheless thought that the money he paid would not go into the pockets of the militiamen, but to the state budget. However, the fine was unjustified, he claimed, because the salespersons had a proper licence. He was confident about this and he went to argue his case at the militia headquarters. After a while, an officer told him to stop making inquiries, otherwise 'we will turn you upside down' (K6).

Kiosk owners are only victims to a degree since they actively try to circumvent existing legislation. The goods sold at kiosks should carry a quality certificate issued by suppliers. Such goods are, however, more expensive and kiosk owners often sell fake merchandise. Andrei was candid about his own fiddling with quality certificates.

Not all wholesalers at the market sell goods with proper certificates, so we are forced to buy goods without certificates. If the militia finds out, we will be fined. A way out for us is to buy some goods with a certificate and some similar goods without a certificate. We sell the ones without the certificate and when the militia comes, we show them the certificate for the other goods (K3).

Fines are a feature of everyday life for kiosk owners, a feature despised and resented because they can bring financial ruin. The various and numerous fines paid by kiosk owners in Visim during the course of their economic activities seemed, for the most part, to be genuine, due to sub-stantiated breaches of regulations. The local militia is seen as a burden for each kiosk owner, who has to give in to their daily requests of goods they do not pay for. These instances of power abuses on the part of the militia were all in the range of rather minor nuisances. The militia requests were greatly despised by kiosk owners because of their arbitrary nature.

Not surprisingly, kiosk owners do not report crimes to the police. According to the Perm police, in 1993 only two cases of extortion were reported by kiosk owners. The number of kiosk owners and street sellers who reported cases of extortion to the police is decreasing: from twenty-two in 1990 to seven in 1992.[30] This evidence matches national data. According to General Gennadii Chebotarev, 'the police uncovered more than 8,000 cases of extortion in the whole of Russia in 1994. However, more often than not, the victims of extortion do not go to the police'.[31]

Since kiosk owners often have 'dirty hands', they try to minimize any interaction with officials. Another reason for failing to report to the police was mentioned by Petr:

If I go to the militia to report that my kiosk was attacked, it will do me more harm than good. If the kiosk is attacked once, they will simply do nothing. But, the more I send reports to the militia, the more likely it is that the militia will close my kiosk, even if I am the victim. This is so because the official crime-rates in the district will increase and the local militia won't have a good image on paper. Since I am the one that signs all the documents, they will say that I am the source of crime and they will go after me, not after the criminal! (K2)

Shop owners also complained of militia and sanitary inspectors' harass-ment and usually paid them off with small gifts.[32] A general attitude of distrust towards courts and militia as suppliers of services of arbitration and protection was present. Respondents either did not trust the system at all, or did not trust it in most cases. These businesses are under great scrutiny because they do have 'dirty' hands and go to great lengths to conceal income from the state. Most interviewees said that they would go as far as possible to conceal their income, although only eight admitted they had succeeded in doing this. Two interviewees (B3 and B6) employed a rather sophisticated system of tax evasion. Fictitious companies were paid for services they never delivered. The nominal transaction reduced the official profit earned by the firm and therefore the tax burden was lower. These fictitious companies returned the money to the firm and kept a 2 per cent service charge. The added convenience of this system was that the firm had unrecorded cash, which could be used without having to be accounted for.[33]

Competitors

Competition among kiosk owners and street sellers is fierce and may take different, and often harmful, forms. A form of placid competition is that of attracting attention to the kiosk through a publicity device: a plastic penis was ostentatiously displayed in the window of Anvar's kiosk, covered with elastic hair-bands for women, both of which were on sale.

Sometimes, competition takes the classic form of a 'price war' for the benefit of customers. One day Inna and Sasha arrived in Dobryanka (a city in the vicinity of Perm) and stopped their truck in the open space where selling was allowed. Somebody they had seen before started selling cucumbers at a lower price than theirs. At first they tried to reach an agreement but the other seller refused. A 'price war' ensued. Sasha and Inna dropped their price even lower and sold all their goods very quickly.

In order to avoid cut-throat competition, kiosk owners and street sellers have a strong incentive to limit new entrants. The ability to do this effectively depends on the individual entrepreneur's ability to mobilize manpower for the purpose of physical violence. Force is also used by sellers in Perm. Sasha and Inna had the following experience:

Once Ploshchad' Druzhby [Friendship Square] was a good place to sell, at the time when no licence was needed. But one day, we had a dispute in that square. We arrived and set up in the special area devoted to selling from trucks. A nearby kiosk owned by a 'black' (a person of Caucasian origin) sold oranges at a higher price than us. He came out and told us to go away. We did not go and shortly afterwards he arrived with two thugs (*balbesy*). So we left (K6).

This was not the only time they experienced this kind of intimidation.[34] Olga also reported conflicts with her neighbouring kiosk owners, of Azerbaijani origin: 'When we wanted to open the third kiosk, the neighbouring Azerbaijani wanted to open a new kiosk as well, and therefore there was a conflict between us. . . . We also clashed over prices: they were charging much cheaper prices than we were' (K9; see also below, pp. 116–17).

Zvezda, Perm's daily, reported that kiosk owners use threats and mugging in order to force a competitor out of a profitable trading area: 'they apply to criminal structures. Confidential sources have informed us that a "fee" can be paid to destroy a competitor's property: it varies from 1 to

5 million roubles, depending on the risk involved.'[35] According to the same article, in July 1995, five kiosks in various parts of the city (including Motovilikha, the area where Visim is located, and Lenin Street, in the very centre of the city) were set on fire for this reason, rather than as a punishment for failing to pay protection money. The technique was the same used in an incident on Cosmonaut Leonov Street: after picking the kiosk lock, bottles with petrol and another explosive substance were thrown inside.

Employees

Sellers have been identified as a potential 'problem' by virtually all of the kiosk owners interviewed (it is interesting to note that the majority of the owners themselves started off as salespeople). They may not turn up to work, get drunk on the job, or embezzle goods. For instance, Andrei once found that he was missing a few bottles of vodka from his stock. The seller claimed that he had been robbed, while Andrei was sure that he had drunk them with some friends. The seller was dismissed but the loss was not compensated for.

Sasha and Inna also complained about their selling agents (we have noted, as well as being kiosk owners, Inna and Sasha travel in the region to sell fruit and vegetables from a truck). They also entrust their merchandise to street sellers (usually women). In order for this to be legal, they now have to buy a selling licence, where the sales site is specified.

Labourers are hired by Inna and Sasha on a daily basis and stand for many hours on one spot. At the start of the day, the two employers take their passports, in order to ensure that the employees do not escape with either the money or the goods. During the day, Sasha drives the truck and passes by those selling spots to check on their employees. 'Most of these people are not professional, although we can count on one or two people who have been working for us for the past year on a permanent basis' (K6). 'Only yesterday', added Sasha, 'I had a new seller lost 55,000 roubles by giving the wrong change. I am not sure whether she is cheating me or not, but I will find a way to punish her. I am still holding her passport. I will either dismiss her or make her pay the next working day, or both' (K6).

More sophisticated sellers have set up a way systematically to cheat their employers. Andrei explained: 'kiosk sellers make a deal to sell the goods brought by somebody else, instead of the goods bought for the kiosk by the owner. When we arrive at the end of the day, the seller tells us that our goods were not sold. In fact, what happened was that the seller sold these other goods!' (K3) By doing so, they get a bigger cut on sales than the usual 5 percent. Andrei had never experienced this himself, though he greatly feared it. Petr reluctantly admitted that he had once caught his salesperson engaging in this practice. He added that she was severely punished, though he supplied no further details. Olga, on the other hand, has established a trust relationship with her selling agents. 'We have been working for a long time with them, they are regular sellers. They work two days in a row, from 8 a.m. to 10.30 p.m. (The kiosks' opening hours), and then take two days off. We pay them 50,000 a day in the summer and 40,000 a day in the winter, when there is less business. Some other kiosks pay them a percentage of the profit, but we got used to this system, it works fine with us, they are quite keen to sell, even without this incentive. They do not really cheat us, we make routine checks. Yes, they might sometime charge their own price, but we think that it is very rare' (K9).

Creditors

Kiosk owners usually have no extra money to lend to other businesses. Other interviewees had lent money and did not manage to retrieve it. 'A person owes me money for eight months,' said Gennadii, '3,000 dollars and so far he has not repaid it. I did not even think of going to the Court of Arbitration. You know, even if they recognize that you have the right to the money, the debtor can always declare himself bankrupt and you will never see it back.' (B6)

The Search for Protection

We now consider to the sources of protection to which business-people turn to in order to minimize harassment. In 1993, Alla, a businesswoman, decided to open a travel agency in Perm and advertised it in the local papers. As she was to find out later, newspapers are used by criminals in search of information on new businesses.[36] After a few weeks, the racket knocked on the door of her travel agency and asked for a sum of money, which she could not pay. Frightened by this incident, she decided to close her office and informed her clients that she was going out of business. Instead, she opened a new travel agency, this time housed inside one of the biggest factories in Perm, which was managed by her uncle. She mainly organized tours for employees of the factory and friends of hers. Alla made a point of keeping her business as secretive as possible, avoiding—among other things—advertising in the papers (B18).

In one incident, she recalled she had organized a shopping tour to Poland, during which some of her customers had bought cars. Once the cars arrived at the airport, she went to pick them up with the legitimate owners, at which point they were asked for a million roubles per car. This they paid. She regarded herself extremely lucky that the racketeers were not the same as those she had encountered before. If she had been recognized, they would have realized that she had lied to them (B18).

Alla consciously decided not to expand her business, in order to avoid the racket. Instead she relied on alternative protection from her uncle. This choice limited the number of clients she could serve. Nevertheless, she accepted the cost. The protection offered by her uncle shielded her from racketeers calling at the door of her agency. It did not reach as far the airport, however, where her clients became victims of extortion. We might expect that next time the same customers might wish to arrange their shopping trip with an agency that, *ceteris paribus*, will protect them at the airport also.

Konstantin is the chairman of the firm Uralbis and former chairman of the sports department of Perm's Komsomol. The firm Uralbis is one of the most successful retail businesses in the city. It owns a store in the centre of Perm. The company also has various shops in the city and employs over 6,000 people. His company employs many private guards full time. They are mainly former sportsmen. He maintains that he is extremely interested in sports and his company sponsors a number of sporting events in the city. He is also a successful politician: at the time of this fieldwork, he is a member of both the city and the regional councils, and sits on the finance committee of both chambers. He denies paying any protection money or ever having been asked to do so. He also claims that his shops had never been the object of criminal harassment (B11). Others also, like Konstantin, maintained that they have never paid protection money to any criminal organization (B1, B3, B13). Mr Leonid Z. supplied the following description of his first, and last, interaction with the racketeers:

One day, a man from the racket came into this office through the very door you have just come through, and asked for protection money. At first, we did not give him any money. Then I went to the militia office and consulted the deputy-head of the Perm Regional Militia. They could have arrested him immediately. We knew his name and address. However, if he had been arrested, we would have had even more problems. Instead, I wanted to reach a compromise. So we agreed with the officer to send for this mafioso. He was ordered to come to the police office where we all had a meeting. I explained to him that he had knocked on the wrong door. He acknowledged that and left. The conversation was civilized and we parted on good terms. He never came back (B1).

Grigorii and Nikolai had a similar experience although they offered less details than Leonid. The militia had always provided effective protection to their businesses, so when they were approached by the racket, they settled 'the matter' through the militia (B3, B13). In neither case did they press charges nor were any arrests made. It appears that the militia and the racketeers in each case came to 'an understanding' and the avoidance of 'unnecessary conflicts'.

Irina Krasnosel'skikh, criminal correspondent for Perm's daily newspaper *Zvezda*, an important source for the present research (J1), related another example of a person who appeared to enjoy selective state protection, even though her activities were unmistakably illegal.

Recently a woman, the daughter of someone from the *nomenklatura*, opened a business, which was a cover for her main activity, smuggling precious metals from the region. She used trucks that were officially carrying washing powder. By accident the police stopped one of her trucks and uncovered the operation. Her flat was searched, but in the end no charges were brought against her. She was not part of a 'criminal' group and did not pay protection money to criminals such as Yakutenok [a well-known criminal figure in the city]. Rather, she was, and still is, protected by some state agencies. According to my sources, she shared some of her profits with them and they protected her activities against honest policemen and greedy criminals (J1).

Corrupt policemen were offering protection to this woman for activities that she was undertaking in the underworld, namely smuggling precious metals. Members of law enforcement bodies formed her 'roof'. Krasnosel'skikh adds a general remark:

The best 'roof' [protection] is the one provided by the state or the KGB. They tend to promote people who were part of those structures and have now become businessmen. For instance, the three biggest firms in Perm (including Uralbis) are headed by former KGB officers and enjoy this sort of 'roof' (J1).

Bogus and Predatory 'Roofs'

Business people sometimes buy bogus protection from swindlers. In a world where there is an expectation of mafia presence, impostors have an incentive to pass as real mafiosi, rip-off the benefits of the mafia reputation for violence, take the money and run. Joseph Serio, a security consultant who works in Moscow, has drawn attention to 'teenage wannabes' (*khuligany*): they 'are 17–20 year-olds who pass themselves as young toughs trying to take advantage of foreigners' well-known fear of "mafia"'. Serio offers an example: 'An American firm was approached by three wannabes in search of easy money. They presented themselves as members of the Chechen criminal community (*obshchina*), knowing that the Chechens have a reputation for being particularly fierce.'[37] The Moscow representative of the firm did not pay and the would-be mafiosi failed to show up again. Similarly, a Russian businessman who testified to the US senate on organized crime in Russia, described his uncertainty over whom to pay: 'As I said, [after 1994] things got out of control. I did not know which "roofs" to pay and which was safe to ignore. Men were showing up regularly asking for protection money'.[38]

The director of 'Muravei', Mr Y. Yakovlev, recalled an instance that occurred to him shortly after he opened his firm in Perm. A man who claimed to be a lieutenant of the Tax Police Department of Perm Regional Administration, Mr A. M. Porublev, approached him. He alleged that the company had broken the law on trading. He then took some official papers out of his briefcase and started to compute the amount of the fine. 'The papers looked official. At first, I believed him' (B8). He then offered to settle the question in an amicable fashion and received two bottles of expensive gin and some cigarettes as a token of gratitude. Porublev returned to the company owned by Mr Yakovlev and offered to protect the company against all possible misfortunes, to inform him in advance of tax police inspections, and to settle potential conflicts with the militia and other businesses. For these services, he asked for a monthly income of 200,000 roubles.

The sum requested was rather substantial, yet Yakovlev paid. Shortly afterwards, however, the payments were becoming too burdensome. He made inquiries and discovered that Porublev was not employed at the tax department. Eventually Porublev was arrested and a criminal case was brought against him at Sverdlovskii district court. He was later condemned to two years and seven months imprisonment in a hard-labour colony for fraud and misappropriation of the title and power of officials (criminal case no. 4025/94). The list of businesses that Porublev managed to swindle in a comparatively short period of time includes more than ten companies and four kiosks. The Tax Police Department of the Perm region informed the public that other people were showing false certificates and obtaining money in a similar fashion.[39] After these events, Mr Y. Yakovlev started to pay a different 'roof'.

The above instance of bogus protection points to the importance of having reliable information on the nature of the protector. Even if the payment of protection money is widespread, it does not follow that effective protection is inevitably acquired. Arkadii opened a shop that sold stereo equipment in Shosse Kosmonavtov, in premises previously used by a book-shop, 'Bukinist'. He did not contact the racket *before* starting the business. Arkadii just opened it. In a matter of a few weeks, the racket showed up. Politely, they asked him whether he already had a 'roof'. They said that if he had not arranged for a 'roof' already, then it was too late to search for a different one. They were going to provide one for him, whether he wanted it or not.

These criminal protectors proved to be extremely unreliable: 'I ended up paying roughly 1,000 dollars a month' (B9). Later on the group became greedier: instead of coming only once a month, they started to ask for advances on the monthly payment. Moreover, when the shop was robbed, the 'roof' was not able to recover the merchandise. Arkadii eventually had to close the shop and considered himself lucky enough not to have any outstanding debts with either banks or unofficial credit channels. Arkadii came to the conclusion that this particular 'roof' was made up of drug-addicts who harassed businesses because they needed a constant supply of money to buy drugs (B9).

In another instance, similar to that of Arkadii, Boris opened a shop selling clothes in a different part of the city without having previously arranged for a 'roof'. When a 'roof' showed up, his first reaction was to call the police. His partner convinced him that the police would not be a sensible solution: 'they come once, and then go leaving the shop in danger' (B10). His partner suggested phoning the lawyer of a prominent criminal, who is said to 'control' the city—Yakutenok. 'This move—said Boris—did not solve much. It just increased the confusion.' Now, there were two groups instead of one, coming in and out of the shop, disrupting ordinary business activities. 'We ended up with the first gang as our "roof", and paid roughly 1,000 dollars a month. However, this "roof" was very ineffective. The shop was robbed twice and they did nothing. They did not want to or could not look after our merchandise. The second robbery was especially severe' (B10). At the time of the interview, Boris's shop was in deep financial crisis and Boris was seriously thinking of giving up his business (B10).

The Search for Effective 'Roofs'

More successful stories of relationships with criminal 'roofs' emerged from other interviewees, in particular B5, B6, B12, and B16. They all explained, in different ways, that the reason why certain businesses were 'luckier' than others depended on their approach to the racketeers. The reason why certain businesses ended up in the wrong hands was because 'they did not arrange for a "roof" *before* opening. This is the best strategy if you want your business to prosper: you get in touch with a "roof" that you trust. You can ask around to find out which "roofs" are most effective. At this point, *they* [i.e. the "roof's" representatives] even tell you *where* to open the shop' (B6). Olga, the owner of a kiosk that has been operating for many years, had arranged in advance for her 'roof'.

I never had any problem of identity with my 'roof', we were in contact with him before opening, we are in good relations with him, for a while he had some problems and disappeared, but now he is back. When other people come and ask us to pay the 'roof', we say that we are already protected by this one, and they do not come back to bother us (K9).

The director of Sever, a private security agency, maintains that the 'rule of the first' applies in Perm.

If a bandit comes to a businessman and is told by him that he has a 'roof' already, the band may either trust the businessman or ask for a proof. In this sense, the question is not so much whether the businessman is telling a lie, but rather whether the 'roof' is strong enough to actually protect the business. If the new bandits want to test this, they organize a meeting with the original 'roof', and this has to prove to be strong enough to retain its right over the firm. If not, then war and blood follow (SF2).

The director of Perm's branch of Alex, a well-known private protection agency, gave me the following advice, when I asked him how I should approach the 'roof', in case I wanted to open a shop in Perm.

If you want to open a shop in Perm, it is better to collect information in advance on the best 'roof' available, check with organs of internal affairs, and with criminal groups. There are in effect three ways to obtain protection: from a state structure, a protection agency or a criminal group. Let's say, you open the shop, in half a year some people will have surely come up to offer you a 'roof'. If you are unprepared, you can make mistakes (SF1).

You cannot leave the choice of a 'roof' to chance, concurs Grigorii. 'It is a crucial business decision, as important as deciding what to sell and how much stock to buy' (B5). If the owner does not arrange in advance for an effective 'roof', the business may be doomed from the start. 'It is better to begin business under the guidance of an experienced "protector" [*brigadir*]. That person, if you can come to an agreement with him, will become your best guide in those difficult affairs you have chosen for yourself' (B16). Vadim added that some 'roofs' are known for being ineffective, full of unreliable individuals. 'The best "roofs" control Komsomol'skii Prospekt [a central street]. There, many shops are owned directly by criminal elements: if you rent a shop in one of these *magaziny*, you are provided with a "roof", which is also interested in protecting its own establishment. This is the best solution' (B12).

Boris V. gave a general picture of 'roofs' in Perm, which further indicates that business people can distinguish among different protectors:

Protection is divided in two broad categories: white and black protection rackets. This division does not refer to the ethnicity of the leader. The white is much more enterprising and reinvests the money it collects in proper business activities, while the black does not think in advance; it collects the money and spends it. The white is much better connected with the administration, via the trade unions. This group is now gaining strength in Perm and is the most powerful. White or black, however, as far as money-raising and violence go, they use the same methods (B16).

There are cases when the relationship between 'roof' and retailer is friendly. Fedor and the head of his criminal 'roof' went fishing together and the two families had become friends. 'You should not get the wrong impression: not all these people are dangerous criminals. Some may be of great help—decent, honest people' (B4). His 'roof' was suggested to him by a neighbour who already had a shop. Fedor was very grateful to him (B4).

Vadim described how he chose his 'roof'. One of his old school-mates, Mikhail, had married the daughter of a rather well-known criminal boss. Mikhail did not have any previous experience in retailing and had been unemployed for some time. Nevertheless, Vadim offered to become his partner. Mikhail eventually agreed and together they used Mikhail's father-in-law to get a 'roof'. However, Vadim had arranged to open a cafe near the Perm's Aeroflot office. The area was very convenient because, opposite the cafe, there is an open-air vegetable and fruit market twice a week. The market is quite busy and Vadim hoped that some customers would be tempted to enter his cafe. The market was protected by a group that would have laid claims to the cafe. Vadim, on the other hand, would rather have had his partner's father-in-law as 'roof'. At this point, a rather complex negotiation started between Mikhail's father-in-law and the gang that occupied the market. Negotiations lasted two months, but the outcome proved to be positive: Vadim was able to start operating and retain Mikhail's father-in-law as his 'roof'. The gang was compensated with some money and won the right to be involved in some of the businesses managed by Mikhail's father-in-law, although Vadim did not know, nor did he want to know, the exact nature of these businesses (B12).

The director of Alex has also some advice on how difficult it is to change 'roof'. 'Let's say you want to change "roof". If it is a state structure, it is easier. If one went to a criminal group of some sort, he has to pay off the "roof", in order to change it. And if one wants to change to a "roof" that is in conflict with the first one, the businessman can be really killed' (SF1).

The evidence presented above indicates that the protection contract for the higher echelons of local businessmen differs from that for smaller entrepreneurs. A 'special' relationship with organs of power and in particular the local militia did emerge directly from interviews with members of the former *nomenklatura* turned businessmen. Entrepreneurs who belonged to the former *nomenklatura* (Leonid, Grigorii, Nikolai, and Konstantin) or were related to its former members avoided low-level criminal harassment and reported that they were well protected by the militia.

Why would individuals in the state apparatus select members of the former *nomenklatura* to protect, instead of simply selling their services to the highest bidder? The answer may lie in the fact the transaction we are concerned with here is not a legal exchange of services. Even if a written contract can be drawn, the content of the exchange goes well beyond the simple provision of guards at the entrance of one's shop. The range of services includes favourable legislation and veiled threats to competitors and to criminal rackets. Rather, the special arrangements enjoyed by these entrepreneurs rely a great deal on 'gentlemen's agreements' and long-term exchange of favours.[40] Similarly, membership in an ethnically homogeneous group facilitates exchanges when the legal framework is non-existent or poorly developed. Only a limited number of 'trusted' traders participates in the network.[41] Direct membership or membership of a close relative in the former Soviet *nomenklatura* is analytically equivalent to membership of a homogeneous ethnic group.[42] The initial question of trust between supplier (officials still in the state apparatus) and customer (former *nomenklatura* person turned business-person) is solved by having had repeated interaction in the past. As in traditional markets, individuals in this market personalize exchange relations as a way of coping with contract uncertainty.[43]

Businessmen who are exposed to criminal harassment are also exposed to swindlers, who offer bogus and predatory 'roofs'. Predatory criminal groups extract vast amount of resources from the businesses they 'protect' and are difficult to send away. The level of the payment is constantly changing and no consideration is given to the demands of the business. Also no service is supplied. The consequences for these businesses are usually fatal: in a matter of few months, they are ruined. This appears to confirm the view that criminal protection is bogus.

The behaviour of predatory groups can be seen in two ways: either they are providing real protection to some customers only, or they are genuinely predatory with all their customers. In the first case, the group appears predatory to one customer, but in fact it is trying to dissuade a new entrant from competing with already existing firms, who are already paying protection money. It is a matter of perspective, as argued by Gambetta: 'From the point of view of the new entrant, [the fee imposed by the criminals] may look like extortion. But from the point of view of those dealers already buying protection, the extra cost imposed on the new entrant is precisely the reason why they pay for protection: to deter new entrants.'[44] Predation is then not a feature of the group, but rather a strategy of otherwise protective gangs.

Nevertheless, groups that are solely predatory might exist. If this is so, we might expect that, over time, predatory groups will deter businesses from opening and the area they control will become poorer. At the same time, predatory groups reduce their own sources of revenues, as pointed out by Leitzel and Pejovich. Such groups will therefore be weak and easily fall prey to better equipped and more efficient criminal competitors.

We have seen that entrepreneurs gather information in advance on the effectiveness of the group that is most likely to protect them and try to avoid ineffective 'roofs'. Rational business-people try to locate their activities in areas controlled by groups that have a reputation for offering better protection. It is also possible to negotiate the protection of a 'roof' in an area that is normally controlled by another 'roof'. This type of negotiation is essential for business people who must open in a particular area, but at the same time have no reason to trust the 'roof' protecting that area. A further reason why businessmen gather information before opening their operation is that a 'rule of the first' appears to be in place. Once a protector approaches a shop, this protector has precedence over subsequent claimants. The victim would find it difficult to change 'roof'.

5

The Contract and the Services

All interviewees who paid protection money to criminals had entered into long-term contracts with their respective 'roof'. Below, I explore the nature of the contract and the services offered, while in this section I concentrate on the supply of one-off protection services.

Although such services were not used by any of the entrepreneurs I interviewed, they do occur. According to one subject (B15), some entrepreneurs 'moved around' and considered it convenient to use criminal groups on a one-off basis.

The criminal group charges from 20 to 50 per cent of the value of what it retrieves for the businessman. Such a way of using the 'roof' enables the businessman to avoid paying a monthly fee. Some consider it very convenient. But they are wrong. Sending a criminal group which is not a permanent protector to settle disputes for you most probably means that the firm will never see its money again and may itself become indebted to the criminals (B15).

The following is a case of one-off service, though it involves not an entrepreneur with a fixed establishment, but an ordinary citizen (Y1).[1]

One of the few people to speak fluent English and Italian, Evgeniya is the granddaughter of a 'Hero of the Soviet Union', a fighter-pilot who died during the Spanish Civil War and to whom a street is dedicated in the city. Her father was a factory worker and her mother a doctor. At high school, she was an active member of the Komsomol and became head of her school committee. In this capacity, she went to the meeting of the

Perm Komsomol executive and met all the future party and city officials. Acquainted with the new entrepreneurial class of the city, she has worked extensively as a translator for major factories and enterprises in the city, including those linked with the so-called 'shady elements'. She has lived in Italy for a number of months and has travelled extensively in Turkey and Eastern Europe.

Evgeniya wanted to buy a flat for her husband to live in once their divorce was finalized. After searching for some time, she decided on a flat that had been recently privatized. A man called Yurii apparently owned the flat. A price that suited both parties was agreed upon. The notary (chosen by Evgeniya) certified all the documents and drew up a contract. The two parties agreed that in the contract the sum really exchanged should not be quoted in order to avoid paying excessive taxes. They quoted a fictitious sum, considerably smaller than the real amount.

Evgeniya started to move her husband's belongings into the new flat, when Yurii's wife and her son, who maintained that they owned the flat, confronted her claiming that Yurii had no power to sell it without their consent. They also added that Yurii had escaped with all the money and that they did not know where he was. At this point, Evgeniya went to a lawyer and found out that the two claimants were in the right: the flat was owned by two persons (Yurii and the son of Yurii's wife, Aleksei), so it had been privatized illegally only in Yurii's name. For the privatization to be legal, the relevant papers should have included Aleksei's name. The lawyer confirmed that Aleksei was entitled to half of the flat and that Evgeniya should compensate him.

Despite knowing that the privatization was illegal, Yurii sold the flat to Evgeniya. He pocketed the money and disappeared. Aleksei, Yurii's son, could reclaim the flat, as long as he paid Evgeniya the (nominal) sum stated in the contract.

Evgeniya was taken to the Civil court by Aleksei and his mother who claimed the flat back. After a number of months, the judge settled the dispute as follows: Evgeniya was to keep the flat but was obliged to buy Aleksei a one room-flat in a similar city location or hand him the equivalent sum in cash. Aleksei was to sign a document stating that he was satisfied with the final arrangement and only then could Evgeniya legitimately possess the flat.

Evgeniya was far from happy about the settlement. She did not know whether Yurii really escaped with the money or was part of a conspiracy with the rest of the family, but at that point it did not really make any difference to her. She had been swindled and intended to do something about it.

Evgeniya decided to turn to a powerful criminal group, which was operating in the city. This group was known to be in charge of the Lenin district, the central part of the city. An old friend of hers, Igor', also active in the Komsomol, was now working as a bookkeeper for this powerful criminal group. He offered to help.

At first she explained the situation to Igor', who reported it to his office. Shortly afterwards, she was granted an appointment and went to present the case herself at the group's headquarters. A clerk, a university gradu- ate, inspected the papers. During a second meeting, she was introduced to a deputy of the group, who called her by name, though they had never met before. At this second meeting, a number of men came along, while during the first meeting only Igor', Evgeniya, and the office clerk were present. It took roughly four months before the criminals decided to take action on Evgeniya's side. According to Evgeniya, the group took so long, because it 'inquired into the other family's standing and found out that it was not connected to any "powerful network" '. She was also confident that the clerk had given a genuine report to the boss and found her to be in the right.

The aim now was to extract a declaration from Aleksei stating that he had received a sum sufficient to buy a one-room flat in a similar location of town. Evgeniya had no intention of paying such a sum to Aleksei. The group went to Aleksei's house, where, according to what Evgeniya was later told, they found Aleksei and his mother having dinner. They explained politely the situation to both and handed over the piece of paper. Aleksei at first refused to sign. He was then beaten up. After a few hours, he agreed to sign. My source for this, again, is Evgeniya, who assured me that the man had only been pushed around a bit, while his mother was not touched. Aleksei was just over 18.

Once the paper had been signed, the group's thugs went away. The party met again in front of the judge. At this meeting, Evgeniya was not accompanied by her lawyer, as before, but by Igor' and one of the thugs who had beaten up Aleksei a week or so earlier. Aleksei was alone and handed the signed paper to the judge. I asked Evgeniya whether she thought the judge had understood what was going on. She replied in the affirmative: 'For sure, but he also knew that I had been cheated by this family, therefore he did not say anything. In fact, he smiled.' After a brief inspection of the papers, the judge issued a sentence that ruled Evgeniya was now the legal owner of the disputed flat.

Evgeniya had to pay a fee for this service. She was told that fees ranged from 55 to 60 per cent of what the customer had saved. In her case, however, a discount was applied, because she was a good friend of one member of the group and a person of importance in the city.

The case of Evgeniya is significant in two respects: the excessive taxation pushed her outside the framework of the law and induced her to sign a fictitious contract. Once she was outside the framework of the law, she fell prey to a swindler. At that point, she could not resort to the services of the state. She had two options: either using the services of a state 'roof' or criminal protectors. Evgeniya did not belong to the former *nomenklatura*, not even via her family: although her grandfather was a 'Hero of the Soviet Union', neither of her parents held *nomenklatura* positions. During the interview, Evgeniya never mentioned trying to explore this channel.

She knew Igor' well enough to ask his advice and help. Igor's group supplied her with a one-off service. A standard price applied in cases similar to that of Evgeniya, however she was offered a discount, or, at any rate, so she was told. It appears that the relative standing of the customer mattered in deciding how much she should pay. The criminals 'kept their word' and delivered the service they promised to Evgeniya. Some years after this event was narrated to me, as this book was going to press, I learned that Evgenya and Igor' married and that they have a daughter together. It might be indeed proof that one-off protection services do turn into long-term relationships.

Long-Term Protection Contracts

All business people who paid protection money had entered into long-term contracts with their respective 'roof'. We first explore the interaction between kiosk owners and the criminal racket that controls the Visim neighbourhood where some of the kiosks were operating (K2, K3, K4, and K5).

Both Sasha's and Inna's kiosks were the only ones that were not open at night, did not sell alcohol, and were not paying protection money. At the time of the interview, Inna had owned her kiosk for almost three months. During this period, she did not receive a visit from the local racket. She did not know why they had not yet come, but offered one possible explanation, that her kiosk was not making enough money to be of interest (K1).

Since Inna did not have first-hand knowledge of the local racket, we have to turn to other kiosk owners for the details of protection in the area. All kiosk owners (K2, K3, K4, and K5) told the same story.

After the first or second month of operation had elapsed, 'some strong athletic gentlemen approach you and say: "I am from such-and-such, and he wants to see you"' (K2). Reportedly, they are extremely polite. The kiosk owner already knows that these men will arrange a meeting with the district boss, the *brigadir*. The meeting takes place quite soon after the owner is approached, invariably during the night, and does not last long, usually ten minutes. The *brigadir* 'comes around with his briefcase and looks like a businessman' (K4). Although the *brigadir* has an office in the district, the meeting is held in his car. This is a puzzle: apparently the office would be a suitable environment, as far as secrecy and convenience are concerned. Moreover, some kiosk owners reported having visited the office during the day. The choice of meeting near the kiosk appears to be a way of showing respect for the new customer. It is also a chance for the *brigadir* to exhibit his fancy car to petty kiosk owners. Andrei said that the *brigadir* drew his attention to the car's high quality music system.

During that meeting a number of questions are settled: first, the amount of the 'fee'. Was it a percentage of the overall turnover, a percentage of profits, or a fixed sum? Various authors have presented divergent data concerning this point. In a report prepared for President Boris Yeltsin in February 1994, the Analytical Centre for Social and Economic Policies claimed that 'three-quarters of private enterprises in Russia are forced to pay a *percentage* (10 to 20) of their earnings to criminal gangs'.[2] Jones and Moskoff document that '[in the last years of the Soviet regime] 75 per cent of Moscow's co-operatives and 90 per cent of Leningrad's co-operatives made payments to racketeers . . . Sometimes racketeers expected their extortion money to be a fixed *percentage* of the co-ops' income'.[3] This would explain, they argue, why many co-operatives want to keep their earnings secret. In fact, some newspapers reported that 'for a fee, racketeers can determine the size of their demands from exact figures about the co-operatives' incomes from the local soviets'.[4]

Other sources point to a different conclusion. *Trud* wrote that in 1988, out of 6,000 reported cases of racketeering, in almost half (2,800) the 'fee' requested was 500r. In 535 cases it clustered at 1,000r. and in 928 instances, protectors tried to extort more than 1,000r.[5]

My findings among kiosk owners in the Visim sub-district point to the conclusion that, during this night meeting in the car, the *brigadir* sets a fixed amount. The kiosk owners are asked to pay a fixed sum at regular intervals, usually monthly. The sum paid was 10,000r. per day, a sum, which they considered rather small, and one, which did not affect their overall earnings (a little more than $US2.00).[6] Kiosk owners praised the 'fair' tax system managed by the *brigadir* and despised the predatory state equivalent (K2, K3, K4, and K5). Olga, who has a kiosk in a different part of town reports the following: 'When the racket comes, my cousin pays to a man called Roma. He comes and asks for my cousin. He decided the date and the sum to pay. It is a fixed amount every month, 200,000r. ($US03.84) for the kiosk in the centre and 100,000r. ($US21.90) for the one in the suburb. This sum of money is not too big. Some people have to pay 200 [dollars] a month. It does not bother us too much' (K9).

There is a reasonable explanation why the sum should be fixed rather than a percentage of profit or turnover. The resources needed to gather information on each kiosk would be exorbitant. Since all these kiosks operate in a similar area, they could be taken to be 'homogeneous' from the mafioso's point of view. And in fact they are so, as far as their location, the goods sold, and the dimension of their establishment are concerned. The differences in profits and therefore the forgone income that the mafioso suffers from charging the same fee to all is negligible compared to the cost of gathering information for each kiosk owner. By choosing a fixed sum, the mafioso saves bargaining time with each kiosk owner. Also, he avoids comparisons among kiosk owners on who got the best the deal. Such comparisons may in turn fuel dissatisfaction. Furthermore, mafiosi seem to settle for round sums of money.

During the night meetings, *brigadir* and kiosk owner agree on the details of the payment. They agree on a date for passing the money over, which is kept secret by the kiosk owner. On that date, invariably at night, an emissary from the *brigadir*, a *boevik*, comes to collect an envelope containing the money. The *boevik* will mention the nickname of the *brigadir* and the salesperson will hand him the envelope. The *boevik* utters a sentence similar to the one he said the first time they met: 'I am from Mr Such-and-such' or 'I work for Mr Such-and-such'. The name given is the *brigadir*'s nickname.

In principle, it might happen that the envelope is handed to the wrong person, but in fact this has never happened to the kiosk owners in Visim. The predetermined date is a safety device: only the real racketeer knows when his man is supposed to collect the envelope. Neither he nor the kiosk owner has an interest in letting other people know about it.

The only other person who knows the crucial date, and might have an interest in cheating both parties, is the salesperson. The kiosk owners reported that they had never had any problem, but three (K2, K3, K4) told me the following story. Once a salesperson gave the envelope to the wrong person, or at least so she claimed. According to her, she was given the right name and so she handed over the money to him. A few hours later, the real racketeer came and was told that his money had been given to somebody else. The kiosk owner was called from home and promised to find the money for the following week. After a few inquiries, the racketeers decided that the salesperson was trying to cheat both owner and racketeer. She was punished for this. The safest strategy, adopted by some kiosk owners, is not to entrust the envelope to the salesperson, but to supervise the transaction directly (K2, K5, K7).

All the other shop owners and business-people I interviewed (and paid protection money) had also entered into long-term contracts with their respective 'roof'. The payment took place once a month and the sum was supposed to be a percentage of the profit of the business, usually within the range of 10–20 per cent of profits. The 'roof', however, did not calculate the exact amount each month. During the first few months of operation, the 'roof' sent an expert accountant to evaluate the profit of the business. Such a person might spend considerable time in the shop during this period, or only few hours, depending on the how complex it was to establish the turnover of the business. The accountant would become the person best acquainted with the ups and downs of the company. He was the person who reported to the 'roof', but was also the one who could obtain delays in the monthly payment. 'These people are very civilized, they understand the problems of the business; they can wait and allow you to raise money. They are not pirates' (B6).[7] Eventually, the accountant could judge what the rough monthly turnover of the business would be and charge accordingly. What was calculated as a percentage of the profit then became, in effect, a fixed monthly payment. Only in case of major expansion of the business would the monthly fee be re-evaluated. The business-person was supposed to inform the 'roof' of any change in profits, but cheating did occur.

Sanctions

Kiosk owners cannot avoid paying for protection. If they refuse to pay, sanctions can be extremely severe. During the night of 14 March, 1994, a kiosk on Cosmonaut Leonov street, in the Industrial District, was burned. The owner and the salesperson—a woman of 24—perished in the fire. According to eyewitnesses, the day before, unknown people had already threatened the seller and had broken glass in the kiosk window. The seller reported the incident to the owner of the kiosk, T. S. Dzhafarov, and refused to continue to work in such an atmosphere of threats and fear. Dzhafarov did not give in and hired a new seller the same day. In the evening, unknown people visited the kiosk once more, but Dzhafarov managed to scare them off. The owner himself stayed overnight in his kiosk, which operated day and night, to help the newcomer. At around four o'clock in the morning, a window was broken and the place was set on fire. The construction, being full of empty wooden boxes, was engulfed very quickly by the fire. The metal door of the kiosk was sealed from the outside, so the two people could not escape.[8] Some kiosk owners agreed that the act of locking the kiosk from the outside signalled that it was a racket's operation (K2, K4, K6).

The owner of five kiosks in Visim also had his kiosks burned down. For two days in a row, masked people set the kiosks on fire and locked the sellers inside. They did not, however, throw any flammable mixture through the window, but simply set fire to the wooden structure. Once the arsonists were gone, the sellers were able to call for help and were released. On the third day, no seller would agree to work for the kiosk owner. Rumours spread that the remaining kiosks would have been set on fire with serious consequences, without allowing the sellers to escape.[9] A further incident that I recorded is that of a kiosk owner who was tortured with an iron and later dropped half-conscious on the side of a street. Later the police picked him up. According to the police officer who informed me of the case, he had refused to pay protection money (M2).

A major case of a business-person who tried to conceal income from his 'roof' took place in Perm in 1993–4. It involved a firm selling alcohol. The business-person in question was a rather well-known medical doctor who stopped practising and started his own business. He opened a commercial enterprise called West-Ur that sold spirits, especially vodka. Alongside this legal operation, he developed an illegal one, acquiring vodka from a factory. The doctor was—according to Boris Sorokin, head of the anti-organized crime unit—'under the control of criminals, to whom he paid hundreds of millions of roubles'.[10] One of the most powerful criminal groups in the city supplied protection to the company and shared the profits (according to Sorokin this amounted to 10 per cent).[11] At the end of the first two years of the operation the business was not so profitable: cheap vodka had entered the market and profits had shrunk. At this point, the doctor decided to start another business, but he did not tell his 'roof'. After roughly six months, the criminal group discovered it had been cheated and a violent quarrel ensued on company premises. Apparently, the criminals were beating the doctor, with the intention of killing him. During this violent discussion, one n.c.o. from the Special-Purpose Militia Unit (OMON), Aleksandr Zuev happened to be passing in the corridor and entered the room. Zuev, who was not in uniform, inquired as to the quarrel and the head of the criminal group turned around and shot him. The killing of the officer upset the *modus vivendi* that the city militia and the criminal groups of the city had reached. At that point, all the most important criminal figures, including the medical doctor, went into hiding, afraid of police retaliation (J1). The death of the policeman led the militia to launch an operation devoted exclusively to combating organized crime in the city, Operation Signal. It lasted several weeks and led to the confiscation of weapons and the arrests of various individuals, including Bari Zykov, the brother of a well-known criminal figure, Yakutenok.[12]

The Services

Protection against Khuligany

Does the racket provide any form of protection to kiosk owners? During the first meeting, the *brigadir* leaves a phone number with the owner. In case of need, the kiosk owner can phone his or her protector. However, there are contradictory stories as to the effectiveness of the racket in protecting the kiosk.

The racket does not really defend us against small *khuligany*. I am afraid that here it is not like St Petersburg. There, the racket punishes even those who dare to break the glass of a kiosk. But here, they do not.

We indeed phone them sometimes to get help, but nobody ever answers. It is always impossible to find them. They intervene only if another organized gang enters their territory. But even then, we have to give them a very detailed account of the event, plate numbers, etc. What they always tell us is that 'you must deal with local people yourself' (K3).

Aleksandr confirmed this. 'Recently, something was stolen from my kiosk so I phoned our *brigadir*. I knew who had taken the stuff but he did not do anything. Anyway, it was really our fault because the two sales-persons were drunk' (K4). Olga had a similar experience:

When we still had links with a factory producing vodka, we had a storehouse in a garage. The storehouse was robbed and there were goods for 15 million rou-bles. We asked the militia first but it did not do anything. Then we tried to find the goods ourselves. You see, it was possible to trace them since they had a specific date and were not sold by anyone else in Perm. We found the liquor in a kiosk, the date also matched and the kiosk owner had no purchase certificate for these goods. We went then to militia again and militia said that there was not a sufficient proof. At this point, we asked Roma [the *boevick*]. We promised him 30 per cent of the 15 million if he was able to retrieve the goods. Then we promised 50 per cent but Roma refused, saying that it is not his business (K9).

In another instance, not only did Roma not help Olga to retrieve the mer-chandise she lost, but appears to have been involved in a minor fraud against the kiosk itself, although it is not clear how 'guilty' Roma actually was. 'Once, somebody came and claimed to be a friend of Roma. We could not check that. He bought a lot of merchandise and paid with counterfeit money (200 dollars). Later, we called Roma and told him what happened; we were very upset about it. After some time, the man came back, brought several kilos of butter as a gift. Maybe it was Roma who told him to come back and compensate us for what he had done' (K9).

Petr displayed a very positive attitude towards the mafia, though he stressed that a man should also be able to rely upon his own force. He praised in particular the mafia's efficacy in returning stolen goods: 'If I go to the mafia, it will take one day to get my merchandise back: the person who stole it from me will come to me on his knees, return everything and also compensate me for the loss of the working day' (K2). Anvar has a similar, positive view of the racket:

The only organization that helps me is the racket. Without the racket, I would not be able to survive. I myself protect the kiosk at night. But if the racket were not present, my business would collapse. Thank God the racket exists. What they do is punish anyone who makes trouble for me. I can report the car plate to them, or describe someone's appearance, and they will make sure these people are punished (K5).

Neither Anvar nor Petr referred to any specific event, although they were very confident regarding the efficacy of the racket.

Kiosk owners do not leave it to the racket to protect their establishments at night. Aleks employed an evening guard, who would spend the night in the kiosk, sitting next to the salesperson. This person was paid to sit in the kiosk and intervene in case his help was required. Anvar and Petr did the night-guarding themselves, spending most of the evening in their own car which they parked nearby. 'I go out at night to check that everything is OK at the kiosk. If there is some danger, I go out of the kiosk, I close the door and deal with it. So, in the first instance, you always rely upon yourself' (K2).

Andrei employed a more elaborate system:

At night I employ a well-built man, his wife and their dog, who do the selling and the guarding at my kiosk at the same time. I pay them a fixed amount for providing security. They do not have guns, just the dog. Some other people use spray. I also let this couple charge whatever price they want so they can make some extra money. They can bargain for themselves at night (K3).

For night-guarding, Sasha relies on a nearby drivers' training organization (STK) called Orbita. This establishment is checked at night by a hired guard. Sasha has struck a deal with the guard, according to which he looks after Sasha's kiosk during the night and Sasha compensates the guard in kind. Nevertheless, he brings home all his valuables from the kiosk every night.

Protection against Militia Harassment

No evidence of the racket being able to help reduce militia and authorities' harassment emerged. Olga, who by 1999 was still operating three kiosks in the city, had developed a special relationship with an official in the militia who would help when needed.

Olga: Each district in the city is run like a different republic, they all have different rules and regulations. For instance in this one there is a special health commission [*medvytrezvitel*'] that comes to check things in the kiosk, but it operates only in this district. When they come they always find something wrong.
Q: And what do you do, do you pay them in order to avoid the fine?
A: No, we let them write the report, then we approach a friend of ours that

works in the militia, a major. He goes to the office and removes the report from the file. Once another militia person came, a woman, and found some faults in our selling centre. We went again to the major and did not go to her office, nor gave her anything. She came once more and showed that she was very upset because we had not gone to her to settle the matter, and found another fault with the kiosk, this time it was very obvious it was a pretext. But we still went to the major and she did not come back.

Q: Do you pay him then?

A: No, he is good acquaintance, he never abuses his position of power with us. Surely sometimes we help him, for instance recently his mother died and he asked to borrow 2,000 r. to pay for the funeral. We lent the money to him and then said that it was OK, there was no need to pay us back. Sometimes he comes, we have a drink together, we offer him a drink (K9).

Olga, in effect, relies on two 'roofs'. One resembles the political protection enjoyed by big conglomerates in Russia and the cosy relationship between sectors of the state appartatus and some businessmen, such as Konstantin and Leonid. On the other hand, she also pays to a *banditskaya krysha*.

Credit

Aleksandr, who was dissatisfied as far as protection against drunken customers and petty thieves (*khuligany*) went, used the services of the *brigadir* in the following instance.

Once I was fined 5 million roubles but I did not have the money to pay the fine. So I decided to pay a bribe to the militia. I approached the militia officer directly, but they asked for a lot of money. I had to borrow money. I met the man who, in the end, lent me the money in the office of the *brigadir* (K4).

The racket arranges for money to be lent and kiosk owners consider it an option (see above, p. 92). Anvar, who did not make use of the system, said:

I did not ask the racket for money because I tried to raise the money I needed [to start my business activity] myself. However, I know that they always charge an interest rate that is lower than the bank's. The main difference is, however, that they want the money back right on time. If you are supposed to give the money back after five months and the sixth month has elapsed and you have not paid yet, then they will either raise the rate of interest or come and ask for the money. In the latter case, they will estimate what you have—such as the kiosk or the flat—and make you pay (K5).

What emerges from Anvar's testimony is that kiosk owners are not forced to borrow from criminal structures and, moreover, they know very well the consequences they would face in case of a delay in the payment. They rationally evaluate pros and cons of each option. Anvar was fortunate enough to be able to utilize other channels.

The racket can help to retrieve loans. Gennadii, for instance, had lent money to a business partner, who had not returned it.

Gennadii: Nobody applies to the court of arbitration to settle disputes. For instance, for eight months, someone, who has yet to return it to me, has owed me 3,000 dollars. I did not even think of going to the court. You know, even if they recognize that you have the right over that money, the debtor can always declare himself bankrupt and you will never see the money again. So I asked my 'roof' for help, but the debtor went into hiding and we have not found him yet.
Q: What happens if you find him and he has no money?
A: It is his problem, let him borrow it from someone else (B6).

Grigorii could fit well the description of the business-person who owed money to Gennadii. He borrowed 15 million roubles to invest in buying a quantity of sugar at a very good price. However, the deal did not materialize and his debt rose immensely. He could not return the money and was kidnapped, beaten up, his house robbed and his wife and child threatened. We met in the sitting room of his flat. There were numerous doors and locks and to get into his flat, one had to go through three armour-clad doors. One of these doors was on the stairs, protecting the corridor from people coming up the stairs, and two were at the door of his apartment. He explained how the underground credit system operates.

To obtain credit from legal banks is extremely difficult. If that channel is unavailable to you, you then turn to 'unofficial' structures, basically criminal ones. They operate in two ways: either they oversee the lending of money that comes from people they know; or, if they want, they can lend their own money. Interest rates are variable. If you are a good acquaintance of theirs, you might even be able to borrow for nothing; they will not charge you anything. The most important thing is that you repay on time (B5).

Grigorii was not running a business when he applied for a loan. He did not have a 'roof', either official or criminal. He had what seemed a good 'business idea' and tried to put it into action. He claimed that not having had a 'roof' is the reason why his business adventure went wrong and why he was now faced with the prospect of further harassment from the criminal world. 'I was a nobody: I had no friends in high places nor among criminals' (B5).

The following is another instance of a debtor, Vitalii, who could not return the money he borrowed. It was narrated to me by Volodya G. (B17). Vitalii was the commercial director of a firm selling Bounty bars in Perm. Vitalii and the owner of the company had struck a deal with a company in Moscow. According to the deal, the Perm company would have received the Bounty bars at a very profitable price, but the deal however was only on offer for a week. After this, the Moscow company would sell the Bounty bars to someone else. In order to obtain the Bounty bars within the time set by the Moscow company, Vitalii and the owner of the company needed to borrow 10 million roubles.

Vitalii explored three different sources of capital. At first he asked the suppliers themselves to lend him the money, but they refused. Then he asked a bank in Perm. The bank agreed to consider his request, but the process would have taken more than a week. Vitalii did not have time to wait for the bank to review his case, and asked some businessmen for the money as a bridging loan. The businessmen lent Vitalii the 10 million roubles and charged him 10 per cent a day. Volodya took the money, went to Moscow and bought the Bounty bars. However, the situation backfired: the bank decided not to lend the money to Vitalii, moreover, Bounty bars were not selling as well as expected. In the meantime, interest rates were skyrocketing. In ten days, the debts had become 20 million roubles. Vitalii, who had negotiated the debt, was left alone to face the lenders. He did not have the money and asked for the debt to be renegotiated. But the deal he obtained was even worse: the lenders were willing to wait, but wanted 20 per cent a day.

In another instance, the debtor was simply killed. Although the people who were eventually convicted worked for a 'private protection firm', they clearly wanted to signal that it was an (Italian) mafia murder. The victim was put into a metal barrel and cement was poured over the body. The barrel was thrown into the river Las'va and it resurfaced not long after.[13]

Elimination of Competitors

The reader may recall Inna's 'price war' at a selling spot in Dobryanka.[14] The day after the 'price war', the same seller started to put pressure on them, by resorting to some thugs (*balbesy*) who tried to scare them away. 'Fortunately', Inna and Sasha had entered a protection contract, so they could continue to sell in that area: '(the second day), we tried to negotiate a common price in a civilized way. But this person refused and called his own *balbesy*. Fortunately, we also had our own people and the matter was eventually settled' (K1).

Anvar recalls another instance of genuine protection against competitors. Anvar recalled the story as if it referred to a friend of his, however his resentment towards his colleagues—and in particular Petr—[15] led me to suppose that it had, in fact, happened to him. Nevertheless, I could not obtain confirmation of this from other kiosk owners.

A kiosk owner, let's call him Maksim, had just opened a kiosk. He was able to sell alcohol at a considerably lower price than his immediate competitors because he was being supplied with newly unloaded, untaxed merchandise by friends. Customers flocked to Maksim's kiosk. In the meantime, the other owners started to get nervous. They approached Maksim who was, by that time, paying protection money, and tried to convince him to raise his prices. He stubbornly refused. Irritated by Maksim's reply, the kiosk owners wanted to punish the 'unlawful' competitor. However, they knew that he had started to pay protection money and could not proceed without informing the local *brigadir*, especially as Maksim would have immediately understood from where the harassment was coming from and would himself have complained to the *brigadir*. So they informed the *brigadir* of their intentions. To their surprise, he did not allow them to proceed. Shortly afterwards, the *brigadir* himself, rather than a deputy, went to Maksim's kiosk and informed him of the danger he had been in. He also asked Maksim to come to a reasonable agreement with the other kiosk owners. In particular, he suggested that Maksim raise the price of the liquors sold at his kiosk. A new meeting with the other kiosk owners took place at a city restaurant, and eventually Maksim raised the price of his alcohol. Olga narrates a similar case.

In one instance the 'roof' helped. When we wanted to open a third kiosk, the neighbouring Azerbaijani also wanted to open a new kiosk, and therefore a conflict between us emerged. The two 'roofs' settled the conflict. The two 'roofs' met and, after the meeting, they agreed that we could open the next kiosk. We also clashed over prices: they were charging much cheaper prices than we were, but now we have come to an agreement.

However, since the incident regarding the opening of the new kiosk, we had no more problem with the Azerbaijani, no more conflict of interest although we had some arguments, like you have with your own neighbours. But we did not need again to use our 'roof'. This is because the Azerbaijani understood that we also are 'serious' people, not just naive (K9).

Community Disputes

According to a respondent, effective 'roofs' may supply a business-person with a 'whole network of services, starting with delivery of goods and ending with the acquisition of privileged credit' (B2). Stepan put it as follows: 'What can you ask your "roof" to do for you? In principle every-thing, even asking them to beat up your wife's lover. You just have to make them *understand* the situation' (B14).[16] The following instance, which derives from the court hearings of a criminal case against a gang headed by a man called Plotnikov (see below, pp. 126–9), testifies to this. On 1 December 1989, a girl called Lena S. was attacked and beaten up by Roman M., her boyfriend. Lena went to Igor' Lun'kov, a friend of hers and member of Plotnikov's group, to complain. Lun'kov phoned Roman and threatened him. He also informed Roman that Plotnikov could not come personally to take revenge on him (the group leader was healing the wounds caused by an explosion at the market) but that he would come as soon as possible. Lun'kov added that it was no use for Roman to go into hiding because they would find him anyway. After a second phone call, and after much worrying on Roman's part, Lun'kov offered Roman a way out: they settled for 5,000 roubles as compensation to the girl. 'We do not want to kill you, said Lun'kov, 'just find the money.' When Plotnikov, Moroz, and Lun'kov visited Roman, he was taken to the hippodrome, where a *razborka* ('discussion') ensued. Moroz said he would kill Roman if he did not pay the money requested. In due course, Roman paid the sum, which was divided among the three men and Lena S.[17]

Uncertainties

Despite an entrepreneur's efforts to foster a lasting relationship with his 'roof', uncertainties always loom on the horizon, as in the event of the sudden death of one's protector. Until a new 'roof' is found, the entre-preneur may run high risks.

Life is not always easy, of course. I will tell you a story. My brother is a busi-nessman in Ufa [a city 200 km. south of Perm] and his protector [*brigadir*] was killed in a confrontation between criminals [*razborka*] over the control of spheres of influence. So he was without protection ['roof'] for a while. During that period, he was robbed and badly beaten up. He was unconscious for three days in hospital. His difficulties were solved when he got another 'roof'. All his goods were returned, except his health, of course (B14).

In another instance, the death of the 'roof' led to a police raid. A bordello was under the protection of Krest, a well-known Perm criminal, until he died in 1998. Not long afterwards, the police raided the bordello. While searching the papers of the keeper, Mrs Alieva, it was found out that she had been paying Krest regularly. In one year (1997), she had paid 270 million r. (almost $US47,000).[18]

The 'roof' is not necessarily advancing the interest of its client all the time. It may decide to switch to another customer and turn against its earlier customer. The consequences of such a switch may be deadly. Mr Suslov, the general director of the Perm company 'Initsiator', was assassinated in 1994. The militia arrested members of a criminal group of eleven people in connection with the murder, headed by a man called Troitskii. Some members of the group proved to be connected to the firm. The police discovered that the group was operating as the firm's 'roof'. The police arrested Suslov's partner, who confessed to having conspired with the group to kill Suslov. He had promised to share a substantial part of the profits of 'Initsiator' with the group and had paid them an extra sum for the murder in advance.[19]

When Two 'Roofs' Meet

Entrepreneurs who are both protected may come into conflict with each other. When they cannot handle the matter on their own, the respective 'roofs' are called in. Leonid Sharov, law correspondent for *Obshchaya gazeta*, reported on how widespread and somewhat elaborate 'outlaw courts' could be in Moscow. 'To my knowledge', he writes, 'fifty such trials took place in Moscow last year. This information comes from a certain Moscow attorney who was invited to participate in several sessions of "outlaw courts" as a legal expert. So in all likelihood, such courts are actually more widespread.' In one instance, a businessman dissatisfied with the *Arbitrazh* court decided to use his criminal connections to settle a dispute. The other party had criminal protectors as well and a rudimentary court was organised, and even outside lawyers were summoned. At the end of the 'trial', the lawyer representing the businessman told Sharov: 'things had not worked all that easily with the criminals. But still, they had worked out.'[20]

Four Perm entrepreneurs among those interviewed resorted to their 'roof' to settle matters with partners or competitors who were also protected. Stepan, for instance, was involved in a bitter dispute over the quality of a shipment of liquor produced by a firm based in the Perm region. The two companies could not reach a settlement and a meeting [*strelka*] ensued. 'We drove to a meeting place outside the city, where we met the other group. The two *brigadiry* exchanged greetings and, almost right after, the group's leader started to insult me. In the process, he was making the most unreasonable demands. My side was doing nothing for the time being and I was quite shocked. Then, my side started to shout and make the same sort of demands on the other businesman. Then, we were made to step aside and the two groups started to negotiate among each other' (B14).

Once the matter has been decided, the two groups perform the 'ritual of hand-shaking': the two *brigadiry* shake both hands, rather than just one, as people do in ordinary situations.[21] Stepan added that the *brigadiry* appeared to enjoy the situation, while he did not (B14). The *strelka* described above was the most elaborate recalled by my interviewees. Other instances occurred in expensive restaurants, where a lavish dinner is served after the matter has been settled successfully. Both groups are invited to the dinner, although the entrepreneurs pay the bill, noted Sergei.

Evgeniya's experience shows how ordinary individuals may end up searching for criminal protection. Excessive taxation led the two parties to draw a fake contract and, when a dispute arose, the actors involved could only resort to private protectors. Business people enter into long-term relationships with their 'roofs', cannot avoid paying, and the money charged tends to be a fixed sum. A round sum provides an obvious 'focal point', just as natural barriers like rivers, mountain ranges, or parallels of latitude are focal points for agreements in international boundary disputes.[22]

Do the criminals offer any protection? The racket of the Visim sub-district does not seem to consider protection against *khuligany* as its duty. The racket does not seem able to protect kiosk owners against militia harassment, and kiosk owners are either victimized by officials or have to develop their own ways to secure special treatment with officials. There is evidence that the racket offers some protection against competitors and assistance in obtaining credit, although at very tough conditions. Also, community disputes have been referred to local criminals and reports suggest that some service has been delivered.

Should we conclude that the protection offerred by criminals is bogus? Even the most efficient police system would find it hard to protect everybody all the time. This does not prevent customers (or citizens) from wishing for increased efforts. Similarly, Hong Kong Triads do not leave their men on the premise of the establishments they protect and customers protest.[23] We might conclude that the *banditskaya krysha* we have been looking at offers protection, which is not entirely bogus but could be massively improved.

We should resist the conclusion that everything works smoothly in a world where the local racketeer becomes a 'stationary bandit', a criminal with a long-term interest in the prosperity of the business he protects.[24] Uncertainties are numerous. Even in the more successful cases of interaction between criminals and business people, unpredictable events, such as the death of one's protector, may occur and disrupt (at the very least) business activities. Furthermore, the 'roof' can decide to switch to another client and dispose of his previous 'customer'. Protection is a private good supplied to a specific individual. If another individual comes along and offers a better deal to the 'roof', the latter might consider the proposition. Individuals in such a world are not 'citizens', with secure rights to protection. They are not even 'customers' in a market with standard rules the suppliers are compelled to abide by.

When a dispute arises between two clients who subscribe to the same criminal group, no problem ensues. The agency enforces a decision that is binding for both. No difficulty arises also in the case where one party is protected and the other is not, as in the case of Evgeniya and the family that sold her the flat. Potential difficulties arise when the disputing parties are protected by different agencies. A rather elaborate interaction ritual among two groups has been described by Stepan. The evidence is not yet sufficient to establish whether 'standard rules' are applied to 'standard cases', or—as in the case of the Sicilian mafia—each case is adjudicated on its own merit.[25] Nevertheless, the meeting of the two 'roofs' described above is evidence of the fact that criminal groups might eschew warfare in favour of arbitration and interagency co-operation. Nothing would stop them colluding with each other at the expense of the customers, as long as they can stop customers from switching to another 'roof'.

PART III

The Russian Mafia

6

The Mafia in Perm

In the previous two chapters we observed the operation of criminal protection rackets from the point of view of the victims. We now turn to the perpetrators and piece together some elements in the history of Perm's criminality at the time of the transition from the Soviet economic and political system to the market economy.

The Gulag Archipelago

Perm is situated in what Solzhenitsyn called the Gulag Archipelago, which extended as far as Kolyma, on the Arctic Ocean. A vast network of labour camps and settlements where criminals and political dissidents where forced to reside was located in the Perm region. Perm-36 is a most infamous camp, where political dissidents were confined, such as literary critic and writer Andrei Sinyavsky and human rights activist Vladimir Bukovsky.[1]

Passport regulations and population policies governed the lives of all Soviet citizens. The residence of Soviet citizens was determined, as pointed out by Louise Shelley, by a 'combination of birthplace, the internal passport system, marriage, and employment opportunities'.[2] Movement between different settlements and cities in the Soviet Union was heavily restricted. The internal passport carried at all times by Soviet citizens had been in existence since 1932. Such passports were given to all citizens at the age of 16: it showed the individual's street address and town or village of residence, the only place where the holder of the passport could legally reside.

The passport is issued by the local police and is updated periodically. If the holder wishes to change his place of residence permanently he must get the formal permission of the militia in his chosen area before he moves in. This is only a formality in small towns and the less desirable spots where there is little pressure on public amenities, but may present a major difficulty in places like Moscow, Leningrad and republic capitals, which have more to offer their inhabitants.[3]

Internal mobility and possibilities for residence were even more limited for former criminals than for ordinary citizens. All previous residences were recorded on the internal passport, including time spent in labour camps or prison.[4] Criminals from major urban centres, such as Moscow, who served minimum sentences of five years, automatically lost the right to register at their former place of residence when they returned from labour camp or prison, a policy in effect since the 1920s.[5] As a result, big cities housed few experienced criminals. This measure was taken in order to prevent major municipalities serving as schools for young offenders. Medium-sized cities, on the other hand, were recipients of a disproportionate number of first-time serious offenders and recidivists. Usually, former convicts were allowed to register in the area of the camp where they had served their sentence.[6]

The Perm region had the highest concentration of labour camps in the Soviet Union and therefore a great number of former convicts resettled in the region after the end of their term of imprisonment. Today, there are more than twenty labour camps fully operating. Among the better-known, Camp 6 (still in operation) was specially devised for dangerous offenders.[7] As of June 1995, the prison population of the region was 31,000 people; 24,000 of them were housed in corrective-labour institutions (ITU) in the Perm region, while 7,000 people were in Perm's Investigation Isolation Cell (SIZO).[8] Many criminals who are released still reside in the nearby under-populated rural areas, as pointed out by Colonel Valentin Gertsen, head of the Department for Combating Organized Crime in Perm (RUOP).[9] According to data from the local militia, 1 in 5 residents in the Perm region (excluding the regional capital) in 1992 had served prison sentences.[10]

Next to the enclosed camps, the Soviet Union authorities devised a system of settlements. In such settlements, former convicts would be forced to live for a number of years, as part of their term of imprisonment. The criminals would not have been guarded as in a proper labour camp, but were forbidden to leave. The inaccessibility of the Soviet countryside contributed significantly to the virtual isolation of inhabitants. As the few privately owned cars were possessed by the Soviet elite, lack of public transport in the rural areas and the poor conditions of roads minimized access to the countryside and reduced the possibility of criminals linking up with fellow offenders in cities. Cherdyn', in the Perm region, was (and still is) the city with the highest concentration of camps and forced settlements. A direct train line between Perm and Cherdyn' does not exist: using public transport, a traveller would have to take a train to Solikamsk and then face a bus ride of 102 km. (the total distance between Perm and Cherdyn' being 518 km.). But, among the many changes brought about by the end of the Soviet Union, cars have become more readily available, making the countryside far more accessible. As a result the settlements are now less remote from the city than in the past.

Vor-v-zakone Yakutenok

How did the legacy of the Gulag affect the contemporary criminal situation? The Soviet prison system was a universe through which as many as 18 million people passed during history of the USSR. As a consequence of resettlement policies, a high number of former convicts resided in the region. They would have been strongly associated with the Soviet criminal milieu, its structure and norms. In fact, a peculiar criminal fraternity, the fraternity of the *vory-v-zakone* (thieves-with-a-code-of-honour), emerged in the late 1920s. The *vory* spent most of their lives in the labour camps, consistently refusing to work. They developed an ideology of monastic purity, a ritual for the initiation into the fraternity and achieved a leading role over the *blatnye*, professional criminals who aspired to become *vory*, the highest possible honour in the criminal world. *Vory* controlled a communal fund (*obshchak*) to support group activities. The *obshchak* was financed both by extortion from inmates and contributions from the outside. The fraternity survived through the entire Soviet period, although in the 1950s camp authorities encouraged a 'war' against the *vory*, known as *such'ya voina* (1948–53). During such a 'war', a new breed of convicts killed many *vory* (see Chapter 7).

Perm also had its own prominent *vor*. Nikolai Stepanovich Zykov, born 8 June 1953, had been convicted eight times for crimes such as rape, drunken driving, and later illegal possession of drugs and arms. At the end of 1970s, he was crowned *vor-v-zakone* in a camp in the Perm region. His nickname was Yakutenok, a reference to the people of Yakutiya and their almond-shaped eyes. Officially he was never employed anywhere, although in 1987, when applying for a passport, he declared to be the manager of a company called 'Selenga'.[11]

Yakutenok and the *vory* of different cities are often portrayed as the apex of the criminal world. For Colonel Sorokin, Gertsen's successor as head of the RUOP in Perm, 'the criminal world has its own hierarchy. It is headed by the so-called *vory-v-zakone*, the lower rank being the criminal bosses [*avtoritety*]'.[12] Regularly, the press and the police pointed to Yakutenok as the person in charge of gathering the criminal *obshchak*, through a deputy referred to as *smotryashchii*. Sorokin maintains that Yakutenok appointed 'supervisors' in all the big cities of the region. These supervisors were responsible for organizing the criminal world of the city and gathering funds for the *obshchak*, to be transferred to Perm. He adds:

In small towns, agricultural settlements, as everywhere, money is collected. All the money gets to Perm, via a so-called *smotryashchii*. For instance, a recidivist B., who had been imprisoned before, was collecting contributions in the city of Osa, and he himself lived in Polazna. Money moved to the *obshchak* from Osa via Polazna to Perm. He tried to cheat and kept a part for himself. B. was killed, his corpse was found in the Kama river.[13]

The Gang of Plotnikov

Although very little is known about criminal groups in the late Soviet period, one was operating at the central fruit and vegetable market of the city, where most of the money could be made by racketeering market sellers, running small black market operations, and playing confidence tricks at the expense of sellers. The gang leader was a man called Plotnikov, to be known as Plotnik in the criminal world. Before entering a criminal career, Plotnikov was a well-known judo and sambo athlete ('master of sport'). He had won a number of competitions but, by the beginning of the 1980s, his sporting carrier had ended and he found himself unemployed. With nothing to do, he hung around the central fruit and vegetables market. After a few months, a group of idle young people answering to his orders had emerged. He was the oldest, kept discipline, and managed the gang's common fund (*obshchak*). A number of the founding members of the group were habitués of Soviet prisons. Moroz entered a colony at the age of 14 and, by 1990, had spent altogether twenty years in prison. Ganiev, another early member of Plotnikov's group, showed evident signs of tuberculosis at a trial in 1990, a disease which he contracted during his imprisonment, which also lasted for some twenty years. On the contrary, Sizov, had never been imprisoned before.

The original group consisted of fifteen to twenty people, with strong group solidarity. The gang members often gathered in a Perm bar that did not sell alcohol. Discipline was strict and included a ban on drinking.[14] Lateness to gang meetings was sanctioned: a fine which ranged from 50 to 100 roubles—a substantial sum of money in the mid-1980s—was to be paid by those who arrived even ten minutes late. During these meetings, the gang's members exchanged news, made toasts with orange juice, and took pictures of themselves, later used by the police to establish the group's membership. Such toasts included promises for those who were 'burned on the job' (arrested): they would receive a constant supply of goods in prison and their family would be supported while the member was behind bars. Also money was set aside in order to bribe officials concerned with the investigation. This money came from the *obshchak*.[15]

At that time, in the mid-1980s, the group's main occupation was thimblerig (*igra v naperstok*).[16] One gang member attracted a customer, another played the part of the lucky player, while a third one guarded the scene, looking out for the arrival of militia. This game attracted the attention of shoppers at the central market. As it was later discovered by the police, market shoppers were lured into believing that windfall profits were possible from the game, and then cheated.

Plotnikov's gang also went on tours 'abroad' in order to work in the Union's newly thriving city markets. After a previous agreement with the local criminal bosses, they settled in an area of the local market and played thimblerig. One of their trips took them as far as Tallinn, where the local militia did not appreciate their presence. The group was ordered to leave the Republic within 24 hours.

Thimblerig was not the only scam that occupied Plotnikov's gang: Zubkov and Batrakov, two other group members, were engaged in car frauds. They bought cars paying with rolls of ordinary paper, with real money on top (*kukly*). But the first major departure from thimblerig, and the beginning of large-scale operations by the group, was the business of smuggling the electric-chain saw, *Druzhba* (lit. 'friendship'), that was produced at the Dzerzhinskii plant. Workers at the plant used to go to the market and illegally sell spare parts for the *Druzhba*, in high demand in a region surrounded by forests. Plotnikov's idea consisted of co-ordinating the thefts of *Druzhbas* from the producing plant and selling the merchandise in various Eastern European countries and Soviet republics. A contraband operation between Perm and Moldavia, Perm and the Ukraine, and Perm and Lithuania was started. Big trucks were taking approximately 200 saws in one trip and bringing thousands of dollars back.

As emerges from letters that Plotnikov wrote to a gang member named Moroz, Plotnikov was in close contact with *vor* Zykov (Yakutenok). In one of these letters, written while Plotnikov and Moroz were awaiting trial in 1990, Plotnikov wrote: 'Yakut went crazy when he knew that I was in prison, because I am his closest friend. You know my friends. They do not speak lightly. If they say "kill", they will do it, 100 per cent.' Yakutenok, who at that time was out of prison, tried to pass a note to Plotnikov through the prison's staff. In the note, he asked if there was something he could do to help. According to Krasnosel'skikh, the only reporter admitted to the trail of Plotnikov,

Zykov exerted pressure on the witnesses who were supposed to testify against Plotnikov. The victims showed great fear of Plotnikov at the trial. They all tried to change their testimony. Even the victims who had got into the situation by chance were not purely honest people. They tried to deceive, they changed their testimony, and you never knew who was trying to pull the wool over the eyes of the court.[17]

During court hearings, a number of new witnesses appeared to exonerate Plotnikov. In his final statement, Plotnikov made a long speech. He expressed his deep offence at being labelled a criminal. In fact, he claimed, he was a protector (*zashchitnik*) of people, especially of women and of the weak. 'I am an honourable man. I just wanted to save people from danger.'[18]

Plotnikov acquired further authority in 1992, when he participated in a serious crime. According to a confidential police report dated 1995: 'he personally killed one boss of the criminal milieu of the city. He was sentenced to six years imprisonment, but served only part of his sentence, and gained authority among both young and experienced criminals.'[19]

As the years passed and with the broadening transition to the market, the group headed by Plotnik penetrated the legal economy. The same police report stated: '[the gang] controls a whole network of retail enterprises and places of public catering. Plotnikov's associates also founded several legal enterprises. They used the accounts of these enterprises to launder big sums of money, which were criminal in origin. With this money the above firms bought privatized shops, restaurants, and cafes. As far as big enterprises are concerned, they bought a significant quantity of shares.'[20]

Other Groups

Plotnik's is not the only post-Soviet criminal group with a permanent nature that emerged in Perm. When public catering enterprises were privatized, the most active was the group under the leadership of Tsiklop, also a former sportsman. Corrupt officials would disclose to him the names of bidders. Tsiklop would visit them and 'convince' them not to bid seriously for an enterprise that was to be privatized. Police reports state that those who refused were victimized 'in the most cruel way'. 'From 1991 to 1995', the police add, 'in Perm and in the Perm region, more than twenty businessmen who did not want to give in to the mafia were killed,' although there is no suggestion that they were all killed by this group. Another strategy pursued by Tsiklop was that of offering services to existing firms. 'He would promise support to existing directors against potential competitors at the future auctions, protection from possible encroachments, delivery of goods, guarding of premises, and support of any type. In such a way, he obtained control over restaurants as Orbita, Galaktika, Kamskie Ogni, and shops like Maksim, Rechnik, and others.'[21]

The picture that obtains at the Central Market in Perm is rather more complicated. Several groups of criminals emerged from the milieu of those who were playing thimblerig. Over the years, these gangs consolidated their resources in better-organized groups. One brigade, founded by a criminal nicknamed Petrus (killed in 1992), controls the sale of agricultural products. For the Perm police,

Petrus and his people had a staff of informers, who supplied information on which type of products will arrive, where from, and at what price. They offered their patronage to the sellers, promised them security, comfortable storehouses, good parking for motor vehicles, free sale of production at the price that they wanted. Petrus possessed outstanding qualities and he ensured protection from other criminal groups, co-ordinated activities, offered advice of a legal nature, and settled problems with tax inspection and militia.[22]

Other brigades operate at the market, each with its own 'specialization'. The same police report maintains: 'One controls the clothes' display area, extorting money, threatening sellers, spoiling their goods, or expelling them from the market. Another brigade is controlling the meat pavilion. They buy wholesale meat at a lower price. In case producers refuse, they create difficult conditions for the seller. The seller cannot obtain a selling point, scales, he can't butcher the meat and give it to the laboratory for health inspection.' All of these gangs are 'under the control of a criminal *avtoritet* named Ibragim. He is 30 years old, cunning and shrewd. Although he has never been in prison and the criminal world is suspicious of him, he leads the most powerful group. For this reason, other criminals accept his authority over the most complicated questions'.[23]

In Motovilikha, another city district, businessmen, sellers of alcohol, owners of transport bureaus, apply to the leader of the district, Popovich. The police believe that 'he takes a certain payment from them and ensures their protection from other criminal groups, but he can't protect them from the administrative organs. Businessmen in the district usually turn to Popovich for assistance in order to settle conflict among themselves'.[24]

A man called Belyaev is reputed to be the *avtoritet* of Ord-zhonikidzevskii district and to have taken under his control a 'significant part of the territory of the district', as emerged at a trial against his organization. Businessmen in various parts of the district (such as the Lev-shino, Golovanovo, and PDK sub-district) and sellers at the local market could not work without paying protection money, often in kind. Reportedly, the band follows a strict daily routine. 'They meet every day in the cafe "Vse dlya vas", where they report the results of their activities. The racketeers are well organized and gather "taxes" more effectively than the state. Every businessman and boy in the district knows the name of Belyaev.'[25] As usual the cases where the victim refused stubbornly to pay surfaced and were investigated by the police. According to one such victim called Subbotin, director of a firm named Kaskad, emissaries of Belyaev visited him in 1993. *Zvezda*, in an extensive report of the trial, writes:

They claimed that his firm needed to be protected, which means that the businessman was asked to pay a contribution to the criminal group. The director demanded a meeting with the head of the group. The meeting took place in a nightclub. There Subbotin met Belyaev and his group. The racketeers demanded that he employ a man from their group in the firm, who would not work but would receive a salary every month. The businessman refused. In a month Belyaev called upon the businessman again and the two decided to meet. Belyaev himself did not go to the meeting, but there came two emissaries [*kachki*], who threatened the businessman. Subbotin refused again. In a few days, there was a fire in his shop. Somebody threw gasoline through the windows and set the shop on fire. The losses were around 20 million roubles.[26]

A second case involved the director of the firm Myaso-produkty Ltd. He claimed he had no money to pay Belyaev's group. After being threatened, he was forced to sell his flat to pay the gang. The director informed the police and a video camera was placed in his office. The Belyaev's mafia group was caught red-handed, while receiving the money from the director. The police started a wider investigation into the activities of Belyaev and found arms and ammunitions in his garage. It also emerged that a police officer involved in some illegal business had paid contributions to Belyaev. Witnesses were at first promised anonymity, a promise that goes against the provisions of the Russian criminal code. When their names were revealed, they became targets of violent pressure: a shop window was broken, a man was beaten, and a woman was raped. One gang member, Borodkin (nicknamed *Raketa*), confronted a police officer, hit him in the face and forced him to reveal the address of an investigator involved in the case.[27]

Inter-group Relations and Conflicts

The headquarters of Perm's criminal world is allegedly the restaurant Gornyi Khrustal' (Rock Crystal). It is possible to meet *avtoritety* there, though the restaurant is not always open to the public. Business-people, local politicians, and criminal *avtoritety* of the city and guests from other cities gather at feasts, picnics, or birthday parties.[28] The police raided one birthday party celebration for Yakutenok on 8 June 1994 and a number of fugitives were arrested. Guests from four CIS states, seventeen regions within Russia, and seven cities of the Perm region had gathered. The total count was 215 people, of whom forty were armed bodyguards. Among the guests were criminals from Perm and Chelyabinsk (Makar, Vasya Tarych, Victor Ivanovich Glushenkov (nicknamed Glunya), Gugutsidze, Khabunaya, Sichinava, Ibragim, and Plotnikov). Also present were a councillor of the Regional Legislative Assembly; the deputy director of a mechanized bakery in Chelyabinsk; the founder of the company Motovilikha, convicted three times; the director of the Central Market; and the head of the firm UralGaz-SI. A fugitive, a singer, an artist, a former football player of the local team, and four students from a military academy concluded the list of guests.[29] Another party took place at a summer resort, *Lukomor'e*, near Perm in July 1994. Approximately 250 people gathered, including a number of business-people and local politicians.[30]

Life in the Perm underworld does not only involve attending parties and victimizing members of the public: inter-group conflicts have emerged. A powerful group of Georgian criminals, headed by Kiknadze (nicknamed Mikho) and Murman Gugutsidze (nicknamed Mirza), both *vory-v-zakone*, was operating at the beginning of 1990s in Perm.[31] Hostilities started to surface. According to one version, the Georgian group had stopped contributing to the criminal *obshchak*, the common pool of resources used to provide for fellow criminals in prison and managed by Yakutenok. According to another version, the businesses protected by the Georgian group had become extremely profitable but they would not agree to share the profits.[32]

In September 1992, a meeting between the most powerful *avtoritety* took place, chaired by Yakutenok. They agreed to resist the growing Georgian mafia. Ovchinskii, who devotes few pages to Perm in his book on organized crime in Russia, writes that, in his fight against the Georgian group, 'He [Yakutenok] was supported by the majority of the criminal contingent of Perm.'[33] Ethnic divisions, however, were not a sufficient predictor of emerging alliances. Some Russian criminals sided with the Georgians.[34] In October and November of 1992, the conflict came into the open, with assaults, attempts on lives, and explosions in flats. The first to be killed was a Vladimir Nelyubin, shot in the suburbs of Perm, while another, Fokin, a criminal close to Yakutenok, disappeared. Three prominent members of the Georgian group also disappeared—the two brothers Mingaleevs and one Gataulin.[35]

While the war was under way, Yakutenok was arrested and jailed at the Nizhne-Tagil'skaya colony.[36] For a while the Georgians prevailed in the struggle, but their superiority was short-lived. Yakutenok, who was given a room in the infirmary and a private telephone line, was in constant contact with his soldiers.[37] While in prison Yakutenok convinced fellow criminals to offer crucial help: three well-armed commandos from the cities of Chelyabinsk and Ufa joined Yakutenok's side at the end of 1992. Another contingent of criminals from Omsk, headed by a criminal *avtoritet* called Beloshanksii, tried to reach Perm by car but was intercepted by the police.[38] As a result, the Georgians lost the war and left the region. Those Permians who had sided with the Georgians escaped. According to newspaper reports, the death toll stands at about sixteen.[39]

Yakutenok was released from prison in March 1993 and, by the end of 1994, was increasingly spending more time in the Russian capital, so that some speculated that he was planning to move there permanently. In Moscow, he worked closely with various Moscow *vory*, such as Mamedov (Miron), Tsitsadze (Mikho), Usoyan (Khasan), and Trofimov (Trofa) from Ekaterinburg. In April 1995, he was arrested in Moscow and charged with illegal possession of weapons and drugs.[40] Although in Moscow, he was able to appoint Vasilii Tarychev to manage the *obshchak* while he was away.[41] According to newspaper reports, Tarychev was made a *vor-v-zakone* at a meeting in St Petersburg and was collecting contributions from businessmen and drug-dealers. In October, Tarychev and his deputy, Permyakov, were killed.[42]

The police believe that these deaths are a consequence of a conflict over spheres of influence between Yakut and a group of criminals based in the city of Kazan', answering to the orders of *vor-v-zakone* Rustam Nazarov, nicknamed Krest. He had made an appearance in Perm in 1995 and started to recruit supporters. A Kazan' gang headed by two brothers, Il'shat and Radik Mukhutdinov, working with Krest was trying to penetrate Perm's criminal underworld, in the wake of Yakut's arrest and consequent weakening of his power.[43] The killing of Tarychev was ordered by Krest and executed by the Mukhutdinov brothers. In turn, Krest himself disappeared on 16 April 1997 and in June and July supporters of Krest were found dead in Perm.[44] Yakut, who was at that point residing in a psychiatric hospital outside Moscow, had managed to enlist the help of other *vory* from the Western Ural region and was behind these deaths. *Vor* Kudinov (Kudin), a deputy of Yakut, emerged as the new leading *vor*, but his 'government' did not last long: in February 1998, he was shot dead just outside the offices of the RUOP. Two months later, one of Kudinov's associates, Viktor Cherkeziya, head of security service of the Gorky Park, was shot point-blank at the entrance of his flat. There was an attempt on Yakut's life as well, his car coming under fire while he was driving in Parkovyi, a sub-district of Perm, where he had a flat. In spite of the danger, Yakut regularly returned to Perm to celebrate his birthday at the Gornyi Khrustal'. At the last celebration, at the beginning of June 1998, nine *vory-v-zakone* from Georgia, Russia, Ukraine, and Moldavia attended. On Friday 19 June 1998, around 10 p.m., Yakut and his two bodyguards entered the night club *Bolid*. Three armed men in masks and camouflage uniform burst into the hall. Yakut and his bodyguards had their backs to the entrance. The bullets hit them in the back. Altogether the police found thirty cartridge cases on the floor. Two people—including Yakut (Zykov)—died on the spot. The third died in hospital that same night, around 3.00 a.m., without regaining consciousness.[45] In one of his pockets, the police found a photo of Perm's *vor* having dinner with Zhirinovsky, the leader of the Liberal Democratic Party of Russia, in a Moscow restaurant.[46] The Mukhutdinov brothers were arrested in Moscow in December 1999 and charged for these murders.[47]

On the night between 26 and 27 October near the hotel Gostinyi dvor, in a restaurant called Yubileinyi, a meeting of the Perm criminal 'fraternity' took place. The meeting was raided by officers from the Perm UVD, who checked documents of all twenty persons present. Famous criminal *avtoritety* such as Plotnikov and Ibragimov were present, guarded by bodyguards from the private security firm 'Legion'. Their status as private security officers allowed them to carry rather sophisticated firearms.[48] Sergei Prokhorov, the vice-director general of AO Kamkabel' and deputy in the Regional Assembly was also present.[49] The purpose of the meeting was to introduce to the local criminal elite a newly arrived *vor-v-zakone*, Aleksandr Serafimovich Burdeinyi, nicknamed Kazachok. He also visited several towns in the region. Speculation was rife over the future role of Kazachok in Perm. Was he going to take the place of Yakut or was he on a brief *tour-d'horizon* on behalf of the Moscow *vory*?

To sum up: from the early to the mid-1980s, the group headed by Plotnikov was involved in low-level swindles and confidence tricks at the fruit and vegetable market. As the transition to the market progressed and the number of criminal opportunity increased, Perm's criminal underworld appeared to be changing. Gangs started to be associated with certain territories of the city or sectors of the now profitable Central Market. Moreover, inter-group fighting and alliance-building were reported. At least three questions emerge from the evidence presented above. First, are present-day groups simply loose networks of criminals or are they organized in a hierarchical manner (and, if so, to what extent)? Second, do they control a territory or a sector of the economy? Third, what is the role of the *vory* in the post-Soviet environment? These are the issues we shall turn to now.

Organizational Arrangements

Two of the major controversies in the study of criminal organizations, and in particular of the Sicilian and American mafias, are whether they are a highly structured or a disorganized entity and whether they are territorially or functionally organized.[50]

The view that the American mafia is an organization, with defined roles and rules of action has a long and distinguished history. It dates back to the testimonies presented before legislative hearings and government commissions in the USA in the 1950s and 1960s. In 1951, Senator Estes Kefauver's Special Committee declared that a nationwide crime syndicate exists in the United States and the Committee identified that syndicate with the mafia. In 1967, the President Commission on Law Enforcement and Administration of Justice described the mafia or Cosa Nostra as a rigidly structured and nationwide organization. It consists of 24 families co-ordinated at the national level by a *commissione*. A boss heads each family. Below each boss, clearly recognizable positions exist: *underboss* (deputy boss), *consigliere* (adviser), *caporegime* (supervisor), and *soldato* (soldier). The *commissione* is composed of the bosses of the most powerful families and its principal functions are judicial.[51]

The structure of a Sicilian family is almost identical to that of an American one. Drawing on judicial evidence produced at the Palermo maxitrials of 1985–6, Gambetta offers the following description. Ordinary members are soldiers or *operai*. The head of the family is the *capo famiglia*, normally elected by the men of honour in his family. He appoints a *vice-capo* and a *consigliere*. Ordinary members are organized under the supervision of a *capo decina*, 'who oversees their "military" operations and mediates their relationship with the boss of the family'.[52] A *commissione provinciale* or *cupola* co-ordinates the mafia within one province. Its members are called *capi mandamento* and each represents three geographically contiguous families. Beyond the provincial level, a *commissione interprovinciale* was tentatively set up towards the end of the 1970s. At the head of the *commisione regionale* is a *rappresentante* or *segretario*, 'the first among equals', in the words of Antonio Calderone.[53] It should be noted that the 'province' is an administrative unit, so defined by the Italian state. Despite the fact that the definition is imposed by an external source, 'province' is a salient definition for the Sicilian mafia too.

Gambetta interprets the role of the *commissione* along economic lines; it is a 'cartel', an association of producers of the commodity 'protection' who co-ordinate in order to discipline each family and restrict competition from alternative suppliers of protection.[54] In fact, it was turbulence *within* each family, rather than inter-family conflicts, that gave rise to the *commissione*. Subsequently, its functions expanded to include the regulation of the activities of all families in the province.[55] The main aim of the *commissione* is to regulate the use of violence. Permission has to be granted by the boss of the territory where a murder is to take place. Also, the *commissione* is concerned with regulating succession when a boss disappears, an event that often triggers disputes, power struggles, and violence. Nevertheless, Gambetta concludes that, 'the arbitration role of the *commissione* has proved far from infallible and families, especially the larger ones, have retained their independence'.[56]

A number of authors, however, challenge this view of both the American and the Sicilian mafia. In an article first published in 1953, Daniel Bell, a distinguished Columbia University sociologist, opposed the Kefauver Committee's description of the mafia as an organization: 'Unfortunately for a good story—and the existence of the mafia would be a whale of a story—neither the Senate Crime Committee in its testimony, nor Kefauver in his book, presented any real evidence that the mafia exists as a functioning organisation.'[57] Other scholars have later questioned the assumption that the American mafia is a *nationwide* formation, pointing to the fact that most major cities outside the North-east are without a mafia family.[58] Ianni challenges the hierarchical and bureaucratic model of organization that emerges from the 1967 Commission report. Instead, he claims that the family structure is a series of social networks based on kinship relationships.

The mafia is not a formal organisation with a membership, hierarchical offices, and a fixed structure, rather it is a behavioural organisation, a cultural model of organisation structured by common values, shared understandings, and an interlocking pattern of mutual obligation . . . Italian-American families are actually biological lineages tied together through blood and marriage into localised clanlike syndicates in various urban centres throughout the country. And these 'families' are linked to each other in an intricate pattern of intermarriage and shared licit and illicit business activities.[59]

Among contemporary scholars of the Sicilian Mafia, Hess is the author that makes the strongest case for the Mafia as a non-organized entity. Drawing on nineteenth-century judicial evidence, he argues that mafiosi are not 'members of a secret society' called 'Mafia', but individuals who 'acted in a certain way, a *mafioso* way'.[60] 'Small clique-like associations' called *cosche* exist, but they do not have an awareness of themselves as a collectivity: 'the *cosca* is not a group; interaction and an awareness of "we", a consciousness of an objective to be jointly striven for, are absent or slight. Essentially it is a multitude of dyadic relationships maintained by the mafioso with persons independent of each other.'[61] Several authors have endorsed Hess's view, stressing that being a mafioso is a 'social practice', and mafia behaviour is guided by a (twisted) notion of honour.[62] A similar view is echoed by the Hong Kong police in reference to Triads: 'Today there are no more than a collection of criminals—far from being controlled by any "godfather" type leader.'[63]

A criminal group may be hierarchically structured but still two possible models may obtain. First, it may be territorially based, taking its name from the area of the city it controls, extracting money from the businesses that operate in its territory in exchange for protection. This is what the American historian Alan Block has called a 'power syndicate' in his book *East Side West Side* and how Gambetta defines the term 'mafia' in his *The Sicilian Mafia*. Second, it may resemble what Thomas Schelling called an 'organised criminal group' and Block termed 'an enterprise syndicate'. The group would be functionally specialized, supplying protection to one or another sector of the economy. If this were the case, we would have the 'kiosk mafia', the 'credit mafia', the 'construction industry mafia', and the 'drugs mafia', rather than a single organization which, in a given territory, protects various businesses.

The case of Sicily fits the first model. 'In Sicily, there is a clear geographical division; individual families have specific areas in which they have sole operating authority.'[64] In New York a different pattern emerges, which is certainly not territorial. Protection tends to be functionally specialized. For instance, the Lucchese and Gambino families have a presence in the carting (waste disposal) industry, while the Genovese family is active in the docks of Manhattan.[65]

Below, I draw on the evidence I collected in Perm in order to establish whether mafia groups are hierarchical organizations or loose networks of criminals. I will also attempt to answer the question of whether they control a territory or a sector of the economy. Similarities and differences with their Sicilian and American counterparts are also explored.

The Structure of Mafia Groups in Perm

For Irina Krasnosel'skikh, the crime correspondent of *Zvezda*, 'the structure of a mafia group in Perm is the following: *torpedy* are at the bottom and take orders from a *boevik*. Various *boeviki* answer to a *brigadir*' (J1). For Viktor, a full-time member of a criminal group, 'the smallest unit is that of a "crew". They are usually five to eight people, fifteen would be a lot, and three too little' (OC2). A number of *brigadiry* would work for an *avtoritet*, although it is not all too clear what is the relationships between *brigadiry* and *avtoritet*. In the case of Ibragim we know that he used to head the most authoritative *brigada* within the market, and his influence grew to the point that other *brigadiry* were willing to obey his orders. According to the head of the RUOP, in 1998 ten *avtoritety* were active in the city.[66]

Fig. 6.1 depicts the internal structure of each group. There is one head of the group, the *avtoritet*, who appoints roughly four deputies, the *brigadiry*. Each *brigadir* has in turn his own deputies, the *boeviki*, roughly in the number of three to four for each *brigadir*. *Boeviki* organize the activities of the *torpedy*, the ordinary soldiers. The average group is between thirty and forty people.

Delicate jobs are assigned to full-time members, rather than to people who have an occasional relation with the group. Igor', a full-time employee of one group, deals mainly with the accounts of the group and works under the supervision of a *brigadir*.[67] He is a *boevik*, but spends most of his time in the group's office. However, he carries a pistol and is prepared to use it. 'As a rule', said Igor', 'it is the *avtoritet* that decides who does what. Of course, he understands that some people are not able to carry out certain tasks. For instance, I am not a violent person. The

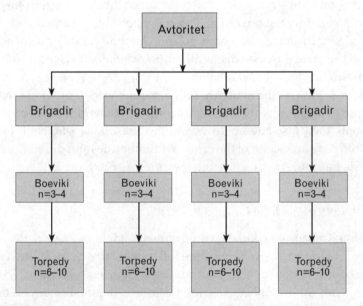

Fig. 6.1 The structure of one organized criminal group, Perm. (total number in group: 47–61. NB 6–10 *torpedy* answer to one *boevik*)

avtoritet could order someone like me to undertake a violent job in order to punish him for a mistake he had made' (OC1). No strict internal division of labour therefore obtains. Any member could in principle be asked to do any job. According to Irina Krasnosel'skikh, 'if you look from the top of the pyramid down, you can see all the functions clearly covered, but if you look from the bottom of the pyramid up, you cannot distinguish among them' (J1).

Igor's testimony points to the fact that the finances of the group are separated from that of the individual members, a sign the groups operate as businesses, with their own accounts. However, the *avtoritet* keeps an eye on how each member spends his earnings. Permission must be obtained for any major personal purchase. Igor' notes that 'even though it is my money, I had to ask permission to buy a Mercedes (permission granted)' (OC1).

When interviewed, Viktor had just been involved in evaluating the value of some wood.

Recently, a debtor could not pay his debt in cash, but could supply three tons of wood. I made the evaluation and saw whether we could make use of it. A sign of a successful settlement is that at the end we all go and have a lavish dinner at the Gornyi Khrustal' and get drunk. The job that I like the most is resolving disputes, so that people can carry on with their work (OC2).

There is a case of a killer who had an occasional relationship with Perm's criminality. Ruslan Kalinin, a petty thief who was escaping justice from Tallinn, was received by the Perm criminal world and forced to work as killer, without having any experience. Also, he was not granted any group affiliation. This implied that anybody could ask him to execute murders. After three (failed) attempts to kill local targets, he was arrested and sentenced to 15 years. He is the only mafia killer arrested for murder in Perm, possibly a sign of little concern for his fate on the part of the local criminal world.[68]

Are the groups organized territorially or functionally? Some groups described above appear to have a firm grip on a certain territory and resemble a 'power syndicate'. The group headed by Belyaev was trying to exert control over the Ordzhonikidzevskii district, and likewise was Popovich over Motovilikha. The gangs at the Central Market are also offering protection within a well-defined physical space. The head of Perm RUOP, Colonel Markanov, confirms this picture: the distribution of spheres of influence is 'territorially based'. However, he adds that criminal groups do not control each and every business in a given territory, giving away the fact that state organs offer selective protection to some businesses. 'They control those places that are not under the control of state structures, such as markets, car parks, discotheques, and so on.'[69] There is no evidence that either Plotnikov or Tsiklop's groups are localized. In fact, it appears that Plotnikov's group started off as gang of petty criminals and then might have evolved into an 'enterprise syndicate' connected to Yakutenok.

The most puzzling feature of Perm criminality is the role of Yakutenok and other *vory* in the city criminal life. According to Viktor, the *vor* is the supreme criminal boss whom a newly established crew would have to pay in order to be allowed to operate.

Let's say some criminal decides to form a criminal brigade and to take under his control some shops. Nowdays, every shop has got its 'roof'. So what do they do? They look around until they find a shop that has a weak 'roof', they organize a confrontation [*razborka*] and hopefully win the shop over. If they do not manage to win any confrontation, they get out of the picture, either dead or in prison. If, on the contrary, they manage to survive by robbing some flats and get one or two shops under their control, then a meeting with the *smotryashchii* would take place. He would claim that they need to pay into the *obshchak*. Behind the *smotryashchii* there are bigger forces, ultimately, at the top, the *vor-v-zakone*, who is in charge of the city (OC2).

This would also imply that the role of the *avtoritety* is rather minor. It could be possible that quite large gangs are *de facto* run by independent *brigadiry*, who in the end answer only to the *vor* of the city. On the contrary, a senior officer of Perm's RUOP sees the *avtoritety* as the crucial power in the city's criminal world. '*Avtoritety* have the real power on the ground, controlling segments of the city. The *vory* are like the Queen of England. A fraction of the contribution collected by the *avtoritet* is then paid by the *avtoritet* into the city's *obshchak*, which is managed by Yakutenok' (M1). Igor' offered the following description of the relationship between each group and the fund kept at the city level by the *vor*.

It is not the case that each group pays into the *obshchak* once a month, as a company does with his employees. The groups pay when they feel like it, as a sort of charity to support the criminal population in prison, or as a sign of respect for the *vory*. The treasurer of the *obshchak* asks for money when he needs it. Alternatively, groups pay into the *obshchak* when the *vor* does something in particular. Also, the *vor* of our city is very respected in Moscow and can get help from all over Russia (OC1).

Irina Krasnosel'skikh's view on the role of the *vory* in Russia and in particular of Yakutenok, coincides with Igor's description. 'Yakutenok is necessary because he has a sustained relationship with the national and international criminal world. Also, without him, they would constantly be killing each other. He does not have a real apparatus, but intervenes when there are disputes' (J1).

Comparisons

The above description of structure, size, and internal division of labour among criminal groups in Perm lends itself to comparison with other gangs and mafias. The internal organization of each group is centralized and hierarchical. This derives from the activities the groups engage in, namely supplying protection services that, at times, require the efficient use of force.[70] Still, the structure of each group differs slightly from the Sicilian and the American mafia groups.[71] Soldiers or *operai* compare to *torpedy*, while the *boevik* would be equivalent to the *capo decina*. If we carry this comparison further, *brigadir* would be the *capo famiglia*. The *avtoritet* is a further level up, a level that does not exist in the hierarchy of the Sicilian mafia. On the other hand, specific roles such as *vice-capo* and *consigliere* (appointed by the *capo famiglia* and without a direct operation on the ground) have not yet been recorded.

A potential source of tension exists between the *brigadiry* and the *avtoritet*. From the stories narrated above it is not clear whether a *brigada* pays the *avtoritet* to operate in a given territory, or is part and parcel of the same group headed by the *avtoritet*. Some of the bigger groups in Perm may follow a pattern similar to the bigger Chicano gangs in Los Angeles.[72] The *avtoritet* could be equivalent to the 'President' of the gang, selected from one of the existing brigades in some way (either elected or chosen). In the case of Ibragim, the mechanism of his career advancement is rather clear, he was the *brigadir* of the most powerful group, rather than a 'political' leader who got elected after mastering the support of the various factions within the gang.

The size of each group is also similar to a Sicilian family. In Catania, a city approximately the same size as Perm, Calderone's family had

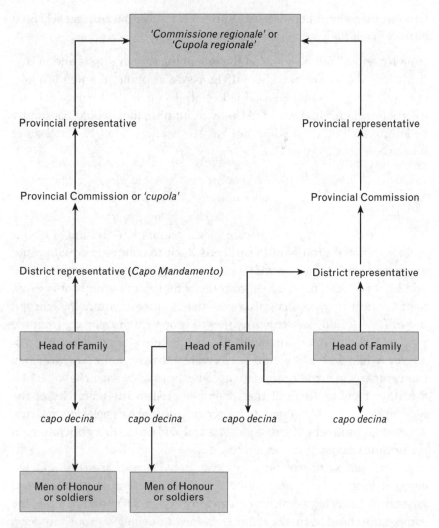

Fig. 6.2 The Sicilian Mafia

Source: Arlacchi, 1992: ch. 2; Gambetta, 1993a: 114–16; Schneider, 1994: 11.
Note: The *capo decina* is the head of a cohort of ten 'soldiers'.

thirty to thirty-five members in 1962. Smaller families have also been recorded, but they were operating in smaller towns: Carmelo Colletti's family in the town of Ribera had about fifteen, and Vincenzo Marsala's in Vicari ten.[73]

No strict roles obtain in each group: every member may be asked to perform any job, notes Igor'. Similarly, Calderone recalls that 'my family in Catania operated very differently from the image presented by newspapers. Rigid roles, such as killer, gunner, accountant, never existed. For a while we had an accountant', continues Calderone, 'but we dismissed him, because he was not honest.'[74] Groups in Perm have accountants, however hard it may be to keep them from stealing the money.

Among Sicilian mafia families delicate jobs are assigned to full-time members, as in Perm. However, as in the case of Ruslan Kalinin, in Sicily too murders have been commissioned to non-members. The individuals involved, however, were also soon killed by made members.[75] Tommaso Buscetta, a prominent mafioso turned state witness, testifies that the American mafia used a black person as a killer in one instance.[76]

The Sicilian mafia families appear to control a territory and fit the description of a 'power syndicate' advanced by Block. Each family extracts protection money from the businesses that operate in the neighbourhood. Even permission to steal must be sought from the local man of honour and, in granting it, he earns a share of the profits.[77] There is a 'logic of protection' that drives the single family to expand over a territory. Gambetta suggests that protection resembles a 'public' (i.e. indivisible) good: once a shop in a given area is protected, the neighbouring shop would indirectly benefit from that protection. 'If the local garage is protected, then other merchants enjoy derived protection by virtue of the fact that thieves are afraid to enter the street.'[78] The Sicilian family tries to prevent free-riders by forcing its protection on all the shops in that street. In the case of Perm, this logic finds significant barriers due to the fact that state organs offer selective protection to some businesses. Furthermore, it is possible that ethnic networks supply protection to some entrepreneurs, as the story narrated by Olga suggests. In conclusion, a crime group finds it harder than in Sicily to have a full control over 'its own' territory.

Did the various *avtoritety* in Perm achieve a degree of inter-group coordination, as the American and Sicilian mafias? The grand parties at the Gornyi Khrustal' described above are opportunities for the *avtoritety* to discuss matters of common interest. As the meetings of the *commisione* were sometimes disguised as hunting parties, a favourite amusement among Sicilian mafiosi,[79] so these meetings of Perm *avtoritety* are disguised as birthday parties. The main difference with the meetings of the *commissione* is that 'customers' here are also invited. Nonetheless, secret meetings among deputies and leaders of the groups have been reported, although little is known about them (e.g. whether they are formal and regular).[80]

Yakutenok may resemble the regional co-ordinator (*rappresentante regionale*) of the Sicilian mafia, and therefore appear as the boss of the bosses, the man that holds the highest position in the mafia hierarchy. Some accounts of the mafia describe the regional commission or regional *cupola* as 'the apex of mafia command'.[81] In the diagrams that sketch the structure of the Sicilian mafia, all arrows lead to the regional *cupola*, chaired by the *rappresentante*.[82] In fact, the regional co-ordinator is—as pointed out by Gambetta—a weak leader, whose task was that of organizing meetings.[83]

Even if the *rappresentante regionale* is a weak leader, he is drawn from one of the families, on which he may ultimately rely. Moreover, Sicilian families do not tax themselves in order to support the entire prison population. Nor would they let an outsider manage such a fund. They simply support each family member when he is arrested. Why would independent gangs pay a non-member to support members who have been arrested? The role of the *vory* needs to be clarified. Chapter 7 is devoted to describing the features of the original society and its origin in the Soviet past, while Chapter 8 assesses the role of the *vory* in the post-Soviet criminal world.

7

Mafia Ancestors: The *vory-v-zakone*, 1920s–1950s

Yakutenok, the most prominent criminal of Perm, was a 'thief-with-a-code-of-honour' (*vor-v-zakone* or *vor-zakonnik*). What is the code and where does it come from? More generally, what are the features of this criminal fraternity that clearly stands at the junction between Soviet and post-Soviet criminality? Although this is an historical question, it matters. The code of behaviour, the rules of interaction among members of the fraternity, and more generally the 'trademarks' of the *vory* still inform today's post-Soviet criminal world, as testified by the case of Perm. This chapter first describes the main features of the society of the *vory-v-zakone*, using archival data that have never been presented before. Second, it addresses the question of the origins of the society, namely whether it was a Soviet or pre-Revolutionary phenomenon.

The Features of the *vory-v-zakone*

Dissidents and political prisoners encountered the *vory* in the camps and described their behaviour. Maximilien de Santerre, a French-Russian 'spy' born in 1924 and confined to the Gulag in 1946 for 12 years, observed that some criminals in the camp adopted a peculiar dress code and mannerisms.[1] They wore 'home-made aluminium crosses round their necks' and waistcoats.[2] They were 'often bearded and almost always wore their shirts outside the trousers with one or several waistcoats above'.[3] They also had tattoos covering their bodies. 'Their chests are often tattooed with a picture of praying angels on each side of the crucifix; underneath are the words: "O Lord, save thy slave!" or "I believe in God",' indicating some respect for religion.[4] They spoke a language of their own (*fenya*), its grammatical structure being Russian, but with a different vocabulary.[5] Santerre came to understand that these were 'symbolic attribute[s] of a *vor-v-zakone*'.[6]

Dmitrii Likhachev, later to become one of the most prominent scholars of medieval Russian language and literature, met the *vory* while he was a convict at the Belomorsko–Baltiiskii canal construction site in the early 1930s.[7] He observed there that the *vorovskoi mir* (the world of the *vory*) was far from anarchical: 'Despite thieves' apparent lack of discipline, their lives are governed by a network of strict regulations that extend to the most minute matters and ultimately by a system of "collective beliefs" that is remarkably uniform among criminals with different ethnic roots.'[8]

Data from the 1930s testifies to the existence of the society of *vory-v-zakone*. A. I. Gurov, deputy head of the Ministry of Internal Affairs (MVD) Research Institute until 1991, concludes in his book on organized crime published in 1990: 'the *vory-v-zakone* were firmly established by the beginning of the 1930s.'[9] According to MVD data, in the 1950s the vast majority of the *vory*, 80 per cent, were professional pickpockets. The percentage of thieves-with-a-code-of-honour did not exceed 6–7 per cent of the total number of professional criminals and recidivists.[10] Gurov also draws on the work of V. I. Monakhov, an investigator at the MVD who published a book—marked 'secret'—for internal circulation in 1957 on organized crime. I have found a copy of this book in the Gulag fund.[11] According to Monakhov, the *vory* were a national fraternity spread 'in all places of imprisonment without exception and in major, highly populated areas'.[12] Specific reports on the activities of the *vory* in the 1940s and 1950s testify to their spread well beyond the Kolyma and Chukotka (Northern Siberia), and refer to the Komi Autonomous Republic, Krasnoyarskaya, Arkhangel'skaya, Molotovskaya (i.e. Perm), Tomskaya, Kemerovskaya, and Sverdlovskaya regions.[13] A report dated 27 July 1955 originating from Ukrainian Procurator's office, states that 'more than 700 people kept in the camps of the Ukrainian Socialist Republic belong to the group which openly calls itself "*vory-v-zakone*"'.[14] *Vory* of Asian, Georgian, and Baltic origins have been identified.[15]

A dress code, tattoos, and even a language of their own would not distinguish the *vory* from any other human group that lives in a closed space, such as sailors, soldiers, and ordinary convicts. The *vory* stand out among such groups because they formed a secret criminal fraternity, with its own code of behaviour and its own ritual for the initiation of new members.[16] Furthermore, the *vory* created rudimentary yet effective 'courts' where members' misbehaviour was judged and wrongdoers punished and which achieved a national dimension.

The Ritual

Monakhov describes the gathering which would 'crown' a *vor*, known as *skhodka* (meeting). Upon the recommendation of at least two members, the meeting accepted the novice into the society and the new *vor* swore an acceptance oath: 'As a young lad, I set foot on the road of a thieves' life. I swear before the thieves who are at this meeting to be a worthy thief, and not to fall for any trick of the members of the CheKa.'[17] Monakhov's version of the initiation ritual is supported by the account given by a *vor* called Ch. of his own crowning in 1951 at the age of 18.[18] After swearing the oath, Ch. was warned by his mentors of the punishment he would incur if he failed to abide by the oath. A *vor* who did so became, in the eyes of the fraternity, a *legavyi*, the *vory* equivalent of *sbirro* (cop) and *infame* (traitor) for the Sicilian Mafia and the most vicious insult a *vor* could have thrown at him.[19]

A police document from the early 1950s describes an initiation ceremony that took place in rather unusual circumstances, in a transit-prison in the Krasnoyarskii Krai, where ten cells had been set aside to house hardened criminals. Confined to isolation cells, the criminals were forced to conduct the ceremony in writing, by pen and paper.[20] The pieces of paper were later confiscated by police, who then wrote a report of the incident. According to the report, a note (*ksiva*) recommending a novice (*malyutka*) was sent from one cell to the others.[21] The authors of the note, *vory* Tolik Pelaga and Vas'ka Kitaets, praised the 'baby', said to possess the right qualities to be admitted into the family of *vory*. In particular, his mentors wrote, 'his behaviour and aspirations are totally in accordance with the *vory* world-view'; he 'defied camp discipline for a long period of time and is practically never let out of the punishment cell'; he, 'at the request of the members, collected money for several months from other prisoners in one of the camp's sub-units' and 'even though still young, his

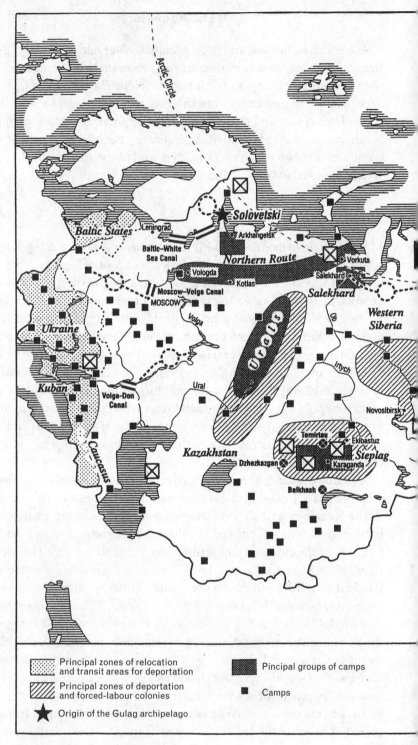

Fig. 7.1 The Gulag Archipelago

Source: Werth (1999), pp. 36–7.

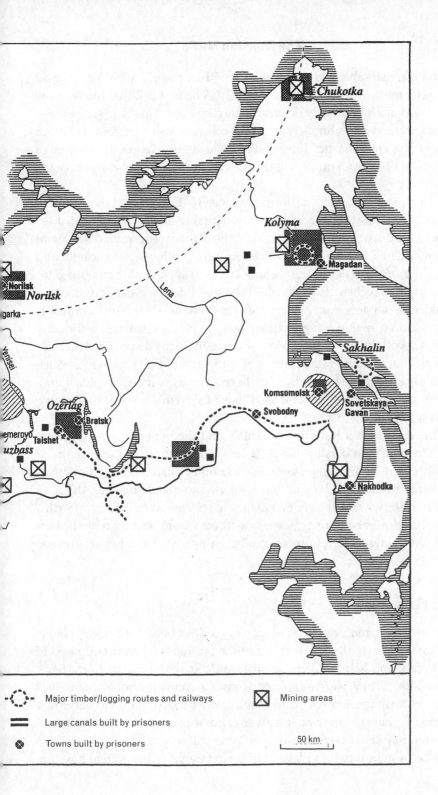

Chukotka

Kolyma

× Magadan

×
Norilsk
Norilsk

garka

Lena

Yenisei

Sakhalin

Komsomolsk ×
Svobodny

Ozerlag
× Bratsk

emerovo Taishet

uzbass

×

Sovetskaya
Gavan

× Nakhodka

mind is remarkable and in accordance with our world-view. We are glad to welcome new thieves into our family'. The first cell that received the note was unambiguously positive in its response: 'This guy will be a *vor-v-zakone*. God bless him.' The second cell was also in favour, although rather less enthusiastic: 'If his soul is pure, let him in.' In the absence of any objections from other cells, the novice became a new member of the fraternity.[22]

A nickname (*klichka*) was formally given in the course of the initiation ritual. The name the *vor* acquired at the ritual arguably was quite distinct from an ordinary nickname. It marked the new life the criminal was about to enter. Thus, following a practice common in other secret societies and religious orders (such as the Catholic Church), nicknaming amounted for the *vory* to a rechristening, as observed by Likhachev 'the adoption of a nickname is a necessary act of transition to the *vory*'s sphere (it amounts to a peculiar "taking of monastic vows")'.[23] Ch., a *vor* crowned in the early 1950s, recollects that at his crowning he could finally dispose of his 'childish nickname *Malysh* (the little one), and get an adult nickname, which I chose myself.' Reportedly, Ch. chose the nickname *Likhoi* (dashing). Through the thieves' prison-based 'postal system', news of the coronation spread in the camps.[24]

The *vory* were a fraternity of equals and the initiation was sufficient to gain a full membership. None the less, a distinction could be identified between junior and senior *vory*. For example, Ch. refers to senior members, the *pakhany*, who could have objected to his young age. Although the fraternity was a society of equals, the *pakhany* were older *vory* with a particular moral authority.[25] New members would be drawn by the *blatnye*, the wider circle of professional criminals who rotated around the *vory*.

The Code of Behaviour

The *vory* were required to follow a strict code of behaviour in their interaction with each other.[26] Members of the brotherhood were supposed to be honest and helpful to one another and always tell the truth to fellow members.[27] They were supposed to avoid conflict among themselves and not to undermine each other's authority,[28] even if they had never met before.[29] A new *vor* arriving in a given camp was granted automatic membership into the local community of *vory*. 'All *vory-zakonniki*, who arrive to a certain locality or a place of imprisonment,' writes Monakhov, 'are automatically members of the thievish community, have certain rights and duties.'[30]

It is instructive to see the rules of the fraternity according to A. M. Bulatov, a former *vor-v-zakone*, as set out in a report sent to The Procurator General of The USSR:

1. A *Vor* should support another *vor* in any circumstances.
2. A *Vor* should not work in any state-owned industry . . . he might be on record as working at some post, but should not fulfil the necessary functions.
3. *Vor* should live only on what he has stolen, seized, acquired by deception, won at cards, only such a *vor* is considered to be honest and independent, a real *vor*.
4. The laws of the USSR do not exist for a *vor*, *vor* does not adhere to these laws.
5. The *vor* despises the members of the CPSU.
6. *Vory* have their own laws and tribunals (*skhodka*). At the *vory*'s *skhodka*, all *vory* pronounce judgements up to death sentences by strangulation, axing, and other methods.
7. A *vor* should not serve in the army.
8. A *vor* should not be a witness in a court, he should not protect the *vory*'s honour in a court.
9. . . . In case a *vor* is under very severe regime [of imprisonment] and has no opportunity to avoid working . . . he could—through the use of deception and cunning methods—become the leader of working *brigada* . . . and . . . rob honest workers of their records of work . . . These stolen records should be shared with the other *vory* who do not earn their ration by working . . .
10. *Vory* should take . . . a contribution from workers . . . who receive parcels, money, goods, etc. According to the *vory*'s law, they have to take the best half . . . the workers know the consequences of not giving to the *vory* what they wish to take. That is why workers are forced to give without resistance and even unconditionally. If the workers leave in solidarity . . . and refuse to pay the 'contribution', *vory* have to kill one or, if necessary, two workers . . .
11. If *vory* in labour corrective camps or prison cannot follow the *vory*'s way of life due to the policies of the administration . . . *vory* have to [resist?] without taking anything into consideration even if it means killing somebody, calumniating and compromising the administration of the camp or prison in front of higher organs, and even the central Committee of the CPSU . . . In general, *vory* should use all their strength to make life easier for themselves . . .
12. Since it is known to the *vory* that each prison or administration fear, with all their heart, prison revolts, for which they could be punished by higher

organs of the Soviet Power ... *vory* 'zakonniki' should play this trump card.

13. All *vory* are obliged to attract and win sympathy of the clever youth both free and when in places of imprisonment, in order to replenish the group of *vory* (*vory* have been giving special attention to this 'paragraph' in recent years).

(GARF, 8131/32/4961/11–13; 7 July 1955)

Vory were supposed to share all they had with fellow *vory*. Those who deviated from this norm would have been punished: a *vor* could have been brought to trial and consequently deprived of his thief's privileges for concealing cigarettes from fellow members.[31] A thief had no right to insult or raise his hands against another thief.[32] Violence, without sanction from a proper *vory* 'court', was prohibited.[33]

The code of conduct also regulated the interactions between the *vory* and the outside world.[34] The *vory* considered the code to be part of their trade, as Likhachev notes in his 1935 essay on the thieves' language. Some elements of the code can be inferred from the notes exchanged at the transit prison in the Krasnoyarskii Krai. Prior to and following initiation, a *vor* was supposed to have acted as a social outcast. Activities that suggested the state had power over the criminal, whether serving in the Red Army, paying taxes, or working in the camps, were strictly forbidden.[35]

The *vory* should have systematically refused to work.[36] In the camps, Santerre observed that they refused to 'take part in the construction of a prison, disciplinary barracks, stretch barbed wire or clean the prohibited zone'.[37] Refusal to work was punished by camp authorities and Soviet courts.[38] Nevertheless, camp authorities generally avoided direct confrontation with the *vory*, at least until the late 1940s.[39]

A *vor* should not, prior to initiation, have been involved in political activities and, upon entering the fraternity, should have severed all links with society, including familial ties. His family was now the *vory* brotherhood.[40] Professional criminals who remained attached to their families were scornfully referred to as *domashniki* and on that basis could be refused entry into the brotherhood.[41]

Despite this prohibition against family ties, the *vory* exhibited an outward cult of motherhood, as seen in the tattoo worn by many *vory* with the words 'I won't forget my own mother'. Varlam Shalamov (1907–82), who spent a total of fifteen years in the camps (1937–53) is well known in West as the author of *Kolyma Tales*. He is also the author of eight essays on the criminal world written in the late 1950s, now printed in the Russian edition of his complete works.[42] In one of these essays, he identified a puzzling contrast between this professed cult of motherhood and the actual indifference shown by *vory* towards their natural mothers.[43] As Shalamov observes, 'there is one woman who is romanticized by the criminal world, one woman who has become the subject of criminal lyrics and the folklore heroine of many generations of criminals. This woman is the criminal's mother.' At the same time, however, 'no criminal has ever sent so much as a kopeck to his mother or made any attempt to help her on his own'. Shalamov thus concludes that the cult of the mother, although surrounded by a poetic haze, was 'nothing but a pack of lies and theatrical pretence. The mother cult [was] a peculiar smoke-screen used to conceal the hideous criminal world'.[44] Monakhov provides a different explanation of the same phenomenon. The 'mother' invoked by the *vory* was not the natural mother but rather a metaphor for the *vory* brotherhood, their new family.[45]

Women had no place in the hierarchy of *vory*. 'A third or fourth-generation criminal learns contempt for women from childhood,' writes Shalamov. 'Woman, an inferior being, has been created only to satisfy the criminal's animal craving, to be the butt of his crude jokes and the victim of public beatings.'[46] A *vor* might have had a wife, but any real attachment to her was viewed as detrimental to the member's dedication to the society.[47] The *vory* code did not preclude monogamy, yet such faithfulness to one's wife was seen as a sign of weakness and 'seldom lasting'.[48]

The wife of a *vor* was allowed practically no social relations with others from outside the criminal world; she was the property of her husband. If he went to prison, she generally would have cohabited with one of his fellow thieves, while continuing to take an interest in his welfare. Although wives were not despised as much as prostitutes and female citizens not connected with the criminal world, they had no special rights. Chalidze (b. 1938), a Soviet lawyer who emigrated to the USA in the 1970s and published an essay on the *vory* in 1977, writes: 'the relation of a thief to his wife is that of a master to his slave, except that the slave has voluntarily chosen her lot.'[49] While the wife may have chosen voluntarily to join the criminal community, she was unable to secede from it. If the criminal's wife failed to meet her obligations, she was warned; if she failed again she would be punished.[50] According to Shalamov, there were no *ménages à trois* involving either lawful wives or prostitutes. Both prostitutes and legal wives could have been told to satisfy the needs of others, but the understanding was that there was always only one 'owner'.[51]

Thieves did not cultivate paternal feelings or care much about children. The *vory* took for granted that 'a thief's son will become a thief and his daughter a companion of thieves, although this does not always happen, especially nowadays'.[52] The son of a thief could therefore benefit from the reputation of his father, even though he was subject to the same initiation ritual as everybody else.[53]

Although passive homosexuality was strictly forbidden, active homosexuality was allowed.[54] Drugs also were allowed and could be freely taken. Yurii Glazov (1929–99), a dissident and former convict who emigrated to Canada in the 1970s, writes: 'Thieves often suffer from epilepsy and drug addiction. In the prison drug stores they get ether, luminal, drugs mixed with cocaine, morphine and opium.'[55]

The attitude of the *vory* towards property seems to have derived from the prohibition against entering into obligations with the non-criminal world. Property bound criminals to the material world, reducing their commitment to the *vorovskoi mir*. The *vory* were supposed to show contempt towards the accumulation of assets. Only short-term use of stolen cash or goods were allowed. The *vory* could use property that was at the disposal of their group but were not to own anything on a long-term basis.[56] A related rule of behaviour concerned stolen property: a *vor* who had found another *vor*'s property was not obliged to return the find to its owner.[57]

As a matter of course, detachment from the outside world included detachment from the most despised officials, law enforcers. A recruit was to have had no connections with law-enforcement agents in his past in order to be eligible for admittance into the society. Even the most insignificant act of camaraderie towards officials would have been sufficient cause for expulsion from the fraternity: Santerre recalls that 'the laws of *blatnye* prevent one to offer any help to a Chekist, and to accept presents or tips from them. For instance, one old *blatnoi* was deprived of his rights as *vor* only because he accepted a pack of tea from a camp guard'.[58]

The rumour that a criminal had contacts with police officers was considered enough to infer that he was bargaining for a softer sentence and intended to betray fellow criminals.[59] The prohibition against contacts with law-enforcement officials thus extended to a prohibition against holding the position of headman or foreman in the camp: 'the *vor* who occupies such a position ceases to be a *vor*. He steps outside the law (*zakon*)', writes Shalamov,[60] although it appears that, under duress, *vory* were allowed to become *brigadiry* and exploit the works of other convicts.[61]

Professional killers were not allowed to enter the fraternity. The *vor* allegedly had a strong code against murder.[62] During his activities he was supposed to refrain from using violence. He should have stolen and robbed without bloodshed. It was acceptable to kill only in order to defend one's honour or one's life.[63] Still, any thief who committed murder had to justify the act to the fraternity.[64]

Monakhov maintains that a *vor* was not allowed to leave the fraternity, and quotes the testimony of a former *vor*. He adds however that cases are known of *vory* who left without betraying old fellows and no punishment followed.[65] *Vor* Ch. challenges the plot of the Soviet film *Kalina krasnaya* (1974) by Vasilii Shukshin. The protagonist in the film, Egor Prokudin, is killed by *vory* because he decided to leave the fraternity and lead an honest life. To this Ch. responds that, 'I respect Shukshin, but he was wrong. This rule never existed. If a thief assassinated another thief because of this, he would himself be accused of unruly behaviour and killed.'[66]

The *vory* were supposed to acquire a leading role in the camps, to rule over criminals 'according to the *vory* rules' and to search for recruits.[67] Indeed, they considered themselves the elite of the criminal world, similarly to the Sicilian mafiosi.[68] 'Candidate members' (usually referred to, in camp jargon, as *patsany*) were asked to perform tasks on behalf of the *vory*, mainly connected with raising funds for *obshchak*, the communal fund to support group activities, bribe officials and care for the families of the imprisoned and for those *vory* who were sick and unable to steal.[69] The *obshchak* was financed both by extortion from inmates and contributions from the outside.[70] *Vory* operating outside collected money and goods, and sent them to *vory* inmates, who in turn distributed them in the prison.[71] *Vory* also sent money they had collected inside to individuals in other camps often via accomplices outside the camps.[72] Once free, the *vor* was supposed to earn his living only through illegal activities and never to work. Because the *obshchak* was supposed to serve exclusively the *vory* in prison, the free *vor* could not rely upon it for support. In fact, the free *vor* was obliged to contribute to the *obshchak*.[73]

An acceptable way to earn money for all *vory*, besides stealing, was by winning at card games.[74] Card playing was widespread in the camps. Shalamov recollects that 'every night the criminal element in the camp gathered . . . to play cards'.[75] Likhachev writes that winning a game was considered a good omen and 'good omens may impel a thief to commit a daring theft, a bad omen stops him from carrying out his plans'.[76] Card playing was also a vicarious form of fortune telling: 'usually the thieves carry one or two packs of cards with them, which they use to tell fortunes, playing *shtos* . . . He will use the cards to decide his future and his next enterprise. If he wins, he is sure to complete his criminal plan in a lucky way. If he loses, he loses self-confidence as well.'[77] Being good at cards was a sign of good fortune and capacity to bring good fortune to the gang: 'a lucky card player will be taken by a thief as a companion for his gang in the hope that he will bring them luck (even if the card player uses sharp practices, since they are acceptable among thieves . . .).'[78]

A thief might have put at stake in a card game anything he had, including his finger, an arm, the promise to carry out a daring act or even his own life. If he lost his stake, it had to be redeemed immediately, no matter what it was. The penalty for defaulting was expulsion from the fraternity or, in same cases, death.[79]

The Vory outside Camp Walls

A *vor* might spend many years of his life in prison. 'To them, prison is their native home,' writes Solzhenitsyn.[80] The length of time spent in prison was a source of prestige and a sign of distinction among the criminals who aspired to become *vory*. For Monakhov, 'it is no chance that *vory* themselves say that—in order to become a *vor v zakone*—it's necessary to go through the Corrective Labour Institutions (ITU), and repeatedly.'[81] In this sense, the *vory* were a peculiar brand of criminal produced by prison culture, a feature that distinguishes them from Sicilian mafiosi.

When free, *vory* were supposed to help fellow members in the camps by sending them money, organizing escapes, and welcoming newly released *vory* into their criminal networks.[82] According to a report dated 1955, newly released *vory* (who had to reside in settlements nearby the camp) had to ask permission of the *vory* still in the camp to escape from the settlement.[83] Indeed, *vory* could count on a network of accomplices outside camp walls, something that worried authorities: 'Information available at the Procurator's office of the USSR shows that *vory-v-zakone* and formations of criminals continue to function at freedom as well. . . . On release from places of imprisonment, criminals belonging to one or another group have the addresses of "their own people", who "help them to settle [down]", render material support to them, so that they could live without working and commit crime together.'[84] Each *vor*, when out of prison, joined thieves' communes known as *shaika*, *malina*, or *kodla*.[85] According to two *vory* who became police informants in the 1950s, N. G. Gubaidulin and V. A. Anfinogenov, the smallest commune consists of two to five *vory*. Each *vor* had his own speciality and would rarely get involved in another sector of the underworld.[86] Santerre writes that *kodla* could reach the size of 20–30 people.[87] Up to ten different specialities, such as pickpocketing, burglary, and motor vehicle theft, could be represented in a single commune.[88] The communes were supposed to be united by ties of solidarity, fraternity, and relatively equal rights, with no single leader.[89] The authorities noticed that the Moscow *vory* were particularly active, organized and able to arrange, rather undisturbed, city-wide meetings.[90]

The Vory's Courts (skhodki)

Questions concerning the brotherhood were discussed, including 'crimes' and punishments, at the *skhodka*, the *vory* meeting. Likhachev refers to courts managed by criminals. These courts dealt with any breach of the *vory* code of conduct: 'behaviour among thieves is regulated and circumscribed by innumerable rules, standards, and notions of propriety and good manners, all interrelated in an intricate hierarchy. Any violation of these rules is punished by a thieves' court, which has its own procedure. The penalty is always severe and is inflicted without delay.'[91]

Shalamov confirms Likhachev's early findings that thieves' courts operated in the camps.[92] For instance, disputes over a woman (usually a prostitute) would be settled at a *skhodka*: 'there are instances when hot tempers and the hysteria characteristic of all criminals will make him defend "his woman". On such occasions the question is taken up in a criminal court, and the criminal prosecutors will cite age-old traditions, demanding that the guilty man be punished.'[93] All participants have the same right to vote, although senior *vory* carry more weight.[94]

Santerre refers to these meetings as *tolkovishcha* (sing. *tolkovishche*), where the *vory* 'discuss all questions concerning them. All the most important decisions are taken there'. As a rule, the meetings were closed, with women and non-members not allowed to attend, although the constraints of camp life allowed non-members to witness the proceedings of the meeting.[95]

Once his honesty is put into question, the fate of a *vor* is decided at the *tolkovishche*. . . . A *tolkovishche* may often go on for several days, during which hot arguments are voiced, the slightest details are remembered, even of things and events that happened many years ago. According to the crime, a *vor* is sentenced.[96]

The *vory*'s *skhodka* was the organ of representation and control of the *vory*'s communes outside camp walls. Any member of the society could ask for a *skhodka* to be held.[97] While local and regional meetings were held,[98] national *skhodki*, where general problems concerning the society were addressed, rarely were. This is not surprising, given the limitation on movement for ordinary citizens of the Soviet Union, let alone former convicts. Still, major criminal *skhodki* took place in Moscow in 1947, Kazan' in 1955, and Krasnodar in 1956. Monakhov reports an estimated attendance of 200 to 400 people.[99]

From the various accounts of such meetings, four types of punishment handed down by the *vory* 'courts' can be identified. First was a prohibition against boasting in public, described by Likhachev. Boasting and storytelling were common among *vory*.[100] According to Likhachev, the purpose of the story was less to convey truth than to portray the characters, especially the victims, in humorous ways and to demonstrate the smartness, shrewdness, and boldness of the *vor* telling it.[101] Likhachev notes that 'to stop and expose the lies of a storyteller is a deep insult. It is considered an infringement of the thieves' force and dignity.' It was an open challenge. Only when the *vor* infringed the *vory'* code, might he be stopped:

It is possible to object to the storyteller only in one case: if he has somehow broken the thieves' ethics, the thieves' rules (laws). One punishment, although not severe, is to be forbidden boasting, which is considered as bad as exile from the [thieves'] sphere. In this case the thief has no longer right to tell stories about his heroic deeds. Everyone has the right to stop him, even if what he says is true.[102]

A second punishment was a public slap in the face, inflicted for minor offences, such as having insulted another *vor*. To slap a *vor* in the face in front of everybody was a severe blow to his reputation.[103] A third and more serious punishment, especially for those living in the camp, was permanent expulsion from the brotherhood. The expelled *vory* would join the caste of the *muzhiki*, the common convicts. The criminal elite in the camps could freely victimize the *muzhiki* and steal their belongings without asking permission from anyone.[104]

A fourth possibility was corporal punishment, usually fifty hits with a stick, according to Santerre. In one such case, a *vor* who had been insulted by another and was supposed to carry out the punishment failed to perform the ritual properly: before starting the execution he should have said, 'I'm not taking responsibility for bruises and blood!' He did not and was himself punished in place of the original perpetrator.[105]

The death penalty was inflicted for grave breaches of the *vory* code of behaviour, such as informing on fellow *vory* or repeatedly cheating them.[106] Santerre saw a sentence carried out according to the following ritual: first the guilty person was 'rotated', thereby taking away his soul. The victim would then be given the chance to die as a *vor* by standing with his back to the wall, tearing his shirt front open, and addressing his several executioners armed with knives, saying: 'take my soul'.[107] Of course, sentences were also passed on non-members and, if they thought it necessary, *vory* had no qualm at 'sentencing' women and children to death.[108]

Punishments of both members and non-members were executed 'without questions', as various camp officials report in their secret memos.[109] A *vor* was obliged to abide by the sentences of the gathering, even against his own will.[110] What is most remarkable is that 'sentences' were carried out across different camps, a testimony to the reach of the fraternity. For instance, a *vory*'s gathering taking place in 1951 in Vostochno-Ural'skii Corrective Labour camp (ITL) sentenced to death prisoner Yurilkin. The camp administration came to know of this and transferred him to Vyatskii ITL, several hundred kilometres away. But even there it was not safe for him, so he was moved to a transit prison in Kirov and then to Mekhren'gskii ITL. And, as a further precaution, he was constantly moved from one sub-unit of the camp to another. On 20 April 1955, four years after the sentence had been passed, two *vory* killed Yurilkin. They were later found guilty and shot by the administration.[111] In another report dated 1955 and sent to the Procurator's office of the Soviet Union, the Procurator of the Ukrainian Soviet Republic notes that a decision taken at a *vory*'s gathering 'at the end of the summer of 1954 in one Siberian camp, reached the Ukrainian camps in September–October 1954'.[112] Alarmingly, the Procurator's office of the Soviet Union writes in a 'note' dated 13 June 1956: 'this criminal formation exists in all Corrective Labour camps and often the decision of the group to murder one or another prisoner who is in a different camp is executed in that camp unquestioningly.'[113]

Origins of the *vory-v-zakone*

The *vory-v-zakone* exhibited a distinct style of dress, had their bodies covered with tattoos and spoke a peculiar argot. The secret initiation ritual and the abidance to a set of rules of behaviour made the society of the *vory* a peculiar and significant criminal phenomenon. 'Courts' existed to make sure members followed the rules and punished wrongdoers across time and space. Although an individual *vor* might have had an interest in punishing a fellow member, that task was the exclusive responsibility and prerogative of the *vory* meeting. We now turn to the issue of continuity and change: are the *vory* a specific Soviet phenomenon or are they themselves a product of pre-Revolutionary Russia?

Jacques Rossi, the author of a seminal work on the Gulag, maintains that the society existed in Tsarist Russia. He writes that *staryi blagorodnyi vorovskoi mir* 'is the old noble thieves' world, the world of real thieves. Many legends tell of the heroics of the old noble thieves' world that existed in Tsarist Russia and even into the 1930s'.[114] Santerre believes that 'the *vory* existed in Russia long before the revolution'. He adds, however, that 'the Soviet reality, and especially its social and economic system, created the specific conditions, in which a criminal world with its completely peculiar features was born and flourished'.[115] Monakhov dutifully writes, 'the Socialist society inherited the *vory* from the capitalist one [that preceded it]'. By this, however, he refers to the remote causes of crime in a Socialist society. For the immediate causes, he points to the NEP years as the period when elements of the capitalist class joined professional criminals and 'consolidated' the *vory*.[116] Gurov, who mostly follows Monakhov, notes that pre-Revolutionary criminologists (such as B. S. Utevskii, S. N. Krenev, and I. N. Yakimov) refer neither to the phenomenon nor to the term *vory-v-zakone*. He comes to the conclusion that the *vory-v-zakone* did not exist in Tsarist Russia and emerged only after the Revolution.[117]

As far as the origins of the term are concerned, Gurov seems to be correct. V. F. Trakhtenberg records in 1908 the terms *urka* (big, daring thief) and *oreburka* (petty thief) in his celebrated dictionary of criminal jargon. Popov (1912) has the words *blatnoi* (criminal), *urka* and *vozhak* (leader). A dictionary published in 1927 contains the word *zakonnyi*, meaning 'real, of good quality', and *vozhak*.[118] Likhachev, writing in a Soviet academic journal in 1935, calls the criminal leaders *vozhaki* and *golovki* (heads), common words with no specific connotation. However, Likhachev uses the adjective *vorovskoi* to refer to the sector of the underworld these leaders control: *vorovskoi prestupnyi mir* (thieves' criminal world) and *vorovskaya sreda* (milieu).[119] Official documents refer in the late 1940s to '*vory-retsidivisty*'[120] and, by 1953, to 'so-called *vory*'.

The expression *vory-v-zakone* is used by officials at least since 1955.[121] Shalamov, writing in 1959 and referring to the 'war' against the *vory* that began in the 1940s (the *such'ya voina*, see below), uses the form *zakonnyi vor* and *vor-v-zakone*.[122] Ivan P. Vorida, the author of 1971 Soviet compilation (*sbornik*) of criminal expressions, records the terms *vor-v-zakone* and *vor-zakonnik* and notes that such criminals ceased to exist in the 1950s.[123] The *vor* Ch., giving his testimony in the late 1980s and referring to the early 1950s, discusses the *bratstvo* (fraternity) of the *vory-v-zakone*. Only at the time when the society was about to disappear, was the form '*vory-v-zakone*' recorded.

The origin of the phenomenon thus must be sought under a different name or names. Prison life during the Tsarist period has been described by a number of sources, including Dostoyevsky's *House of the Dead*, based on the author's experience as a convict in Omsk from 1850 to 1854.[124] Dostoyevsky portrays the criminals' passion for card playing, boasting, and vanity.[125] He also describes the practice of swapping places: one convict would pay another to take his place and serve his sentence. Once the prisoner had agreed to swap and had already spent the money, he could not change his mind. If he tried to, he would be punished by the other convicts for not keeping his promise.[126] The fact that other prisoners took upon themselves the burden of punishing somebody with whom they had not been dealing testifies to the existence of norms of behaviour ('keep thy word') and collective punishment. Rossi also mentions that professional criminals in Tsarist Russia would 'keep their word'.[127]

Vlas Mikhailovich Doroshevich (1864–1922), who visited Sakhalin penal colony at the end of the nineteenth century, writes of a type of prisoner 'who wanted to gain the respect of his comrades and become an "Ivan", the hero of the colony'. Such prisoners would do so by defying prison rules and bravely enduring the ensuing punishment.[128]

There is also evidence that senior prisoners forced newly arrived convicts to pay them a tribute. In 1900, prisoners Averkiev, Utkin, and Bashmakov were terrorizing new convicts, and extorted food and money from them in the Nikolaevskaya corrective prison in Ekaterinburg, as detailed in a report dated 24 October 1901 of the prison head to the prison inspector of the Perm region.[129]

Individual and sporadic defying of prison rules and forcing newly arrived convicts to pay a tribute are near-universal features of prison life. Neither the writings of Dostoyevsky, Doroshevich, nor the archival evidence I have been able to consult refer to organized groups of convicts that systematically refused to work or collaborate with the authorities and, most importantly, that possessed an initiation ritual, strict rules of behaviour and criminal 'courts' to enforce such rules across different prisons.

Outside camp walls, however, a fraternity more similar to the *vory* existed at that time. Russian juridical literature refers to *arteli* (guilds) of ordinary thieves, including horse thieves, from the middle of the nineteenth century onwards.[130] Horse thieves belonged to criminal groups with a rudimentary internal division of labour and spread across different districts and even provinces, although one source stresses that thieving would be done in a given place and accomplices would sell or hide the horses afar.[131] Yakushkin, the author of a reference book on customary law published in 1896, describes a beggars' *artel'* as follows:

All the beggars here and for some distance beyond make up a regularly organised association known as the 'beggars' guild', with an elected guild-master and its own laws, custom and language. New members are nominated by their comrades and must accept the obligations of the guild. A person entitled to practise as a beggar by reason of physical deformity or disablement is apprenticed for a time to a fellow beggar, after which he is enrolled on a list and has to pay a subscription. As a rule, the term of apprenticeship is six years and the subscription is 60 kopecks; but an apprentice may elect to serve a shorter term and pay a higher subscription. Membership in the guild is effected by a special ceremony. The aspiring member is brought into the assembly, and after mutual greetings, the guild-master tests his knowledge of the prayers, beggars' songs, and the special language of the fraternity. The apprentice bows and kisses the hand of each person present and is then admitted as member and assigned an area where he can beg. A feast is given in his honour, and, on this occasion, he is allowed to sit with the others for the first time. The guild-master is elected for an indefinite period and is generally a blind beggar; he convokes the guild for necessary business, including the punishment of transgressors. This used to take the form of a beating but is now usually a fine for the purchase of church candles. The most ignominious punishment consists of slitting the offender's wallet, signifying that he is no longer entitled to practise as a beggar. A steward is elected to look after funds and expenses. Both extraordinary and annual assemblies are held, the latter on the first Monday of Lent or on Whitsunday, when a new candle is placed in the Church on behalf of the fraternity. The funds accumulated by the guild are generally devoted to church purposes . . . The beggars have a language of their own, which they endeavour to keep secret from outsiders.[132]

The *artel'* described by Yakushkin was a group operating independently, in competition with other groups. This does not exclude the possibility that *arteli* at times joined forces or maintained relations with one another. Sergei Maksimov, for example, reported in 1869 a case in which some beggars' *arteli* joined together to exclude a rival group from a fairground.[133]

The *arteli* resemble the *kodla*, the thieves' communes described above. Yet, four significant differences can be identified between the *vory* communes and the nineteenth-century *arteli*. First, the *artel'* was a group of people involved in the same business, who organized and accepted the leadership of a fellow member. It exercised a localized monopoly over a certain sector of the underworld. This feature qualifies them as a form of organized crime group. If we accept that each *vor* in a *kodlo* would work with accomplices and stick to a given sector of the underworld, then the *kodlo* amounts to a coalition of leaders of criminal *arteli*. Such a coalition of underworld godfathers had some control over their own 'soldiers' and accepted a sector-based division of labour. No doubt, a *vor*-led group of criminals entered into conflicts with criminals who did not work under the protection of the *kodlo*. Pre-Revolutionary *arteli* never formed a fraternity of leaders of individual groups.

Second, no one could 'buy' the title of *vor*, although it might have been the case that young criminals worked under the protection of a *vor* in a *kodlo*, and entered a sort of apprenticeship relation. Third, the *kodla* apparently were associations of *primi inter pares*, meaning no recognized hierarchy existed above the *vory*. The *skhodka* was the collegial organ that discussed matters and settled disputes among *vory*. The fourth and most significant difference relates to the national scale of the fraternity of the *vory*, which far exceeded that ever achieved by *arteli*. There is no evidence that pre-Revolutionary *arteli* had created a systematically organized structure with the purpose of co-ordinating their activities. Nor is there evidence that the *arteli* merged into a single national organization or that entry into one *artel'* meant automatic recognition by other *arteli*. Likhachev, Shalamov, Santerre, and many others met organized criminals in camps that were as far apart as the Belomorsko–Baltiiskii canal construction site in European Russia and Kolyma in the Arctic, facing Alaska. This is a formidable achievement for a criminal fraternity, considering the vastness of the country and the scope of its activities: devising rituals, policing behaviours, settling disputes among members, and protecting insiders from outside challengers.

A question follows from the above: how could such a society succeed where the *arteli* failed, namely in forming a national network? In order to answer this question, one must consider both the *arteli* and the *vory* as organizations offering some privileges to their members. The crucial condition for such organizations to exist is the ability to distinguish members from non-members and to punish both those who faked membership and those who misused the organization's privileges or violated its code of behaviour. This in turn requires close proximity, potential for repeated interaction among members, and the presence of information channels.[134] The localized nature of the *artel'* provided these conditions and enabled its leadership to levy a fee on entrants, distinguish members from non-members, and punish wrongdoers. Despite appearances to the contrary, these conditions were also well provided by the Gulag system. Furthermore, the scale of the Gulag archipelago allowed for the spread of the fraternity's rules and punishments, enabling the society to reach a national dimension.

The camp system was a fairly integrated system: it supplied a source of contacts for criminals and an opportunity to share experiences and devise ways of promoting common interests. By the middle of the 1930s, the network of the corrective labour camps was already fairly extensive. The northern camps, situated in the former Komi-Zyryanskaya oblast', held some 41,000 prisoners. In the far eastern camps, some 15,000 people were engaged in the building of the Boguchinskaya railway, as well as fishing and forestry. The Visherskie camps, which were chiefly involved in chemical, paper, and timber production, held a further 20,000 prisoners. There were 24,000 prisoners in the Siberian camps and 40,000 in the oldest of the Solovetskie camps, building the road from Kem' to Ukhta.[135] A recent estimate suggests the total number of those repressed in Gulag camps and colonies in the period 1934–52 reached over 18 million.[136] Prison numbers were not static within and between camps: inmates entered the camps, left the camps, and were transferred around the camps. Recently disclosed data places the number of intra-Gulag camp transfers for the period 1934–47 at around 3 million.[137]

Intra-Gulag transfers allowed not only repeated interaction but also the spread of information, another crucial requirement for the group to persist. The sharing of precise information was necessary in order to inform the prison population about new entries into the *vory* brother-hood, check reputations, expose frauds, and monitor convicts' transfers. In fact, news spread quickly among the different camps, as in the following story taken from the memoirs of General A. V. Gorbatov, a Soviet Army general detained in 1939 in a camp in Maldyak, Kolyma region, containing 400 political prisoners and some fifty criminals:

Boris is nicknamed 'The Careerist'. He got his name in one of the northern camps because he made himself out to be a big criminal, with six murders and five major robberies to his credit. He is believed and is appointed a senior prisoner. Then it turned out that he is simply an independent, petty thief. There is a great fuss and he is demoted and given his nickname.[138]

In another incident, Yadviga Iosifovna Verzhenskaya learned the fate of her husband through the criminals' information network. Arrested in 1938 as a member of the family of a traitor of the Motherland, she was very anxious to know the fate of her husband, arrested the year before. While discharging her duties in the camp hospital, she befriended some criminals, who offered to help her find information about her husband. After some time, she received 'a tiny piece of paper' with news about his fate.[139] Apparently, a sophisticated system for transmitting coded information between different camps existed, perfected by many generations of criminals. The system attracted the attention of the police, who claimed to have broken the code and that it consisted of a cryptographic language.[140]

As the population of the camps grew in size, the Gulag became an even more significant source of contact between criminals scattered across the Soviet Union. The camps quickly became the best possible medium for the swift dissemination and maintenance of *vory* rituals and traditions.[141] While the fraternity surely drew upon the rich pre-Revolutionary under-world culture, such a milieu never produced a national organization. A crucial factor for the existence and the endurance of the *vory* was the Gulag system, as it developed from 1920s onwards. This by itself does not answer fully the question of the emergence of the *vory*; rather it points to the presence of a crucial and necessary condition.[142]

The *vory* society was almost entirely destroyed by the end of the 1950s during what came to be known as *such'ya voina* (bitches' war). Various sources evidence their downfall: Gurov writes that by the mid-1950s, 300 *vory* were known to reside in Soviet prisons; by the end of the 1950s, the *vory* had 'virtually disappeared'.[143] According to Bukovsky, a political dissident who served his sentence in a camp in the Perm' region in 1973–4, only a 'few dozen' survived in the whole Soviet Union.[144] Perushkin uses a similar figure: 'the number of thieves-in-law who survived the bitches' war did not exceed two dozen.'[145]

The *vory-v-zakone* bore tattoos and spoke a language of their own. They followed well-defined rules that regulated interaction among members and between *vory* and outsiders, such as family, strangers, and officials. Most importantly, a ritual marked entry into the brotherhood. 'Made' members who did not follow the rules were summoned to a rudimentary tribunal, where their crimes would be discussed and, if the defendant found guilty, a sentence passed. The sentence was carried out on the behalf of the society as a whole, not of the single member who had been insulted or put in danger by the rule-breaker. In places of confinement, their main aims were to avoid working and to victimize and rob other convicts (especially political prisoners), most likely with the tacit support of the prison authorities. The Gulag system allowed the fraternity to spread across different camps and acquire a national dimension. Most likely, the *vory* evolved from pre-Revolutionary criminal *arteli*. Outside camp walls, they operated as a coalition of criminal leaders each exercising control over a sector of the underworld but allied with each other. And it is outside camp walls that we find the *vory* when the Soviet Union came to an end.

8

The Russian Mafia

The fraternity of the *vory-v-zakone* survived the *such'ya voina* into the 1970s. Soviet dissident Vladimir Bukovsky recalls that *skhodki* took place in his camp in 1973–4.[1] Seventy-three *vory* were investigated in the early 1980s by Soviet police.[2] Since then their numbers have increased significantly. A book written in 1993 and published in early 1994 claims to have the *complete* list of 266 names of the *vory* operating in the former Soviet Union.[3] By the end of 1993, the official figure of the Ministry of Internal Affairs was that of 600 *vory* operating in all of the CIS, 200 of whom were thought to be active in the Russian Federation.[4] According to data supplied by the same department on 1 April 1994, there were 740 *vory* in Russia.[5] The number of *vory* in prison also increased. In 1993, twenty-nine were arrested and twenty were sentenced. A total of about 100 *vory* were behind bars in 1994.[6] The Russian police reported that 800 *vory* were operating in the CIS in 1999, 387 of these being active in the Russian Federation, a significant drop from the 1994 figure.[7] The number of *vory* went from less than one hundred in the late eighties to 740 in 1994, and then declined sharply to 387 in 1999.[8] What does account for this trend? Below, we offer some reasons for this outcome. These reasons will in turn shed light on the role of the *vory* in the post-Soviet criminal world.

The new *vory* have less of a prison background. Eleven out of seventy-three *vory* investigated in the early 1980s had never served a prison sentence, a departure from the past, when prison terms were regarded as an essential part of the *vor*'s reputation.[9] The head of the Moscow anti-organized crime unit (RUOP), Igor' Zakharyan, declared in 1994: 'Recently the *vory-v-zakone* and the *avtoritety* have been getting younger.

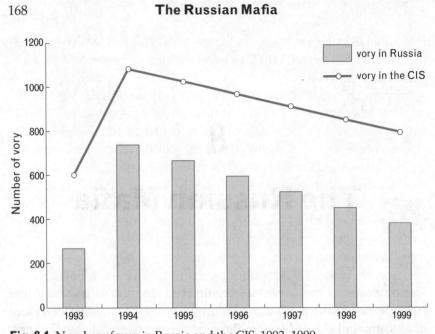

Fig. 8.1 Number of *vory* in Russia and the CIS, 1993–1999

Source: Gurov, 1990, 174: 200; *Moskovskie Movosti*, 9 May 1993; Podlesskikh and Tereshonok, 1994: 239–53; Afanas'ev, 1994: 22; *Izvestiya*, 27 Jan. 1994; *Zvezda*, 3 June 1994; Handelman, 1994a: 18; Razinkin, 1995: 12–15; *Komsomol'skaya Pravda*, 18 Feb. 1999. Data for 1995–98 is projected.

Before, a title could only be gained after being imprisoned for a certain time; now many young criminals simply buy it for money.'[10]

Reports of *vory* who acquired their title by paying for it date to the late 1980s. In 1990, Gurov writes that 'cases of paid entry into the association were common [since the mid-eighties] and led to a division between "new" and "old" *vory*'.[11] He refers to a closed conference held at the MVD of the USSR on 16 December 1986, where evidence of the thieves-with-a-code-of-honour who had a reputation for strictly following the old rules being paid to arrange initiation rituals was presented.[12] Newspaper articles from the early to mid-1990s confirm that some *vory* paid for their title. According to the crime correspondent for *Komsomol'skaya Pravda*, 'Now [in 1994], in order to become a *vor-v-zakone*, it is not necessary to have been in the camps. The process [of becoming a *vor*] is easy: three *vory* who hold the title already gather together and baptize the new recruit. They allocate a sphere of influence to him and take a fee.'[13] Prices were quoted in the press: *Kommersant-Daily* reported that in May 1995 the fee for *vory* initiation was 150,000 dollars.[14] At a gathering in the Tyumen' region, the novices paid for their 'crown' in kind: they gave foreign cars to the *vory* that attended the gathering.[15] Maybe in an effort to save money, Gordelidze, a Georgian criminal who operates in Yoshkar-Ola, simply declared himself *vor-v-zakone*.[16]

The rapid increase in the number of *vory* between the late 1980s to the mid-1990s can be attributed to four related factors. The numerous criminal opportunities that accompanied the transition to the market economy attracted more individuals into the underworld and a fraction of these individuals sought the title of *vor*. The new criminals had more financial resources at their disposal than the *vory* who had survived the Gulag system. The temptation to accept money was too strong to resist. Some *vory* agreed to drop a crucial requirement of a true *vor* (a lengthy prison sentence) and initiated younger criminals. Once this requirement was not considered any more a requisite of a 'true' *vor*, the barriers to enter were significantly lowered. Furthermore, the prison system was not functioning any more as a check on who was eligible to enter, as in the past: at this point in time, the fraternity was operating outside camp walls and any three *vory* could arrange a ritual and grant the title.[17]

We now turn to the reasons that might account for the decline of the number of *vory* in the second half of the nineties. Below I will refer to three reasons. First, a *vor* who aspires to organize significant criminal activities and even to act as a provider of protection in the underworld cannot rely simply on the label of *vor*. Such label is meaningless unless it is backed by the ability to display violence. *Vory* with a chance to succeed had to join or form territorially based criminal groups. Those who did not, faced the threat of being killed or marginalized in the underworld. Even those who joined criminal groups, however, were not insulated from the likelihood of being killed. Once admitted into the newly formed crime groups, they would find themselves involved in mafia wars, like any mafioso in Sicily and North America. These combinations of factors provided the best check on the proliferation of the number of the *vory* in the second half of the 1990s.

The *Vory-v-Zakone* and Territorially Based Groups

The case of Mordak—a distinguished *vor* from Saratov—shows how personal authority is not sufficient to enforce decisions over parties with stronger military power: Mordak earned in the past the reputation of being a 'supreme judge', able to adjudicate conflicts among *vory* by applying the rules and traditional precepts of the fraternity. In August 1994 he interfered in a conflict among two younger *vory*, Makho and Ded Khasan. One of the two parties disagreed with the decision reached by Mordak and resorted to violence. Makho was almost killed as a result.[18]

The ability to mobilize a number of well-armed individuals is a crucial requirement for survival in the underworld. Since the early 1990s, the post-Soviet criminal landscape started to be populated by territorially based groups with this ability. By 1995, writes Perushkin, the crime correspondent for *Argumenty i Fakty*,

The picture is reminiscent in some way of a classic Italian Mafia family. As a rule, these are groups formed on a territorial basis, such as Solntsevskaya, Dolgoprudnenskaya, Izmailovskaya, Lyuberetskaya . . . All the members of such a family are called *bratva* [brotherhood]. Every group is divided into brigades headed by a *brigadir*, who is linked to the *avtoritet*.[19]

Below we shall review the organizational structure, the activities and the inter-group relations of these units.

Organizational Structure

In a 1995 interview, a deputy of Egor, the leader of the Izmailovskaya group, told Cesare Martinetti, a Moscow-based Italian investigative journalist: 'The leader of the group, Egor, is surrounded by six to eight people, not more, otherwise the structure becomes difficult to manage. Then we have people in charge of different crews and the foot soldiers (we call them *shestyorki*).' According to Egor's deputy, the entire brigade was composed of 1,000–1,500 people.[20]

The image of a hierarchical but flexible internal structure seems to apply to the Solntsevo (or Solntsevskaya brigada), the largest and most powerful of the Moscow *brigady*.[21] The Solntsevo takes its name from the Moscow suburb where it originated from. For Iosif Roizis, a former member turned state witness for the police of various countries, it consists of roughly 9,000 members.[22] The leading figures are Mikhas' (Sergei Mikhailov) and Avera (Viktor Averin), both with Israeli passports.[23] Sil'vestr (Sergei Timofeev) was also a leader of the group until he was killed in August 1994. Boroda (Sergei Kruglov), another prominent figure, suffered the same destiny as Sil'vestr. Other prominent figures are Yura Samosval (Yurii Esin) and Yaponchik (V. K. Ivan'kov), who was regarded as the American link of the Solntsevo until his arrest in June 1995, while Semen Mogilevich is an emissary based in Hungary.[24] The younger brother of Averin, Sasha, is gaining authority.[25]

The Solntsevo is as an umbrella organization of different crews (probably twelve) active in different countries. Thanks to an investigation by the Italian police, the structure of Esin's crew is rather well documented.

At least until 1997, Esin was leading a crew based in Moscow but with significant criminal interests in Rome.[26] Only ten people have been identified with certainty as being members of the Russian sub-unit, two of them Italians resident in Russia, but the Italian police believe the group to be larger. These people went regularly to Italy and committed crimes in both countries. They included a member of the State Duma and a former KGB officer. The police identified twenty people belonging to the second unit, based in Italy. They included eight women, and six native Italians (most of the others were born in the former Soviet Union but acquired Italian citizenship). Three Russians have been identified as 'deputies' of Esin, a fourth, Dmitrii Naumov was a close collaborator but tried to set up an alternative group and was killed on 23 September 1996 in Moscow. Women turned out to be very active in the day-to-day working of the organization in Italy. They also managed the common funds of the group, discussed sensitive operations, including punishment, and directly threatened other members. Some of them spoke both Russian and Italian and their role as interpreters gave them a crucial role as go-betweens.[27]

Esin's crew in Moscow operated with a degree of independence from the overarching Solntsevo. For instance, in a May 1996 conversation, Esin was discussing the final details of a shipment of fish to Moscow with two businessmen from Vladivostok. He told them that, in case they had any problem in Moscow, they should contact his 'boys': 'If someone does not pay or tries to cheat you, Sasha must call the boys immediately.' Most interestingly, he adds, 'It is not necessary to call Solntsevo or Ismailovo . . . although we are all friends, it is not necessary to stir the waters.'[28]

Within the Solntsevo a supreme council operates, formed by twelve people who have 'great power' and are the leaders of individual crews.[29] The council meets regularly to discuss important matters for the organization. Only made *vory* can attend the meeting, although there are no special rituals to join the *brigada* at the lower end of the pyramid.[30] Roizis was informed in detail of one such meeting that took place in Miami in 1993, just after the arrival of Ivan'kov in the USA. Among others, Boroda, Sil'vestr, Averin, Esin (Samosval), Mikhas', and Ivan'kov were present. Reportedly, the matter discussed was the expansion of the Solntsevo abroad.[31] The Italian police concluded that at this meeting the Solntsevo decided to start its operation in Italy under the supervision of Esin.[32]

Some of the proceeds from criminal activities of each crew converge into a communal fund of the entire *brigada*, the *obshchak*, which is managed by several banks. Various instances point to the fact that the *brigada* has its own accounts, separate from those of the members; for example, in May 1994 Averin reminded Semen Mogilevich that he still had not paid into the Solntsevo common fund the sum of 5 million US dollars.[33] The evidence is still insufficient to assess in greater detail the financial flows from each crew to the central *brigada*, although one suspects that crew leaders try to minimize their contribution to the collective fund. This might explain why Esin was wary of informing the *brigada* of one of his deals.

In St Petersburg the structure of criminal groups does not seem to differ dramatically from that of Moscow *brigady*. Andrei Konstantinov, a crime correspondent for *Komsomol'skaya Pravda* and the author of several books on organized crime in St Petersburg, writes that various *brigady* (from two to five, the most notorious being the Tambovskaya, Malyshevskaya, Vorkutinskaya, and Kazanskaya) form a larger unit (*zveno*), which in turn is affiliated to either one or another of the larger criminal groupings.[34]

Activities

An investigator at the Moscow Procurator's Office, Mikhail Slin'ko, pointed out in 1993 to the importance of collecting protection money for established crime groups in Moscow, such as Solntsevskaya, Ostankinskaya, Lyuberetskaya, Dolgoprudnenskaya, Podol'skaya, Koptevskaya:

These groups are not simply involved in ordinary crimes, such as stealing and killing, but also they extort money in a certain district for 'protection' of places of public catering, commercial kiosks, co-operatives, consumer service enterprises, prostitutes. Often the leaders, once they have accumulated sufficient money, enter legal business and become directors of commercial enterprises and banks. They also bribe politicians and law-enforcement agents.[35]

This picture matches the one that emerges from the interview with the deputy of Egor: 'We make money in the old way, through the racket, this is the basic activity that allows us to raise capital. But then, one needs to make this capital grow, so we put the money into business, banks, import–export ventures.'[36]

In Moscow, the Solntsevo is involved in dispute settlement and protection in sectors of both the overworld and the underworld, in particular drugs, prostitution, retail, oil and gas. In one instance, a businessman, P.A.K., needed to retrieve 90,000 dollars from somebody who was under the protection of the Solntsevo. P.A.K. contacted his own protector, who in turn tried to contact various Solntsevo representatives, including Esin in Italy. Esin sent some of his immediate associates to talk with another Solntsevo member, Borya. Esin added, 'the matters must be solved positively. We cannot dishonor the name of the Solntsevskie.'[37]

Esin was directly involved as the *krysha* of both businesses and individuals in Moscow. The director of a diamond company who needed to retrieve a loan turned to Esin for help.[38] In another instance, an under-secretary of state in the Russian government owed money to the Medvedkovo *brigada* (named after a Moscow suburb), a *brigada* of 'independents' according to Gavrilov, a deputy of Esin in Moscow. Esin's group in Moscow protected the politician. The two groups met and reached an agreement: the politician would earn the money by working for Esin and pay his debt, Esin being the guarantor of the deal.[39]

The mafia world is agitated by anomalies and uncertain borders, as the following cases show. A major food retailer in Moscow paid 200,000 dollars every month in protection money to the Solntsevo, although he complained that more than one group was trying to extract money from him.[40] A businessman who was protected by Esin complained that members of both the Podol'skaya and Leninskaya groups had been taking money from him to the value of 200,000 dollars. Esin asked why the businessman did not get in touch before and asked his deputy to contact the rival groups in order to clarify the matter.[41] Similarly, a banker was forced to pay protection money twice: to Esin and to a 'person from the Party', somebody described as having been very influential in the past. Esin was extremely upset by the fact.[42] He understood that his credibility as a protector was put into question if he could not prevent this other person from extracting money from an individual (the banker) he was suppose to protect.

In another instance, the Solntsevo decided to victimize a person who had turned to the *brigada* for help. Aleksandr Abramovich, a Moscow jeweller, opened a shop in the center of Moscow in 1993 and with his partner Vlasov entered into a dispute with a supplier protected by the Taganskaya *brigada*. They turned to the Solntsevo for help. A meeting with Mikhas' and Averin was arranged in the gym of a school in the Moscow district of Solntsevo and the shop was 'officially' accepted under the 'roof' of the group. Between 1993 and 1995, Abramovich paid 1 to

1.2 million dollars as protection money to the group and eventually was forced out of business.[43] Maksimov suggests that Taganskaya and Solntsevskaya are allied.[44] This might explain why Abramovich was eventually forced out of business. The Solntsevo decided to side with the Taganskaya at the expense of their client Abramovich.

Even criminal groups specialized in a given sector of the underworld pay protection to larger groups. Mikhail Slin'ko observes in his 1993 interview that smaller gangs of robbers, pickpockets, and even professional killers, with either a rudimentary hierarchical structure or no structure at all, pay protection money to the gang that controls the area in which they operate.[45] One such instance is reported by *Kommersant-Daily*. A criminal gang, active in the period between 1991 to 1994 and dedicated to the production of explosives, included both explosive experts, an engineer working in the defence industry, and criminals. According to *Kommersant-Daily*, 'during two of those four years, these producers [of explosives] had found a reliable 'roof' with one of the biggest criminal groups [of the city]'.[46] Relations are not always smooth, as testified by the following instance: Sergei Pridanov and Evgenii Ivanenko teamed up with Sergei Agal'tsov, a member of the Malyshevskaya criminal group, in order to run some criminal deals. Between 1992 and the end of 1993 business ran well. By autumn 1993, Pridanov wanted to get rid of Agal'tsov and thereby stop paying dues to the Malyshevskaya group. Together with other members, they set a trap for Agal'tsov and killed him. The reaction was swift and harsh: both Pridanov and Ivanenko were almost killed in an ambush and then arrested by militia, a success that could not but have pleased the Malyshevskaya group.[47]

Inter-Group Relations

Some evidence of inter-group co-operation emerges from the police report on Esin and his crew. Esin, although connected to the Solntsevo, was on friendly term with members of the Kurgan brigade and 'the boys of the Izmailovo'. Members of both groups were his guests in Rome. He watched the Juventus–Aiax final of the Champions League with 'the boys of the Izmailovo', with whom he planned to open a shop selling arms in Moscow.[48] When planning to punish one of accomplices, Esin suggested that the man should be kept in a 'prison' managed by 'the people of Ul'yanovsk' in Moscow (it turned out that the 'prison' was already full).[49]

The Role of the Vory-v-Zakone

We now return to the role of the *vory* in the post-Soviet environment and the questions we posed at the start of chapter, namely why the number of *vory* decreased from the mid-1990s and what role the *vory* played in the Russian criminal underworld in this period.

First, the evidence presented above testifies that *vory* such as Sil'vestr, Mikhas', Yaponchik, Boroda, and Esin had joined territorially based *brigady*. Others deserve to be mentioned. *Vory* Frol and Starostin, known as Gera, were affiliated to the Balashikhinskaya group, Sukhorukov, known as Sukhoi (Dry), was the leader of Zheleznodorozhnaya band until his death,[50] while A. D. Petrov, nicknamed Petrik, was part of Mazutka group.[51] The most powerful Georgian group operating in Russia, the Kutaisskaya group, was led by *vor-v-zakone* Tariel Oniani, and, as of 1994, included fifty *vory* and criminal *avtoritety* among their number.[52] In the city of Komsomol'sk-na-Amure in the far-east district of Khabarovsk, the most prominent criminal is Evgenii Petrovich Vasin, nicknamed Dzhem, who set up a rather mysterious 'Far Eastern Association of *vory*' (DVAV).[53] Reportedly, Dzhem was crowned *vor-v-zakone* in the Tobol'sk prison, at the suggestion of Yaponchik.[54] *Argumenty i Fakty* concludes that, 'having felt that their influence in the criminal world is gradually weakening, the *vory* elite at present [1995] tries to enter into alliances with the most influential criminal *avtoritety*.'[55]

Second, the title of *vor-v-zakone* is still bestowed on deserving criminals. The wife of Esin told her son in 1994 that Sergei Aksen, member of the Izmailovskaya *brigada*, had just been crowned *vor-v-zakone*. Her son, speaking from Moscow, commented: 'He is a good guy, full of bullet wounds and one of the Izmailovo guys.'[56] Two years after, Serezha (phoning from the Far Eastern city of Khabarovsk) told Esin that Vitya [a.k.a. Kisel'] had just been 'crowned' in Komsomol'sk. Esin approved of the choice and added: 'They have [also] crowned Sergei Aksenov. The more Russians the better.'[57] Respect for *vory* appears in a conversation referring to the presence in Italy of *vor* Dlinnyi: 'A crown is a crown.'[58] Obtaining the title of *vor* in this new environment signals a promotion within the group.

Third, *vory* can also lose their title and are killed in mafia wars. In 1991 the thief Masya was blown up by a radio-controlled mine near Bratsk.[59] In 1992, twenty-nine armed clashes were recorded by the Moscow

Procurator's Office, and 800 *boeviki* were involved. Seventeen *vory* were killed and forty-seven wounded.[60] Prominent *vory* died, such as Sukho-rukov, known as Sukhoi (Dry) and Starostin (Gera).[61] The *vor-v-zakone* Kalina (Viktor Nikiforov) was one of the most distinguished victims of that year, allegedly killed by Aleksandr Solonik, a former militia sergeant turned contract-killer.[62] In 1993, sixteen *vory-v-zakone* were killed, includ-ing Boroda, Lesik, Sultan, Frol (S. Frolov), Leva Tbilisskii, Arsen, and Abo so Shramom.[63] *Vor-v-zakone* Globus (Valerii Dlugach) was murdered in the spring. He was shot at 3 a.m. while leaving the discotheque U Lis'sa in Moscow. The shot was fired from a Simonov rifle with a telescopic sight, at a distance of 30 metres, from the canopy of the neighbouring building. Seconds later Arkhilashvili, alias Ital'yanets, a friend of Globus, left the discotheque and was also slain. A few days later, another close associate of Globus, Rambo (Anatolii Semenov), was killed with three shots from a Makarov pistol, near the porch of his house in Stroitelei street in Moscow.[64] Apparently, Globus had been killed because of a dispute over drug trafficking.[65]

A *vor* from Tomsk, Rostom, and Sultan Balashikhinskii, the only *vor* of Chechen origin, were ambushed and slain in February and April 1994, respectively.[66] *Vor* Zaostrovskii was killed in Ekaterinburg.[67] Makho—who had escaped death twice before—was killed while driving a car in the city of Sochi, on 28 August 1994. In the same ambush, Vako, a prominent Georgian *vor* allied to Makho, also died. A few weeks earlier, *vor-v-zakone* Avtandil Chikhladze, nicknamed Kvezho, was shot.[68] Sil'vestr, first leader of the *brigada* neighbouring the Solntsevo, Orekhovskaya,[69] and then of the Solntsevo, was murdered in August 1994.[70]

Although Esin moved to Italy as a result of a decision taken by Solntsevo's 'council of twelve', he was afraid for his life. Both Esin and Gavrilov were closely associated to Sil'vestr and Boroda and, according to Roizis, were afraid to be caught in the war if they had stayed in Russia.[71] When Gavrilov informed Esin in May 1996 of the death of another man associated with Sil'vestr, Drakon, he added 'all those who were with Serezha [Sil'vestr], they will kill them all'. Gavrilov insisted he wanted to attend the funeral, while Esin suggested that it might be wiser not to go because the police would be taking pictures of the mourners.[72] Esin and his immediate associates also discussed a newspaper report suggesting that Esin escaped to Italy because he was afraid of being killed. He immediately asked himself why such a version of events should have been published.[73]

In a February 1996 phone call, Esin told one of his associates in Moscow that a *vor* was 'born with the crown hanging from his ears'. He referred to a *vor* who had secretly plotted to kill an associate of Esin (Dmitrii Ivanov) and had lost his title.[74]

Vory are killed in what appears to be ordinary gang warfare and intra-group conflicts. Rather than indicating the end of the fraternity, the high number of murdered *vory* testifies to the fact that *vory* are playing a role in the post-Soviet criminal world. What is their new role?

A crucial requirement for a criminal organization is the ability to enforce decision, if necessary with the use of violence. Territorially based criminal groups, with an elaborate internal structure and the ability to resort to violence, dominate the Russian criminal landscape. A national society of criminal supremos, with no ability to sanction its decision, would not be viable. The view of the *vory* as dispute settlers of criminal matters devoid of military power does not stand to reason.[75] Still, the traditions of the *vory* have not disappeared: their rich apparatus of rituals, rules of interaction, and mythology is being used in the new environment. After a period of transition, when entry into the fraternity went virtually unchecked, territorially based groups resurrected the *vory* rituals. The *vory* ritual now marks the entry of powerful crew leaders into the 'governing body' of the biggest criminal groups in Moscow. (Contrary to what happens in the Sicilian Mafia, initiation is reserved for the leaders, rather than being a requirement for each group member.) The governing body of the Solntsevo is a coalition of *vory*. A number of other crime groups are said to be in broad agreement with the Solntsevo. We have discovered relationships of co-operation between Solntsevo and Izmailovskaya. Newspaper reports point to at least seven Moscow crime groups connected in some form with each other, but still retaining their independence.[76] *Vory* have leading roles in these seven groups. It is likely that crew leaders who in turn have gone through the ritual govern the majority of the Moscow *brigady* along similar lines as the Solntsevo. Thus the groups that share *vory* rituals and norms of interaction and are federated with each other constitute the Russian Mafia.

Chechens and Cossacks

The account we have given of the criminal landscape of Russia is not exhaustive. We have already seen a member of the Solntsevo referring to a *brigada* of 'independents'. More significantly, other criminals do not share the rituals and traditions of the *vory* and count as their competitors. Below we discuss two such competitors, the Chechens and the Cossacks.

The *vory* traditions never influenced ethnically based criminality. A Chechen criminal, interviewed by *Argumenty i Fakty*, maintained: 'We have nothing of this sort. We do not accept laws of the *vory*, we recognize only our national traditions.'[77] Only one Chechen is on record as a *vor*, Sultan Balashikhinskii.[78] He campaigned for a compromise with the existing Russian gangs, but his fellow countrymen were not convinced. Eventually, Sultan broke away from them and headed his own brigade in Balashikha, and divided territory with Sergei Frolov, who was killed at the end of 1993 (Sultan was killed in March 1994).

The history of Chechen criminality can be written almost without any reference to the *vory*. According to information released by the national anti-organized crime unit (GUOP), Chechen criminals established themselves in Moscow in the middle of 1987.[79] Ruslan, Lecho-Lysyi (the bald) and Khoza were at the head of this embryonic centrally organized group. The Chechens found a niche by winning some crucial battles with rival criminal formations, such as Solntsevskaya, Balashikhinskaya, Lyuberetskaya, and Dolgoprudnenskaya. At the end of 1991, Ruslan, Lecho-Lysyi, and Khoza were arrested. What was until then a unified entity, broke down into a number of separate gangs, each headed by its own leader. Notable among them were 'Richard', the Talarov brothers, Gennadii Arakelov (his group numbered 100 people), and Sultan Balashikhinskii. The three main Chechen groups are Tsentral'naya, Ostankinskaya, and Avtomobil'naya.[80] These groups control areas of the city of Moscow and extract protection money. 'Even Azerbaijani flower peddlers and fruit merchants in Moscow—there are 5,000 to 7,000 in the capital—must pay 500 rubles a day [$US 2.25 in 1992] to the Chechen group,' reported in 1992 Joseph Serio, a security expert in Moscow.[81] Traditionally, the Chechens control the north-east of Moscow and a section of the centre.[82]

When in a given country there is an expectation of terrorist attacks from insurgent groups, every bomb blast tends to be blamed on those insurgents. A bomb was found on a bus in March 1996. In the summer of 1996, a wave of explosions hit Moscow, including two blasts in Moscow trolleybuses (11 and 12 July) and the bombing of the Tul'skaya metro station (11 June; four dead). Another bomb exploded in April 1999 in an elevator shaft on the upper floors of the Intourist Hotel near the Kremlin, leaving eleven people injured and sending shattered glass raining down on Tverskaya Ulitsa and the Patio Pizza restaurant.[83] On 22 June 1999 a powerful bomb exploded outside the offices of the Ministry of Internal Affairs.[84] The most shocking terrorist attacks in Russian recent history were the apartment bombings in September 1999, when about 300 people were killed in Moscow (two explosions) and in Buinaksk and Volgodonsk in southern Russia.

The government has blamed all these explosions on Chechen terrorists, helped by the Chechen Mafia. The hypothesis that Chechen organized criminals are involved in terrorist attacks in Moscow and other cities of Russia is rather weak. (Indeed even the hypothesis that Chechen terrorists are involved at all in bombing attacks outside their region is far from certain.) Chechen criminals greatly resented Dudaev's nationalistic policy and opposed the war, as pointed out in various reports ('there is no information that any Moscow-based Chechen gangs are preparing terrorist acts in the capital', Mikhail Suntsov, of Moscow RUOP, told *Kommersant-Daily*, 18 Aug. 1994).[85] Timur, a medium-level criminal attached to a Chechen group in Moscow mainly involved in flat and automobile scams, was asked in 1994 whether Dudaev could use the Chechen Mafia in Moscow to plant bombs in the capital. The answer was: 'It is out of the question. This conflict has forced the Chechen Mafia to keep a low profile in Moscow. And our rivals, Georgians, Daghestans, Russians, all take advantage of the situation to nibble away our territory. If this state of affairs continues, the Chechen Mafia will take action to bring peace in Chechnya. Forget about planting bombs in Moscow.' Clearly, the Chechen criminals failed to convince their brothers in the Caucasus to scale down their nationalistic demands.

Cossacks are also powerful competitors of the Russian Mafia. The Federal government, faced with an understaffed and demoralized army, is increasingly resorting to the services of Cossack units in various parts of the Federation, such as the Caucasus and border areas.[86] In 1997, they were granted special permission to carry weapons and they use these powers to operate as suppliers of private protection.[87] In the Rostov region they patrol streets, maintain law and order, punish wrongdoers, usually by traditional public flogging, and extract fees from the local population;[88] in Moscow, they have been recruited by the mayor Yurii Luzhkov to patrol some of the city railways stations and market places. They are also reported to be running private protection rackets in a purely criminal fashion and several Atamans have been arrested on organized crime charges.[89] After a confrontation between Cossacks and local racketeers in the city of Volgodonsk, the latter asked to join. Reportedly, the local 'godfather', a man nicknamed Captain, is among those who did. The nearby Tsimlyanskii district is under the control of a former criminal turned Cossack, who served a sentence for murder in Magadan region, and twenty-seven other former convicts.[90]

Representatives of the Union of Cossacks told *Kommersant-Daily* that 'criminals have started to penetrate the Cossack movement. In Russia there are at least twenty pseudo-Cossack organizations, headed or heavily infiltrated by criminal bosses [*avtoritety*]'.[91] In order to acquire credibility, these organizations lure into their services retired army generals and reputable Cossacks, who grant them an aura of authenticity. A reason given for such criminal penetration is that Cossacks obtain tax privileges, and rights to land and to carry arms. According to *Izvestiya* (20 June 1993), they guard the Danilovskii market in Moscow, while a Moscow city official later revealed that the market is under the control of *vory-v-zakone*.[92] This may be further proof that professional criminals penetrate Cossack units. Pudel', reputed to have been the keeper of the *vory*'s communal fund (*obshchak*) in Khabarovsk in the 1980s and a former protégé of *vor* Dzhem, is Deputy Chief Ataman of the Cossack forces of Russia.[93]

Cossack units have been extremely successful at negotiating a pact with the Russian state. They have been given the right to carry arms and have been tacitly allowed to run protection rackets in exchange for some policing and military services in the border areas of the country and in some cities like Moscow. A possible development is that Cossack formations become an umbrella uniting different brands of criminals, supplying these individuals with common and recognizable 'trademarks', such as a patriotic mission, ideology, uniforms, and rituals alternative to those of the *vory*.

Profitable Relations: Criminals, Politics and the Church

A pact between fragments of the political elite and established criminal organizations could be in the interests of both. It would assure political leaders a degree of stability in the underworld and clear boundaries to the penetration of the criminals in the overworld. It could also deliver politicians easy and quick results in the fight against crime. Some gangs would be singled out for persecution, while leaving the bulk of the 'certified' groups undisturbed. Furthermore, specific covert operations could be carried out in co-operation, for instance, against Chechen 'terrorists'. The Cossack movement, although significantly penetrated by criminals, have already struck a pact with the Russian State. Is there evidence of such a pact with the Russian Mafia?

Prominent Russians from both sides of the law have spoken in favour of striking a deal between established criminal groups and the state. The singer Iosif Kobzon, a man closely associated with shady figures in Russia, has emerged as a prominent speaker in favour of such a pact.[94] In an interview Kobzon granted to *Komsomol'skaya Pravda* on 17 May 1994, he called for a truce between the state and the criminal structures: 'Maybe, it is necessary to have a dialogue. It is necessary to sit down at the table, so to speak, and negotiate through mediators, public councils, or the press.'[95] Vladimir Petrovich Podatev, nicknamed Pudel', is the founder of *Svoboda* (freedom), a private protection firm. The firm has been involved in instances of extortion and kidnapping and is reputed to be a front for the criminal activities of Pudel'.[96] He suggested that entrepreneurs pay his protective association a fee. In return, *Svoboda* would undertake some public duties, support the prison population and ensure order and safety in the city.[97] This scheme appears equivalent to legalizing his protection racket. A criminal *avtoritet* writing in the respected weekly *Argumenty i Fakty*, maintains that the fight against the Chechen Mafia undertaken by the Slavic criminal world is equivalent to fighting Chechen terrorists and urges the police to join forces against a common enemy.[98]

Criminals can send menacing messages to the political elite of a country, if their offers of co-operation are ignored. The Sicilian Mafia planted various bombs in historical sites (such as the Uffizi Gallery) in the summer of 1993 in order to signal its disapproval of the newly introduced article 41 *bis* of the prison regulations.[99] On 11 and 12 July 1996, two bombs went off in Moscow. These events happened just after Alexander Lebed, then newly appointed Security Council Chief, had announced an impending crackdown on crime. Lebed was to increase the ranks of the police (18,600 more officers), the tax police (1,000 more officers), and the judiciary (650 more judges); build four new prisons; and create a witness protection programme. At the time, both Duma Speaker Gennadii

Seleznev and Konstantin Cherkasov, of the Moscow mayor's office, believed that the explosions were a message sent to Lebed.[100] After only a few weeks in his job as Chief of the Security Council, Lebed was dismissed: although one should resist the temptation to link the two events, none the less his policies were dropped.

On the other side, journalists, businessmen, officials, and politicians have also called for a truce. Yurii Shchekochikhin, a prominent journalist of *Literaturnaya Gazeta*, suggested that a secret agreement should be reached with the more sensible sectors of organized criminality. Such an agreement would keep the more ruthless gangs under control. Shchekochikhin's voice is not an isolated one in Russia. Igor' Gamayunov—also on the staff of *Literaturnaya Gazeta*—witnessed a similar appeal broadcasted on TV: 'I saw a programme on Russian Television a couple of months ago devoted to a discussion of the crime problem. One of the panellists seriously proposed that we gather up all *vory-v-zakone* and try to come to an agreement with them. He suggested that they might be persuaded somehow to end their bloody conflicts.'[101]

In 1995 a group of businessmen asked Moscow Mayor Yurii Luzhkov to petition for the return of Yaponchik (Ivan'kov) to Moscow. Only Yaponchik could bring order to the city.[102] Sergei Dontsov, the head of the Moscow mayor's legal and law enforcement department, said of the official contacts he had with criminals: 'They are civilized and intelligent people. As I found out, they were *vory-v-zakone*. They told me very clearly that no other structure would be allowed into the Danilovskii market without obtaining [their] permission.' Mr Dontsov suggested that lawmakers draft a special legal act (to remain secret) allowing for negotiations between law-enforcement and organized criminality.[103]

Among the political leaders with national significance, Vladimir Zhirinovsky, the leader of the Russian Liberal Democratic Party (LDPR), is the one that has made the most significant gestures towards the criminal world. Several times he said that open collaboration with figures from the shadow economy would help the Russian economy. In September 1999, he welcomed shadow businessmen into his party: 'We would like to see members of the shadow economy among us because they represent the real and powerful economy.' In 1998, in order to attract voters, he described his party as one able to promote the interests of 'bureaucrats, bankers, and criminal structures specializing in economic crimes.'[104] In the pockets of dead Nikolai Stepanovich Zykov, nicknamed Yakutenok, the most prominent *vor-v-zakone* in Perm killed on 19 June 1998, a picture of the Perm criminal having dinner with Zhirinovsky in Moscow was found.[105] According to Hungarian newspaper *Nepszava* (26 Sept. 1998), 'several Russian mafia leaders' met in Budapest with Zhirinovsky, a meeting monitored by the local secret services. Zhirinovsky reportedly met with Semen Mogilevich, a businessman closely connected to the criminal world.[106]

Any meaningful discussion of a pact between the political elite and criminal organizations must consider the fact that criminals penetrate politics directly. No self-imposed rule prevents the *vory* or criminal leaders from entering politics.

Zhirinovsky's LDPR has opened its doors to individuals with a dubious past.[107] Mikhas' (Sergei Mikhailov), one of the leaders of Solntsevskaya, was number 16 on the LDPR list for the 1999 Duma elections. Eventually, the Central Electoral Commission forbade him to run.[108] The LDPR is reportedly allowing other individuals with a dubious past to contest local elections. In Chuvashiya, the LDPR candidate to the Presidency of the Republic has, according to *Nezavisimaya Gazeta*, 'ties to the criminal world' and a criminal past. Two of his main aides were each convicted of twenty-four criminal charges.[109] According to a recent lengthy article published in *Versiya*, in the autumn of 1999 Zhirinovsky met M. Skripnik (nicknamed Skripa) and A. Pugachev (nicknamed Pugach), the leaders of a criminal group operating in city of Bratsk. They discussed the possibility of Pugach standing as a candidate for the Duma.[110] According to another paper, Duma deputy Valentin Filatov (LDPR) enrolled criminals as his assistants.[111]

The LDPR is not the only opportunity offered to criminals to enter politics. Many reports point to candidates linked to crime groups standing as independents or put forward by local political associations. Andrei Skoch, reputedly a prominent member of the Solntsevo group, entered the Duma as an independent representing Novooskol'skii one-mandate district (Belgorod region).[112] In the city of Chelyabinsk, a deputy of the Regional Duma and former athlete, a certain Morozov, is the leader of a 'brigade' controlling several liqueur and vodka distilleries. He ran an aggressive electoral campaign and is now under investigation.[113] In the Kamchatka region, one of the most remote parts of Russia, the newly formed 'Our Kamchatka bloc' is standing in the elections for the Regional Duma. The party is filled with candidates charged with theft and tax evasion, as well as former convicts, and is rumoured to be closely connected to a local crime syndicate, headed by a man known as Shaten.[114] Notwithstanding the above, accusation of 'ties to a criminal syndicate' should be taken with caution, since they can be used strategically by other candidates.[115]

Penetration of politics is not, however, as easy as is often reported. Frol, the *vor* attached to the Moscow Balashikhinskaya group spent a great deal of money in order to have his own candidate elected in the December 1993 Duma elections, but he was short by 300 votes.[116] In a well-known picture, Otari Kvantrishvili, killed in 1994, sits a few metres away from President Yeltsin at a tennis match in Moscow in 1990. Otari's Party of Sportsmen has now disappeared. Despite the effort of the Uralmash Public and Political Union (the legitimate face of Ekaterinburg's most powerful crime group), its candidate, Aleksandr Khabarov, was defeated again in the December 1999 election.[117]

No doubt some politicians have close links with criminal figures and some people with criminal pasts have entered politics. It cannot be said however that Russian politics is filled with hardened criminals, to the extent that Georgian and Armenian politics are (in Georgia, *vor-v-zakone* Dzhaba Ioseliani, the founder of the military organization Mkhedrioni, was, until his arrest in November 1995, a government minister and very influential political figure[118]). There is no evidence of an open and general pact between politics and crime. Tacit pacts between fragments of the political elite and segments of the criminal world might however be in place. In various instances, criminals themselves have pointed to certain sectors, or certain areas and businesses as being under the protection of state agencies. Criminals seem to respect this division of labour. The fact that some criminals have directly entered politics should serve to ease communication between state and criminal structures, in order to avoid misunderstandings. Moreover, the way the Russian government has handled the Chechen conflict was surely welcomed by Russian criminal organizations. It is most likely that Chechen groups—powerful competitors of Slavic criminals in Russia—have been weakened in the underworld as a consequence of the conflict.

The Gun and the Cross

The association between the church and the mafia has been noted in the Sicilian context. As in the case of Sicily, Russian criminals are attracted to the church and display a deep religiosity. The police in Perm regularly videotapes the funerals of leading criminals. In a video shown to me, the various *boeviki* attended the funeral of a group member and showed signs of profound religiosity while in church, bowing and reciting prayers.[119] Pudel', who met Yaponchik in the US, told *Izvestiya*: 'we have a lot in common, we both believe in God and carry in the pocket the same prayers.'[120] Yurii Esin, the first *vor-v-zakone* with an Italian passport, also appears to be deeply religious. When he was arrested in March 1997, he was celebrating his birthday in an exclusive skiing resort in Northern Italy. His guests from Moscow had just brought him a birthday present: a precious edition of the Gospel, which was found in his hotel safe. Within the book, the police found the text of a gospel written in Church Slavonic copied on a strip of black cloth. The text refers to God as one's 'protector and shelter'.[121] There is even the case of a criminal, Sergei, turned monk. Sergei confirms that criminals and the church are close to each other. 'You might be surprised at how many guys with guns in their pockets cross themselves every time they drive past a church.'[122]

Russian mafiosi are keen to build ornate tombs and mausoleums for themselves. In Ekaterinburg, a 3-metres-high gravestone to Mikhail Kuchin, boss of the Tsentral'naya gang killed in 1994, dominates the most prestigious part of the Shirokorechenskoe cemetery. His portrait is engraved on a vast slab of dark green stone made of malachite and serpentine. He is depicted holding the keys of his Mercedes and on the top of the edifice is a giant cross. In the same cemetery, one can admire the tomb of *vor* Aleksei Selivanov and various other criminal bosses.[123]

A traditional Russian custom is to leave food on the grave of the deceased and even to pour vodka over the grave; also, the wife of the deceased would be given envelopes with money. At funerals of criminal bosses in Ekaterinburg, friends and close relatives of the deceased threw bank notes in the grave, so that the dead will not be without means in the afterlife. Throwing money in the grave, before it is covered by earth, is an expensive innovation.[124]

Criminals are also generous donors. Sergei, the criminal turned monk, accepts their donations to his monastery.[125] The head of Perm RUOP maintains that the main restoration work for the Feodos'evskaya Church, a church in the centre of Perm, was paid for by a company which is a front for one of the criminal groups in the city.[126] The leader of the Tambov crime group, Nikolai Gavrilenkov, asked to be buried in the prestigious Pskov Caves Monastery, a stronghold of conservative theology, offering £40,000 to the monastery as an accompanying donation. Killed in 1990, his remains are now in a gilded shrine in the monastery caves, alongside the resting places of saintly monks.[127] Mikhas', the boss of the Solntsevo group, offered to make a generous contribution for the construction of the Church of Christ the Saviour in Moscow, although he wanted the donor's name to be inscribed in gold letters on the marble slabs that were to adorn the church.[128]

In times of hardship, the church can flourish with the money coming from donations, even if they are tainted. There is a further reason why the church might want to mingle with criminal protectors, namely to collect its own debts. Each monastery and congregation pays a fraction of its income to the central offices of the Diocese. Although bishops have absolute canonical power in their dioceses, they are financially dependent on parishes, which sometimes fail to pay up. The bishop may in turn be tempted to use rough methods to collect. This is what happened in Ekaterinburg. After Bishop Nikon (later involved in a sexual scandal) increased the transfers due to the diocesan treasury, a number of local congregations rebelled. In response, Bishop Nikon, as reported by *Moskovskie Novosti*, resorted to 'extremely harsh collection methods, sending special "inspectors" around to shake down every congregation in the diocese. "Money is the blood of the church," he would say to explain his severe financial policies.'[129]

Criminals pursue an association with the church as a form of self-promotion. An impressive burial monument is a memento to the reputation and the career of the criminal. Furthermore, the church is a respectable institution and, by association, criminals gain public recognition. As Gambetta put it, this association 'signals to the world at large that Don Peppe's "protection firm" is so powerful as to offer its earthly protection even to a protector par excellence.'[130] In the case of Russia, the church can directly benefit from such association by having access to muscle to collect its own debts.

Conclusion

The Russian Mafia is not a single crime group. One national organization did not emerge from the collapse of the Gulag system and the increase of criminal opportunities that accompanied the end of the Soviet Union. There are several reasons why this should have been the case. First, information gathering becomes more complicated as the number of people one needs to gather information upon increases; as a result of this, a mafia group might have to 'subcontract' part of the work to individuals it trusts—but then the chain of authority stretches and the risks increase. As a consequence, recruitment into the organization becomes more risky and uncertainty over the identity of members higher. Like any other organization, a mafia group is based on a chain of hierarchical relationships, and problems of asymmetric information, imperfect monitoring, and opportunistic behaviour arise. But the longer the chain, the harder it is to monitor agents. On the contrary, the shorter the chain, the easier it is to solve the governance problem.

Second, a mafia group stretched across a vast country would find it difficult to operate. As the range of operations increases, the number and the complexity of disputes also increase. It will be harder to oversee all transactions and extract a cut from each of them. It also becomes more likely that clients both in the overworld and in the underworld will make deals without the intervention or the knowledge of the mafia group. Criminals in the underworld, as individuals in the overworld, might develop relations of trust and reciprocity that escape the mafia as a guarantor of transactions, thus bypassing it. Such an overstretched mafia would need to rely on an army of enforcers able to intervene in troublesome spots around the country, protecting the 'legitimate' representative of the organization, in ways that do not differ significantly from sending troops to crush a rebellion in a breakaway region. *Ceteris paribus*, such a 'foreign' legion would be at a disadvantage compared with the locals.

The picture that emerges from post-Soviet Russia is one of many gangs with a grip on a specific bit of turf, such as a neighbourhood or a number of 'clients'. Each group is organized hierarchically and has its own army of enforcers who are recruited from a pool of trusted aspirants.

Some Russian crime groups have succeeded at forging common trademarks. The trademarks derive from past Soviet criminal history, the rich baggage of norms and rules that the *vory-v-zakone* developed over the Soviet period. Leaders of single crime groups are initiated into the fraternity of *vory-v-zakone*. The marks of the *vory* are shared across different crime groups, even if each one enjoys a high degree of independence and may even compete with another over territory and businesses.

The Russian Mafia is the sum total of the criminal leaders who went through the *vory* ritual. The *vory* initiation is reserved to the leaders, not recruits. It is a marker of quality and commitment to the underworld, and evokes—in the eyes of other criminals—an honourable and distinguished tradition. Thus, the Russian Mafia shares crucial similarity with the Sicilian Cosa Nostra. Sicilian crime families have been highly successful at forging shared marks of identity, while at the same time maintaining the independence of each family. Moreover, although some lesser opponents exist on the island, the Sicilian Mafiosi have been able to prevent the formation of powerful competitors, who do not share their marks of identity. Have the Russians been equally successful? The answer is no. Competitors are the ethnic crime groups that do not share the *vory* marks. These groups can be best described as *non-Russian mafias*. I have also argued that the Cossack brotherhood is likely to emerge in the future as another competitor, also grounded on a rich baggage of rituals and norms, alternative to the *vory*.

The peculiar Russian transition to the market has allowed legal and semi-legal providers of protection to flourish. Private protection firms, police departments, fragments of the security services moonlighting on their working time on behalf of private employers, respond to market incentives and offer protection to legitimate and non-legitimate businesses. Thus, they all compete with the mafias of Russia. These protectors are only partially independent of the state. Although they do not qualify as autonomous suppliers of protection, the state itself is hardly a unitary entity in Russia.

The Russian Mafia has been able to forge political alliances, for instance with the LDPR of Vladimir Zhirinovsky, and has penetrated politics to a degree.

What is the future of the Russian Mafia? First, one should not exaggerate its role. It has not dominated the transition to the market. Powerful economic lobbies of the Soviet era and newly formed conglomerates run by the 'oligarchs' have captured the state, aptly defined by Janine R. Wedel as a 'clan state'. Colossal economic concerns control property and resources and are identified with particular ministries or institutional segments of government to the point that agenda of the administration and the clan overlap.[1] This state of affairs is likely to continue. Police forces, security services, and private protection firms are likely to dominate the market for protection.

The privatization of protection need not be an entirely unwelcome outcome. State protectors turned private suppliers will be less inclined to stage a *coup d'état* to turn the clock back to Soviet-era economic planning and state socialism. A by-product of the fragmentation and privatization of protection, however, is that disputes between clients will not be adjudicated by an independent third party, a liberal state. The conflict will transfer right at the heart of the state machinery. When an entrepreneur protected by an FSB unit has a dispute with a competitor under the wings of the MVD, sensitive files, confidential information, state secrets, compromising materials (the well-known *kompromat*), and state military resources will be used in the fight. Such conflicts among state agencies are potentially destabilizing and further reduce trust in the administration as a fair supplier of dispute resolution and protection for all.

For its part, is the Russian Mafia a bad for society? Criminal groups collect debts, settle business disputes, at times help businessmen obtain special credits, and have even shown the ability to restrain their demands and take into consideration the ups and downs of the economy. Entrepreneurs in Perm complain that criminal protection is far from perfect: in the Visim sub-district of Perm, the racket is not always able or willing to prevent theft and retrieve stolen goods. Still, shopkeepers and kiosk owners resent the police and tax inspectorate the most.

Some criminal protectors do behave in a predatory fashion. Predation, however, can be a matter of perspective: what looks predatory from the

point of view of the new entrant in a market, may well be a genuine protection against competition for those who are already in that market.
None the less, predatory criminals do exist. They extract a vast amount
of money from the business they protect and lead the business into bankruptcy. Over time, these groups are likely to disappear, since they destroy
their own source of revenue. In the meantime, entrepreneurs in Perm
know that, once they have opened a shop, they might come under
the spell of predatory gangs and choose the protector in advance, before
starting their business operations. Such a choice reduces uncertainty
and ensures better protection. When disputes arise between protected
businesses, rudimentary tribunals with embryonic judicial rituals
adjudicate.

Prima facie, criminals perform a function and one might be tempted to
conclude that, 'the net impact of organised crime in Russia today is ben-
eficial'.[2] This is hardly the case.

Criminal protection includes protection against competitors or business rivals and the acquisition of soft credits. In a world protected by the
mafia, sellers compete, not by improving quality or reducing prices but
by acquiring more efficient violent skills in order to enlarge their share of
the market. This is an hazardous and uncertain environment, 'perturbed
by anomalies, uncertain borders, incongruent circumstances, breached
norms, and biased information'.[3] Also, no absolute rights are established
and enforced in the mafia world. In one case, a Perm criminal group
switched client and started protecting somebody else. As a consequence,
the first client was murdered. In the case of Evgeniya, the group protecting her first inquired into the standing of the family she had a dispute
with. Only when they discovered that this family had no significant connections in the city, did they freely victimize it. *Banditskaya krysha* does not
supply protection on the basis of universal criteria.

The criminal tribunals are a parody of the justice system: intricate legal
disputes cannot be evaluated and adjudicated in such settings. Ultimately, the military standing of one's protector is the strongest legal argument. Some entrepreneurs might decide to *exit* the Russian market, either
by emigrating to a different country or by choosing a different profession.
In the dry language of economics, 'human resources' are wasted in the
process. Those who continue to do business in such a world must be prepared to face potentially severe consequences. Alternatively, an entrepreneur can decide to limit the expansion of operation, as in the case of Inna
and Alla described in Chapter 4. A limited activity is less likely to come

under the scrutiny of criminal rackets, but also hampers economic growth.

One need not ask whether the Russian Mafia is a bad for society: that we know. One should ask rather whether the remaining institutions of authority, which are supposed to enforce universal rights and secure protection to the Russian people, behave according to a logic entirely different from those of the mafias. Doubts remain.

Appendix A

Aliases in the Soviet and Russian Underworld

Nicknames have long been considered a special feature of the underworld and have been recorded in Europe since at least the early fifteenth century.[1] The Russian and Soviet underworld is no exception. In the following I analyse nicknaming among the *vory-v-zakone* of the Soviet and post-Soviet period.

Vory of the Soviet and post-Soviet period were (and are) given what all sources call nicknames (*klichki*), formalized in the course of the initiation ritual. I have collected and analysed 279 nicknames of crowned *vory*. The greatest number (223) of nicknames derives from a list drawn up by Ministry of Interior Affairs (MVD) and circulated to the militia in the early 1990s.[2] The MVD list provides, for each *vor*, full name, nickname and date of birth. (Thirty-eight entries do not record the nickname: these entries qualify as 'missing values' in Table A2.) In most cases, it also specifies the type of crime committed, the prison regime and the end of the term of imprisonment. I have supplemented this list with nicknames of *vory* found in the press and in specialized literature.[3] I have also interviewed a member of an organized criminal group in city of Perm, Mr Leonid K., who willingly commented on nicknames among the *vory*. Although he is not a *vor* himself, he spent five years in prison and came to know a number of *vory* (OC3).

There are reasons for trusting the general accuracy of the list, besides the reliability of the authority issuing it. Thieves and non-thieves alike refer openly to the *vory* by their nickname. Likhachev had already noted: 'every thief has his own nickname. He tattoos it or its symbol to his body and does not change it even if the criminal investigators know it. This practice is followed even though it is obviously risky. For instance, his whole prison history can be known by just looking at it.'[4] A *vor* does not hide his identity. It is therefore plausible that police officers were able to record, with a fairly high degree of accuracy, the nickname by which the *vor* was known in the colony.

In the following, I introduce some conceptual distinctions in the variegated world of aliases; I then analyse the *vory*'s nicknames according to their source, conferring mechanism, motive, and semantic content. I argue that the *vory*'s nicknames are best understood as 'second names', in many respects similar to the new name acquired by a novice who joins the ranks of the Catholic or Russian Orthodox Church as priest or nun. Nicknaming in this case is a form of rechristening.

Aliases Defined

Some preliminary conceptual remarks are necessary in order to distinguish among different types of alias. Gambetta and Pizzini, in a study of Sicilian mafiosi's nicknames recorded in the files of the Palermo maxi-trial (1986–7), introduce useful analytical distinctions. They distinguish between code-names, *noms-de-guerre*, and nicknames. Ordinary first names, used instead of the person's real first name, qualify as code-names of the kind adopted by spies. They analysed twenty-five such names used by mafiosi in telephone conversations that were recorded by the police. It is possible that mafiosi suspected that the conversations were being recorded and used code-names. Code-names are coined for instrumental purposes, to conceal the bearers' identity and to give them a new one. Code-names can be chosen either by the bearers themselves or the agency they work for (arguably, it depends on the degree of centralization of the latter). The conferring mechanism is informal, no instance of ceremonial granting of code-names has been recorded. The content of a code-name should be as neutral as possible. A code-name that becomes too well-known and invariably connected to a specific person—as in the case of James Bond's *007*— is a liability in the real world of spies, as opposed to the fictitious world of movies and novels.

Noms-de-guerre are a type of alias usually adopted by partisans and guerrilla leaders, and share some features with code names: both are attributed for reasons of secrecy and prudence. However, *noms-de-guerre* remain connected to a person's reputation and identity as well as being a means to disguise it.[5] A partisan may become famous with his *nom-de-guerre* and then will be reluctant to give it up. Soviet revolutionary leaders, such as Stalin, Lenin, and Trotsky, are well-known examples. The semantic content of the *nom-de-guerre* may be either neutral or appreciative. 'Lenin' (supposedly after the river Lena, in the Russian Far East) is neutral, while 'Stalin' (Steel) is supposed to capture a feature of the bearer's qualities. While the *content* of the *nom-de-guerre* may be appreciative, the *motive* for adopting a *nom-de-guerre* is instrumental, contrary to what Gambetta and Pizzini argue.[6] It is the covert nature of the individual's activities that motivates the adoption of a *nom-de-guerre* rather than the pleasure of finding a biting equivalent for the individual's salient feature.

Nicknames are chosen by others. Morgan, O'Neill and Harré define nicknames as 'the names [a person] acquires informally, often contrary to his wishes'.[7] Why do people not give nicknames to themselves, either positive or negative? Why people would not give themselves demeaning aliases is self-evident, while further exploration is required to account for people not giving themselves high profile aliases. In the case of the Sicilian mafiosi, Gambetta and Pizzini offer an explanation based on the norms and conventions that obtain in Cosa Nostra. Mafiosi have a convention which rewards understatement and deems bragging as a sign of weakness. This would account for their reluctance to give themselves exalted aliases.[8] However, the phenomenon appears to go beyond the Mafia subculture and to be a feature among individuals more generally. One needs to address the credibility of the source: the source of the exalted nickname (the bearer) is in this case not credible for the nickname to be repeated by other individuals. Praise is of little effect and short-lived if it is self-praise.[9]

Though the literature on nicknames is divided on the functions nicknames serve, anthropologists and folklorists have in general come to the conclusion that nicknames provide a source of amusement for the name-givers.[10] Nicknames 'are bestowed primarily for expressive reasons, because of the mischievous *fun* derived from finding an amusing, biting and concise way to capture a person's salient feature'.[11] The irregular pattern and imaginative variety of nicknames of Sicilian mafiosi is an indicator of this motive: standardization would not be conducive to fun.

The content of a nickname may be either appreciative or mocking, though authors have tended to stress the latter feature of nicknames, viewing them as a form of 'verbal aggression'.[12] The offensive content of most nicknames has been acknowledged in certain societies, where nicknaming is regarded as uncivil. In most Japanese schools, nicknaming is formally prohibited.[13]

Noms-de-plume should be added to this list of aliases: their source is unmistakably the writer and the granting procedure is informal. The motive is expressive: for instance, Aleksei Maksimovich Peshkov chose a *nom-de-plume* that was supposed to capture a feature of his writing: Maksim Gorky ('Bitter'). An interesting phenomenon may however take place in countries where ideas cannot be freely expressed: writers adopt pseudonyms in order to disguise their real identity and avoid persecution, as in the case of A. Sinyavsky, who signed his works as Abram Terts. It is hardly ever the case, however, that the pseudonym is completely neutral. To the extent that some positive associations (though not intended to refer to the identity of the author) are suggested by the *nom-de-plume*, an expressive motivation emerges. If no association is intended by the writer, we should classify the pseudonym as a code-name, regardless of the fact that it is used for concealing the identity of a writer rather than that of a spy (this is indeed a matter of perspective: an illiberal regime such as the Soviet Union considered the dissident writer a spy).

A further phenomenon in the world of aliases is *renaming*. It is practised by the Catholic and the Russian Orthodox Churches and by some secret societies when a novice is accepted into the ranks of the organization. Priests and nuns bear two names, the worldly name (*imya v mire*) and the faith name (*imya vo vere*). The source of the new name is the bearer. He or she has a limited amount of freedom in the choice of the church name. The name is then conferred on the bearer by an external agency (the church) and the procedure is marked by a ritual. Table A1 orders the features of aliases according to source, conferring mechanism, motive, content, and typical bearer.

Table A.1   Types of aliases

	Source	Conferring mechanism	Motive	Content	Typical bearers
Nicknames	others	informal	expressive	mocking/ appreciative	Sicilian Mafiosi
Code names	self/others	informal	instrumental	neutral	spies
Noms-de-guerre	self/others	informal	instrumental	neutral/ appreciative	partisans
Noms-de-plume	self	informal	expressive	appreciative	writers
'Second' name	self	formal	instrumental	appreciative	priests

Source: Adapted from Gambetta and Pizzini (1995). It differs from theirs in some respects: it adds two columns (granting procedure and typical bearers) and two rows (*noms de plume* and 'second' name). Also, *noms-de-guerre* are given only as instrumental motives, rather than both instrumental *and* expressive.

Source and Granting Mechanism: The Ritual

Code names, *noms de guerre*, *noms de plume* and 'second' names can be their bearer's creation or choice, while mafiosi's 'nicknames tend to *fall* upon individuals regardless of their intervention and whether they like it or not; nicknames are a manifestation of the way others see us'.[14] The nickname of a *vor*, on the contrary, appears to be chosen by the bearer, is a formal requirement, and its retention is promoted by a ritual.

Soviet and post-Soviet *vory-v-zakone* obtained their nicknames at a ceremony which marked their entry into the *vory* brotherhood (see above, Chapter 7, pp. 147–50 for a description of the ritual). Ch. recollected that at the crowning he could finally dispose of his 'childish nickname *Malysh* (the young one), and get an adult nickname, which I *chose* myself' (emphasis added). Ch.'s new nickname was *Likhoi* ('dashing').[15] The new ritual is more verbose and intricate than the old one,[16] but similarly the one who is accepted into the criminal fraternity is given a nickname.[17] Leonid K. befriended a *vor* in a labour camp and was informed of the crowning procedures. Crowning took place in the 1970s in a labour camp in a region of the Russian Far East. The *vor*'s nickname is the diminutive of that region's geographical name. The *vor*'s mentor had previously discussed the nickname with him and had come to an agreement about what it should be. At his crowning, the officiating *vor* ended the ceremony by saying: 'we shall call you *such-and-such*' stating the agreed nickname. The ceremony sanctioned what had already been agreed (OC3).

The granting of a nickname marks the 'new life' the criminal is about to

Table A.2   Structure of nicknames

Structure of nicknames	Frequency	Percentage
Two-word nicknames	36	11.4
Two-word second nickname	2	0.6
One-word nickname	218	68.8
One-word second nickname	22	6.9
One-word third nickname	1	0.3
Missing values	38	12.0
Total	317	100.0

Source: Podlesskikh and Tereshonok (1994: 239–53) and various newspapers, 1990–5.

embark on. Nicknaming among the *vory* therefore shares an important feature with the ritual of renaming practised by the Russian Orthodox Church. Nicknaming as a form of rechristening has been noted by Likhachev: 'The adoption of a nickname is a necessary act of transition to the thieves' sphere (it amounts to a peculiar "taking of monastic vows").'[18] The ritual makes the nickname a rather stable and reliable signal of the bearer's identity. This is the more so if the *vor* tattoos it on his body, a practice also noticed by Likhachev.[19] A feature of ordinary nicknames is that of not being exclusive: a bearer may have several nicknames.[20] In the Sicilian mafia also, multiple nicknaming is present and some individual may be known by different nicknames in different groups. Examples include *Mario Agliaro* who is also *Salamandra*, *Il Falco* also known as *Il Principe di Villagrazia*, *Lucchiceddu* is *u'Piccirdu*, *Fifu Tsuni* is *Milinciana*, *u' Viddanu* is *u' Tratturi*, *Il Ragioniere* is *Il Corto* and so on.[21] The second nickname does not share any resemblance to the first.

The presence of two nicknames is comparatively rare among *vory*. Table A2 captures two aspects of nicknames among the *vory*: their structure (one-word nickname, such as *Amir*, and two-word nicknames, such as *Roma Abkhazskii*) and the number of bearers with multiple nicknames (one-word second nickname; one-word third nickname; two-word second nickname).

Twenty-five (9 per cent) cases qualify as second or third nicknames, i.e. the bearer appears with two or three nicknames in the MVD list (usually the two nicknames are separated by an 'and'). In a number of cases, the second nickname greatly resembles the first and does not seem to qualify as an altogether different nickname. Rather it seems the product of uncertainty on the part of the police as to the content and form of the nickname. For instance, Boris Fedorovich Arustumyan is *Borya Bakinskii* (from Baku) and *Boka*, David Guramovich Katsiashvili is *Dato* and *Dato-Ryzhii* (the Red-haired), Murat

Borisovich Koloev is *Murat* and *Murik*. David El'gudzhevich Chatrikashvili is the only case to have three recorded nicknames: two however are a slight variation of the same theme: *Chita* a city in Siberia, and *Chitrak*, which appears to combine aspects of both his surname and the Siberian city. The actual cases of double nicknames that stand a second look are therefore reduced to a handful (20 out of 278).

Leonid K. offered some comments on the cases of multiple nicknames. I pointed out to him that some *vory* appear to have two nicknames. He strongly denied that two nicknames would be given at the ceremony. He added: 'It may be the case that the criminal circle where the *vor* was known by a certain nickname continues to refer to him with an old nickname, acquired before being crowned. This, admittedly, causes confusion' (OC3).

The ritual reduces the likelihood of finding Russian *vory* bearing two nicknames. Furthermore, nicknames are less likely to change in the context in which the *vor* operates.

Motive

The motive for granting nicknames to full members of the *vory* brotherhood appears to be instrumental. Rather than the 'mischievous fun' derived from finding an amusing proxy of one's qualities or characteristics, the nickname marks entry into the brotherhood. As in the case of the church bestowing new names on its priests, the nickname among the *vory* appears to be a 'second' name, a name that marks their new life. Various sources have pointed this out. The *vor* was supposed to live by completely different values than the ones advocated by the Communist regime. Engaging in activities that suggested the state had power over the criminal, whether it involved serving in the Red Army, paying taxes, or working, were forbidden. A common saying among thieves was: 'I should be considered a *legavyi*, if I do [one or another of these forbidden acts].' A proper *vor* should have severed all links with society, have no binding family attachments or be involved in political activities. His new family is the *vory* brotherhood. Monakhov and Gurov stress the importance of total and selfless dedication to '*vory* ideals'.[22] It is still part of contemporary *vory* ideology to stress human values and dedication to society rather than material possessions and family bonding.[23] The transition into the fraternity calls for a new identity and therefore for a new name.

Content

Given the above, we should expect that the content of *vory* nicknames also differs from those of the mafiosi analysed by Gambetta and Pizzini. According to their findings, 'most nicknames . . . pick on oddities of sort, large and small, physical and psychological'.[24] Also they tend to be mocking, as is the case for nicknames in general. The very word *'nciuri*, Sicilian for nickname, means abuse. Gambetta and Pizzini found nicknames such as *Il Cornuto di Buffalo* (the Cuckold from Buffalo) and *u 'Scemo* (The Fool). They conclude that 'mockery more than admiration, ridicule more than appreciation, are triggers for nick-names'.[25] Though some clear cases of mocking nicknames are found in our list, they are few; the majority refer to other names.

The majority of nicknames in Table A3 (178 out of 279, 63.8 per cent) are derived from the original name/patronymic/surname (either alone or com-bined) of the bearer or from someone else's name. Sixty-six nicknames do not contain any reference to any name out of a total of 279 (23.7 per cent).

Nicknames derived from either the first name, the patronymic or the sur-name of the *vor* are 126. For instance, Arutyun Lyudvigovich Arshokyan is *Arutik*, Yurii Dzhafarovich Amirov is *Amir*, Boris Fedorovich Arustumyan is *Boka*. In the case of Razmik Bagratovich Guluasyan, his nickname is simply patronymic—*Bagratovich*. Twenty-three *vory* recorded in the list carry a nickname which combines (a variation on) their real name and a place-name. For example, Vitalii Yur'evich Kozyrev is known as *Vitalik Osetin* (The Osset-ian), Boris Fedorovich Arustumyan is *Borya Bakinskii*, Roman Ivanovich Agroa is *Roma Abkhazskii*. Ossetia, Baku or Abkhazia are not necessarily the *vor*'s place of birth, but may refer to some aspects of his criminal past. For example, David El'gudzhevich Chatrikashvili is known as *Chita*, a remote city in Siberia, site of the labour camp where most probably he had been incarcerated. Vladimir Matevosovich Martirosyan is known as *Vova Vetlag*. Vova comes from Vladimir, while Vetlag refers to a *Vet-Lager'*. (In Russian *lager'* means camp.) In one case (that of Sergei Ivanovich Timofeev), we know that his nickname (*Serezha Novgorodskii*) refers both to the place of birth and to the area of his early activity as a criminal. Timofeev was then stripped of his title as a *vor* and appears in the press and in police reports as having acquired a second nick-name, Sil'vestr.[26] We may speculate that, along with his title, he had been stripped of his *vor* name.

In twenty-two cases, the nicknames have come from someone else's name. According to Leonid K., the acquisition of a totally new name is no accident.

Often, people decide to give someone the nickname of a *vor* who has recently died in order to keep his memory alive. But this in no way implies that the new *vor* has to operate in the same sector or city. He is free to do what he wants, though he should feel obliged to keep up the memory of the dead *vor* (OC3).

This practice has a parallel in the church: the choice of a name is a tribute to a fig-ure of the church's past, to whom the novice wishes to pay homage. A similar phenomenon has been noticed among the Japanese Mafia. The new gang's Boss *adds* the name of the previous Boss to his own one. 'Often, if a group is power-ful, the subsequent bosses keep the founder's name and add onto that name the generation they represent.'[27] Both instances are different solutions devised in order to honour the reputation of worthy criminals.

Table A.3 Content of nicknames

Semantic content of nicknames	Frequency	Percentage
Non-name based nicknames		
Animal	7	2.5
Place name[a]	14	5.1
Famous Character	4	1.4
Psychological feature	12	4.3
Foreign nationality	8	2.9
Object[b]	7	2.5
Physical characteristics	9	3.2
Kinship (such as dad, grandpa)	4	1.4
Religion	1	0.4
Sub-total	66	23.7
Name-based nicknames		
Other name	15	5.4
Other name + place name	2	0.7
Other name + nationality	1	0.4
Patronymic	2	0.7
Patronymic with a meaning[c]	1	0.4
Personal name	98	35.1
Personal name with a meaning[c]	7	2.5
Personal name + place name	23	8.2
Personal name + psychological features	2	0.7
Personal name + physical features	7	2.5
Personal name + relation	1	0.4
Personal name + surname	1	0.4
Surname	17	6.1
Surname with a meaning[c]	1	0.4
Sub-total	178	63.8
Not identified	35	12.5
Total	279	100.0

[a] City, region, mountain or place of confinement located in the former USSR.
[b] includes plants.
[c] The nickname, though derived from a name/patronymic/surname, carries an autonomous meaning in Russian.

Source: Podlesskikh and Tereshonok (1994: 239–53) and various newspapers, 1990–5.

The nicknames that refer to the bearer's name or to someone else's name can be considered appreciative or at least neutral. The bearer may have good reasons to try to keep his old name: he has probably risen to some fame in the criminal world with his ordinary name and does not want to lose the reputation that is attached to that name. Adding a place-name may either signal the territorial boundaries of his future operations or some events of his past. References to places are not unusual in Russian names and are a form of distinction. Famous historical figures have added to their original name a place-name, which refers to a notable deed of theirs. For instance, Dmitrii, grand prince of Moscow in the fourteenth century, added *Donskoi* after having won a crucial battle against the Tatars in the vicinity of the river Don, on 8 September 1380. Aleksandr Nevskii, who was in fact the prince of Novgorod, was awarded his place-name (*Nevskii*) after the brilliant military victory against the Swedish army (1240), fought on the banks on the river Neva.

Several nicknames in the sample (9) originate from one of the *vor*'s names but have a second independent meaning: for instance, Murad Ulievich Burchu-ladze is known as *Murashka*. Instead of the simpler form *Mur*, the nickname sounds like the Russian words *Murashki* (shivers, creeps) and *Muravei* (ant). Sergei Alievich Gafarov is on record as being nicknamed *Seryi* (instead of the diminutive Serezha), a word which derives from his first name which also means 'grey' and, in the figurative meaning, 'dull, dim, uneducated'. Another case in point is that of Vladimir Kirpichev, an influential *vor* from St Petersburg who has been advocating a truce between state and mafia. He is known as *Kirpich* (brick). Valerian Borisovich Dzhanashiya's nickname, *Valter*, is also derived from his first name but it is the name of a widely used pistol as well as the name of a sadist Gestapo character in a famous Soviet TV movie titled *The Variant Omega*, shown in the 1970s. *Vor* Konstantin Leonidovich Granin's nick-name is *Kot* (cat), which refers to his real first name (Konstantin) and also means 'a swindler who uses his partner as allurement' in criminal jargon.[28]

Psychological features are referred to in thirteen cases such as *Beast*, *Little Evil Spirit*, *Bold*, *Energetic*, and *Strong*. Supposedly a psychological attitude is captured in the nickname *Banzai*, granted to Pavel Anatol'evich Romanov. Gennadii Aleksandrovich Mikhailov is known as *Salty* (*Solenyi*). Two appre-ciative nicknames are *The Hero* and *The Prince*. Ruslan Sokolov is known as *Rus-lan* and *the Expert*. Physical features inspired sixteen nicknames such as *Beard*, *Bald* (in two variants *Lysak* and *Globus*, the latter being a colloquial expression), *Gibbous*, *Anzor Stump*, *Givi-the nose*, *Paat the little*, not to be confused with *Paat the big*, *Ruslan the Grey-haired*, and *Dato the red-haired*. Valera Sukhumskii is also known as *The Beauty*. References to part of the body are found in *Ivan The Hand* and *Lenchik* (diminutive of Leonid) *The Shaking Head*. The animal kingdom con-tains *Hog*, *Beast*, *Cat*, *Little Dog*, *Eagle*, *Lamprey*, and *Fly*. Religion is openly found only for one case (B. M. Krasilovskii is called *Zhid*). Among these nicknames only *Zhid* may be considered as demeaning: to the Russian ear, *Zhid* (as opposed to *Evrei*) is an abusive way of referring to Jewish people.

The name the *vor* acquires at the ritual differs substantially from nicknames as defined by Gambetta and Pizzini. In the Sicilian case, nicknames are bestowed by others and their retention is not promoted by a ritual. Also, nicknames are not a formal requirement and are often demeaning. *Noms-de-guerre* and pseudonyms appear to be, to a degree, closer to the *vory's klichki*. They may be acquired for instrumental purposes and their content may be (though not exclusively) positive. The crucial difference between *noms-de-guerre* and the *vory's klichka* resides in the conferring mechanism. In the case of the *vory*, the *klichka* is bestowed upon the new *vor* at a ritual which marks his entry into the *vory* brotherhood. This very feature makes the *vory's* 'nickname' analogous to the *imya vo vere*, the faith name acquired by priests and nuns in the Russian Orthodox Church. The *klichka* is a 'new name'.

The future evolution of nicknaming in the Russian underworld should be seen in the light of the discussion presented above (Chapter 8). If leaders of powerful groups retain the *vory* ritual, the *klichka* will continue to be a 'second name'.

Appendix B

The Destination of the Soviet Elite in Perm

Below I give a sociological profile to those who benefited most from the transition to the market in Perm. In particular, I explore the destination of the Soviet economic elite in the new market society. In order to do so, I use a survey on the 1993 destination of those who were members of the Party elected assemblies in 1988.[1] The survey covers 297 members of the CPSU who held elected positions in the Party's committees (*gorkom* and *obkom*) in 1988, as a result of the 19th Party Conference. It also specifies date of birth and a fairly detailed description of the members' occupations in 1988 and in 1993. The 297 names represent the total of elected officials to those bodies. The individuals elected in those bodies were not just members of the *nomenklatura*.[2] The City Party Committee (*gorkom*) and the Region Party Committee (*obkom*) were supposed to represent the different strata of Soviet society. Therefore candidates were selected and elected to these positions on the basis of various demographic criteria (such as sex, age, marital status, occupation, and other personal details) with the intention of reproducing a microcosm of Soviet society. The phenomenon of the so-called 'token' candidates was more generally typical of the Soviet Union's political system. The 'token' deputies frequently served only one term in office and rarely contributed to the decision-making process. 'They sat passively in their respective soviets: their arms were the only bodily parts required—to vote unanimously on decrees.'[3] The survey at our disposal gives a picture that extends beyond the *nomenklatura* and includes manual workers, peasants, and school teachers. Table B1 summarizes the distribution of occupations of those elected to the Party's in 1988. Data were then collected on the position held by the same people in 1993. Table B2 shows the outflow data and percentages, which record the distribution of destinations for each category of origin. The image is that of individuals flowing out of their 1988 occupation.

Of interest for the present discussion is the destination of the Party *apparatchiki* (coded as I). Institutional changes occurring in Russia in the past years have been so far-reaching that a major institutional arena, the Party, has disappeared. Full-time Party workers have been forced to move in one or another direction. The data above show that most of those in category I in 1988 flowed to category II in 1993. Forty-seven individuals out of 92 (51.1 per cent) were found to be top managers of economic enterprises in 1993. Another destination

Table B.1   Members of Party Assemblies
(*Gorkom, Obkom*) 1988 (N = 297)

Code	Occupation held in 1988	%
I	*Apparatchik*	31.0
II	Top manager	13.1
III	Top manager (agriculture)	3.0
IV	Army	1.3
V	State	4.0
VI	High intelligentsia	8.1
VII	Middle/Low Manager	11.1
VIII	Low Intelligensia	1.3
IX	Manual worker	25.1
X	Peasant	1.0
Total (N = 297)		100.0

of many Party *apparatchiki* was the top layers of the State bureaucracy: 22 cases out of 92 (23.9 per cent) appear in category V.

Almost all the members of the economic elite retained their positions, despite the transition to the market economy (34 out of a total of 39 individuals, or 87.2 per cent); 23 out of 24 members of the city intelligentsia (formed by university professors, two newspaper editors, the director of the local theatre, one artist, and one writer) retained their posts: only the editor of the daily *Zvezda* retired.[4] The numbers in other categories are very few, such as top managers of sovkhoz and kolkhoz (N = 9) and Army officers (N = 4), therefore it is not possible to draw conclusions of any great consequence. Nevertheless, in both cases a high degree of stability exists: 7 out of 9 directors of agricultural enterprises and 2 out of 4 officers retained their posts. One officer retired and no data are available for the other.

The data for the lower spectrum of occupations (VII, VIII, IX, and X) are for the time being rather defective. There is a great deal of data missing in these categories (respectively, 72.7, 50, 50.6 and 100 per cent). The only categories with a noticeable number of cases are VII and IX (respectively, N = 33 and 77). Nevertheless, some clear trends are observable and even the missing data reflect an interesting sampling bias. Thirty-three out of 77 (42.2 per cent) of individuals classified as manual workers were still manual workers in 1993; only 3 moved into category VII, while 2 retired. For category VII (a person with responsibilities over subordinates), data on 1993 occupations were only collected in 9 cases:

Table B.2　Occupational mobility of members of Party Assemblies, 1988–93

Occupation in 1988	Occupation in 1993											Row tot.
	II	III	IV	V	VI	VII	VIII	IX	X	XII	99	Col. %
Count Row %												
I	47	2	1	22	6					8	6	92
	51.1	2.2	1.1	23.9	6.5					8.7	6.5	31.0
II	34			2						1	2	39
	87.2			5.1						2.6	5.1	13.1
III		7								2		9
		77.8								22.2		3.0
IV			2							1	1	4
			50.0							25.0	25.0	1.3
V				9	1					2		12
				75.0	8.3					16.7		4.0
VI					23					1		24
					95.8					4.2		8.1
VII		1				7				1	24	33
		3.0				21.2				3.0	72.7	11.1
VIII							2				2	4
							50.0				50.0	1.3
IX						3		33		2	39	77
						3.9		42.2		2.6	50.6	25.9
X											3	3
											100.0	1.0
Col. N =	81	10	3	33	30	10	2	33		16	79	297
%	27.6	3.0	1.0	11.1	10.1	3.4	0.7	11.1		5.4	26.6	100.0

Note: XII = retired; 99 = missing data.

7 remained in category VII, while only 1 moved from VII to III. 50.6 per cent and 72.7 per cent of the data for categories IX and VII are missing. This in itself is worth noticing. It is easier to trace the occupational destination of those who held top positions, because they were more noticeable and conspicuous within the city. By contrast, it is very hard to trace the occupational destination of workers who moved to low-level occupations.

Two findings of the survey deserve special attention. First, the success of the Soviet economic elite in the new market situation and, second, the lateral movement, rather than dramatic downward mobility, of the old Party elite into the new economic elite.[5] Cadres are reaping the benefits of the transition to the market. They are not experiencing a relative loss, nor do they seem to be in any way disadvantaged.

The data for Perm in Tables B1 and B2 are consistent with what has been documented for Russia and other post-Communist societies, namely that the majority of the former Party cadres have joined the local economic elite, while the old Soviet economic elite is still, to a great extent, in place.[6] Though the data are far from satisfactory, they support the conclusion that the old *nomenklatura* forms a portion of the new economic elite.

List of Respondents and Interview Content

The first column reports the coding of each interview. The second column present features of the interviewees and the date of the interview. Some respondents were interviewed more than once. Unless otherwise stated, all interviews took place in Perm. Several names have been changed or omitted.

Kiosk Owners and Kiosk Sales Persons

K1   Inna, female, Russian, aged 37, owns one kiosk in the Visim sub-district selling various consumer goods, except alcohol. The kiosk closes at night and has been operating for three months. Formerly a housewife. Does not pay protection money. (9 Mar. 1994)

K2   Petr, male, Non- Russian, aged 41, owns one kiosk in the Visim sub-district selling various consumer goods, including alcohol, open at night and operating for ten months. Has a criminal record and was formerly an underground trader. Started paying protection money after a month of operation. (15 and 16 Mar. 1994)

K3   Andrei, male, Russian, aged 32, owns a kiosk in the Visim sub-district selling various consumer goods, including alcohol, open at night and operating for 11 months. Former employee of state sector (industrial sector). Started paying protection money after 50 days of operation. (18 Mar. 1994)

K4   Aleks, male, Russian, aged 30, owns a kiosk in the Visim sub-district selling various consumer goods, including alcohol, open at night and operating for one year. Former employee of state sector (military or industrial sector). Started paying protection money after a month of operation. (19 Mar. 1994)

K5   Anvar, male, Non-Russian, aged 34, owns a kiosk in the Visim sub-district selling various consumer goods, including alcohol, open at night and operating for five months. Formerly a trader, has a criminal record. Started paying protection money after fifteen days of operation. (8 Apr. 1994)

K6   Sasha, male, Russian, aged 40, owns a kiosk in the Ordzhonikidze's district, 20 km. from the city centre. The kiosk sells various consumer goods, except alcohol, is not open at night, operating for five months. He sells fruit and vegetables from a truck he owns and with the help of Inna, his business associate. Former employee of state sector (industrial sector). Does not pay protection money. (10 Apr. 1994)

K7   Lyuba, female, Russian, aged 46, kiosk sales person. Employed for thirty-six months (part-time) in a kiosk open at night, selling various consumer goods, except alcohol. Receives a percentage of the profits. Formerly worked in the retail sector and had previously worked in the Visim sub-district as Anvar's sales person. Shortly after this interview, she left the job and to operate a stall at a market near the city Circus. The kiosk owner pays protection money. (12 Jan. 1995)

K8   Marina, Russian, aged 24, kiosk sales person. Employed for sixteen months in a kiosk specializing in books, not open at night and located in the Visim sub-district. She is paid a percentage of the profit and does not pay protection money. Formerly a housewife, she has no criminal record. (7 Feb. 1995)

K9   Olga, female, Russian, aged 46, owner of one pavilion and two kiosks. (2 Mar. 1995, 5 Jan. 1998, 24 July 1999)

Other Business People

B1   Leonid Z., male, Russian, aged 57, general director of 'Uralimpex' (import–export), employs 15–20 people. Former Militia colonel and chief manager of prison factory. Does not pay protection money. (18 Mar. 1994)

B2   Vasilii E., male, Russian, aged 38, retail, employs less than 10 people. Formerly an employee in a state factory, pays protection money. (21 Mar. 1994)

B3   Grigorii B., male, Russian, aged 47, import–export, mainly auto parts, employs 10–15 people. Formerly chief manager of state enterprise producing machine equipment, pays protection money. (24 Mar. 1994)

B4   Fedor, male, Russian, aged 47, owner of a bakery, employs less than 10 people. Formerly employee of state bakery firm, pays protection money. (6 Apr. 1994)

B5   Grigorii T., male, Russian, aged 28, ruined businessman, involved in the retail sector. Formerly student of a culinary-technical school. (13 Apr. 1994)

B6   Gennadii, male, Russian/Tatar, aged 35, experienced businessman, now involved in the oil sector. Formerly a technician in a chemical factory, pays protection money. (16 Jan. 1995)

B7   Sergei, male, Russian, aged 29, computers/retail, employs 10–15 people. Formerly a university student, pays protection money. (18 Jan. 1995)

B8   Yurii Y., male, Russian, aged 49, general director of Muravei (retail), employs 4 people. Formerly employee in state retail sector, pays protection money. (20 Jan. 1995)

B9   Arkadii, male, Russian, aged 34, owner of a stereo equipment shop, employs less than 10 people. Formerly a technician in state enterprise, pays protection money. (22 Jan. 1995)

B10   Boris, male, Russian, aged 36, owner of a clothes shop, employs less than 10 people. Formerly employee in a state factory, pays protection money. (25 Jan. 1995)

B11   Konstantin, male, Russian, aged 38, general director of a company involved in commerce and industry. Employs several thousand people. Formerly, of the CPSU. Does not pay protection money. (26 Jan. 1995)

B12   Vadim P., male, Russian, aged 29, manager of coffee house/catering, employs 4 people. Formerly a student, pays protection money. (1 Mar. 1995)

B13   Nikolai K., male, Ukrainian, aged 51, owner of three pharmacies, employs more than 20 people. Former CPSU Official, does not pay protection money. (4 Mar. 1995)

B14   Stepan, male, Russian, aged 34, Owner of a shop selling spirits and liquors, employs less than 10 people, Formerly employee in the retail sector, pays protection money. (10 Feb. 1995)

B15   Iosif, male, Russian/Jew, aged 32, retail, employs 10–15 people. Formerly an engineer in state enterprise, pays protection money. (13 Feb. 1995)

B16   Boris V., male, Russian, aged 27, retail/import export, employs 10–15 people. Graduated recently, pays protection money. (14 Feb. 1995)

B17   Volodya G., male, Russian, aged 31, retail, employs 10–15 people. Formerly an employee in a motor-car service, pays protection money. (28 Feb. 1995)

B18   Alla, female, Russian, aged 32, owns a travel agency and employs 2 people. Formerly a medical student, does not pay protection money. (3 Mar. 1995)

B19   Eleonora, female, Russian, aged 50s, shuttle trader. (11 Mar. 1995)

B20   Larisa, female, Ethnic Korean born in Tashkent, trader at the central market. (23 Mar. 1995)

B21   Safar, Tadzhik trader at the central market. (26 Mar. 1995)

B22   President, Investment Bank Kauri. (12 Feb. 1998)

Judges and Police

A1   Tat'yana A. Trapeznikova, Judge, Perm Arbitration Court. (9 Feb. 1995)

A2   Nonna E. Grebneva, Advisor to the President of the Supreme Court of Arbitration. Moscow. (1 July 1999)

M1   Lieutenant and Senior Investigator, RUOP. (28 Jan. 1995)

M2   Major and Senior Interrogator, RUOP. (28 Mar. 1994)

M3   Head of Perm police. Interviews took place both in Oxford and Perm. (9 Oct. 1998, 5 Aug. 1999)

M4   Head of RUOP. (1 Feb. 1995)

M5   Senior Investigator, Perm police, murder investigation department. (14 Mar. 1994)

Security Firms and Criminals

SF1   President of security firm Alex. (14 Jan. 1998)

SF2   General director of security firm 'Sever'. (April 1994)

OC1   Igor', male, Russian, aged 30s, Criminal. (1994 and 1995)

OC2   Viktor, male, Russian, aged 30s, Criminal. (1994 and 1995)

OC3   Former convict and currently political figure on the extreme right. (30 Jan. 1995)

Various

Y1   Evgeniya, female, Russian, aged 32, interpreter, used the services of a criminal group. (1994 and 1995)

J1   Irina Krasnosel'skikh, crime correspondent, *Zvezda*. (1994 and 1995)

J2   A. Korabel'nikov, crime correspondent, *Permskie Novosti*. (6 Mar. 1995)

G1   Rudolf, sculptor and Gulag survivor. (19 Sept. 1997)

G2   Ford Foundation Representative, Moscow. (10 Mar. 1998)

P1   V. Fil', mayor of Perm 1992–94. Managing director, Bank Menatep. (3 Feb. 1998)

P2   City councillor. Formerly LDPR. (15 Feb. 1998)

P3   City councillor. Independent. (17 Feb. 1998)

P4   Igor' G. Yakovlev, president of the entrepreneurs association Edinstvo. (29 July 1999)

Interview Content: Items Presented to Kiosk Owners

Age. Sex. Marital status. Ethnic background. Educational background. Location of residence. Income level (as compared with other sectors, private/public). Occupational history. The effects of local and/or national government policy on the interviewee's activity. The interaction between agents of policy implementation and enforcement and people in the same business. Common offences incurred by people in the same business and arrests. Conflicts with enforcement agents. Factors governing spatial distribution. Types of agglomeration. Responses to spatial intervention. Information sharing. Labour utilization (unpaid family labour, paid family help, wage employment, commission wage workers). Capital requirement (fixed and variable costs). Sources of capital and credit (bank loans, rotating credit association, black market loans, credit from suppliers or wholesalers, credits from friends or relatives). Access to supplies. Working hours. Economic competition. Alliances and hostility. Businesses' associations. Type of customers (regular or occasional). Price of commodities as compared with nearby/distant shops. Newcomers. Methods of dispute settlement. Criminals' interventions. Interactions with the racket: how people in the same business are approached; amount asked for; threats; services provided by the racket.

Notes

Introduction

1. Drawing on Posner (1992; 1995), I take 'right' to mean a claim or entitlement enforceable through courts or equivalent state agencies.
2. North and Thomas, 1973: 20.
3. From 1812 to 1860, the number of landowners of large estates in Sicily went from 2,000 to 20,000; from 1860 to 1900, the number of hectares in private hands increased from 250,000 to 650,000 (Sereni, 1971: 276–7; Gambetta, 1993*a*: 91).
4. Lupo, 1984.
5. Gambetta, 1993*a*: 94.
6. Ibid. 77; Putnam, 1994.
7. Gambetta, 1993*a*: 94.
8. See J. A. Davis, 1988.
9. Sabetti, 1984: 104.
10. Gambetta, 1993*a*: 78.
11. Hess, 1973: 17–18. In 1750, one nobleman, for instance, is reported as employing a 'company of twenty-four dragoons' (Blok, 1974: 90).
12. Hess, 1973: 19; see also Blok, 1974: 61.
13. Gambetta, 1993*a*: 80.
14. See e.g. Rawlinson, 1997: 51.
15. Although this point appeared obvious to Schelling, definitions of 'organised crime' as 'a group of people who act together on a long term basis to commit crimes' abound (for a review, see Levi, 1998).
16. Schelling, [1971] 1984: 180–3.
17. Gambetta, 1993*a*: 1.
18. Schelling, [1971] 1984: 182.
19. 'Justice removed, then, what are kingdoms but great bands of robbers? What are robbers themselves but little kingdoms? The band itself is made up of men; it is governed by the authority of a ruler; it is bound together by a pact of association; and the loot is divided according to an agreed law.' Augustine, *The City of God against the Pagans*, iv. 4 (Eng. trans. Dyson, 1998: 147–8).
20. I have discussed these issues also in Varese 1994 and 1996.
21. See Reuter 1983 and 1987; Chu 2000; Hill 2000.
22. This is an expression used by Sartori (1991: 32–5). On the comparative method see also Sartori (1971).
23. A. Cohen, 1995: 37. See also Handelman, 1994*b*: 89 and 94; Shelley, 1997: 131 and 137 n. 20; Leitzel, Gaddy, and Alekseev, 1995: 28; Leitzel, 1995: 43.

24. See Hendley, Murrell, and Ryterman, 1999*a*, 1999*b*, 1999*c*, 1999*d*.
25. The only English-language study of Perm is a journal article by McAuley (1992, later in McAuley, 1997: 156–73), that compares elite realignment at the end of the Soviet Union in three cities, St Petersburg, Perm, and Arkhangel'sk.
26. An exchange programme exists between students and staff of the University of Oxford and Perm State University.
27. See *South China Morning Post*, 27 Nov. 1990 quoted by Chu (1996: 7). Mak, author of *The Sociology of Secret Societies* writes: 'Ironically, the danger [for the researcher] does not stem from the member being interviewed, but from members of rival societies who are still active' (1981: 159, quoted by Chu, 1996: 13).
28. See e.g. Oakley, 1981: 35; Brannen, 1988: 553; McCracken, 1988: 9–11.
29. See McCracken, 1988.
30. Brannen, 1988.
31. Quoted in Tentler, 1977: 94.
32. Chu: 1996: 25; Mak, 1981: 158.

Chapter 1

1. For the most persuasive recent analyses, see Stiglitz, 1998 and 1999; and Hellman, 1998.
2. Shleifer and Treisman 1998; Åslund 1999.
3. Johnson, Holmes and Kirkpatrick, 1999: 331.
4. Chernina, 1994. Adult mortality rate increased from 341 males per 1,000 in 1980 to 472 per 1,000 in 1995 (World Bank, 1998: 105). A US–Russian study presented in Moscow on 3–4 June 1995 reported that male life expectancy declined from 64.9 to 58.3 years since 1987, and the downward trend is expected to continue. The study also predicted that the number of suicides and cancer cases would continue to rise and that tuberculosis cases would remain at the level they were in developed countries 30 to 40 years ago (*OMRI*, 5 June 1995).
5. Frydman, Rapaczynski and Earle, 1993, quoted in Varese, 1994: 242.
6. Pistor, 1997: 176.
7. Naishul', 1993, quoted in Varese, 1994: 242.
8. See Lazarevskii, 1994 and Varese, 1996: 21–25.
9. Almakaeva, 1995: 41.
10. Morozov, 1996: 43; see also *Moscow Times*, 25 Mar. 1994 and 19 Mar. 1994.
11. Charap and Webster, 1993: 305.
12. Morozov, 1996: 43.
13. Ibid. 45.
14. The report offers the following example: 'For instance, M. Kabakov, director of the Kalinin Machine Building Plant, calculated that the doubling

of profits that this plant achieved through very tight economising on resources and staff reductions allowed it to increase net profits by only 2 per cent' (Filippov, 1994: 1–2). A St Petersburg entrepreneur calculated that 80 per cent of his gross revenues has been taken away by taxes. If one combines VAT at 28 per cent with the profit-based excess wage tax at 32 per cent, the marginal tax on value added is 60 per cent, of which less than half is potentially refundable. Even the amount that is refundable, would lose most of its value in the face of high inflation (Charap and Webster, 1993: 305).

15. Until 1995, tax authorities could keep ten per cent of income that was hidden from taxation and 30 per cent of imposed penalties (Morozov, 1996: 44).

16. Morozov, 1996: 44.

17. See Hood and Sparks, 1970: ch. 1.

18. Zablotskis and Zvekic, 1994: 40.

19. Alvazzi del Frate and Goryainov, 1994: 8.

20. These estimates are from the Research Institute of the Russian Interior Ministry, reported in Ponomarev (1996: 1). Aleksei Kazannik, the Russian Federation Prosecutor General in 1993, said that his office is in a position to complete no more than 50 per cent of the bills of indictment in the already investigated cases (*Nezavisimaya Gazeta*, 28 Oct. 1993).

21. See Åslund, 1997: 84.

22. Since March 1999, *Corriere della Sera* has reported widely on this case. See e.g. 18 Mar. 1999 and 13 Sept. 1999.

23. *AP*, 9 June 1998.

24. He was removed in March 1998. *ITAR-TASS*, 9 Nov. 1995. (In 1996, Kulikov set up an Internal Security Dept., the UVB, to root out police corruption. His so-called 'Clean Hands' operation resulted in the dismissal of 21,347 officers. *Moscow Times*, 28 Dec. 1998.)

25. Transparency International, 1996.

26. 'By the beginning of 1996, 17,937 industrial firms, 72 per cent of large and middle-sized enterprises, had been privatized, accounting for 88.3 per cent of the industrial output of the Russian Federation. Roughly 82 per cent of small shops and retail stores were also privatized' (Blasi *et al.*, 1997: 2, 26). Housing stock has been privatized at spectacular speed (Struyk and Daniell, 1995). Land is the only sector where the privatization process is lagging behind (Wegren, 1993 and 1994).

27. Barzel, 1997: 4. What I call 'natural control' is akin to an Hobbesian 'natural right'. Barzel (1997) calls it an 'economic' right and distinguishes it from a 'legal' right. Following Barzel, the term 'asset' is intended here in the widest possible sense, including: physical assets, people's control over themselves, brand names, and reputations (see Barzel, 1997).

28. Broadly defined, co-operation takes place when two or more people 'engage in a joint venture for the outcome of which the actions of each are

necessary' (Williams, 1989: 7). Most human undertakings, therefore, are forms of co-operation, from driving cars to play, from marriage to international relations. 'Even [economic] competition, rather than being an alternative to co-operation, rests on co-operative arrangements' (Gambetta, 1993*b*: 678). The greater the number of assets in the private domain, the greater the co-operation among owners. It is an often unrecognized phenomenon that the advent of private and competitive markets should require not less but more co-operation.

29. In fact, the opportunities for cheating are positively correlated to the opportunities of exchange.

30. Binmore and Dasgupta, 1986: 3; Gambetta, 1993b: 678–9.

31. See Posner, 1995: 73; Getzler, 1996: 654; Ryan, 1987: 1029–31.

32. 'If, for instance, nobody could leave land to their children, or sell a freehold in it, or raise a mortgage on it, we should be doubtful whether individuals could be said to "own" it at all' (Ryan, 1987: 1029).

33. Posner, 1995: 73.

34. Smith, [1776] 1986: 380. North and Thomas (1973) have stressed the importance of credible property rights for economic growth. Torstensson (1994) is an empirical study of the relationship between the structure of property rights and economic growth. He finds a significant and negative correlation between growth and arbitrary seizure of property. See also Johnson, Holmes and Kirkpatrick, 1999.

35. In other words, the contract is self-enforced outside the scope of the state. See Barzel, 1999.

36. See Kiser and Barzel, 1991.

37. Barzel, 1999: ch. 9, 29.

38. By corruption I refer to an exchange that takes place between two actors, the *corrupter* and an official, but involves a third actor, the *principal*. The official is an *agent* employed by a principal in order to implement rules set out by the principal. Typical examples of agents include bureaucrats who oversee the issuing of permits, policemen who patrol a neighbourhood, or lab scientists who check the quality of retail food products. The principal is usually thought of as the state administration, which employs individuals to undertake such tasks. The corrupters are members of the public or of another organization who want to bend in their favour the rules laid out by the principal. See Gambetta, 1999.

39. See Gambetta, 1988*a*. The following instance testifies to this problem. Corporal Elena Troshina, a telephone operator in an army unit, paid up to $US4,500 to by-pass the queue and get a one-room flat in Moscow. The recipient of the money, Vladimir Solomonov, an army general, claimed he could deliver but in the end pocketed the money and did nothing. Eventually he was sentenced to four years imprisonment. In recent years, thirteen army generals have been found guilty of corruption and fraud, mainly connected to housing allocation. All of them have been given sus-

pended sentences or granted an amnesty by the State Duma. Vladimir Solomonov appears to be the only one who will actually serve his sentence. See *Komsomol'skaya Pravda*, 3 Dec. 1998; *Moskovskii Komsomolets*, 14 Nov. 1998 and 23 Oct. 1998; and *Kommersant*, 14 Nov. 1998.

40. See Gambetta, 1999. Such a demand is the greater if the official is the only one who has control over the resources. On the contrary, if the number of officers is so great that they cannot co-ordinate and enforce a common price for the bribe, the corrupter can shop around for the cheapest bribe.

41. Posner, 1995: 72. Posner concludes 'the distinction between positive and negative liberties blurs'. For instance, the right to abortion is a negative right for an affluent person, but for a poor person, who cannot purchase an abortion, it must be a positive right, a state-supplied service, for that right to be meaningful (ibid.). Although this conclusion may be correct from a normative point of view, it clearly is not true descriptively. States such as the USA and the UK provide individuals with negative rights without dedicating themselves to provide them with the resources necessary to exercise those rights. I share with Lord Goldsmith the negative right to freedom of speech and to run for office but the state is not dedicated to ensuring that we both have a positive right to the financial means to exercise these rights effectively.

42. Petrova, 1996: 70.

43. Dornbush, 1991: 7.

44. The size of groups in connection to collective action is a classical question explored first by Olson, 1965.

45. Hay, Shleifer, and Vishny, 1996: 564.

46. See Hunt, 1936.

47. Raeff, 1983.

48. Barzel, 1999: Ch. 7: 41. See also Olson, 1982.

49. See Nove, 1977; Ledeneva, 1998a.

50. This is the 1988 Law on State Enterprises. See Brown 1998, and Shleifer and Treisman, 1998.

51. Åslund, 1999: 66.

52. Ibid.

53. Ibid. 67.

54. McFaul, 1996: 291.

55. Olson, 1995: 452.

56. Frye, 1997: 89.

57. Wallach, 1994; Shleifer and Treisman, 1998: 64.

58. 'The enterprise management could buy 5 per cent of the shares at the book price', while 'employees were to receive 25 per cent of their enterprise free of charge as nonvoting shares; they could buy another 10 per cent in voting shares, at a 30 per cent discount of the extremely low book value' (Shleifer and Treisman, 1998: 65).

59. Shleifer and Vasiliev, 1996. See also McFaul (1996: 293) and Boycko *et al.* (1995: 98).
60. McFaul, 1996: 294. The official unemployment rate—which includes only those who register as unemployed—was only 3 per cent of the labour force in 1995 (Kotz and Weir, 1997: 180).
61. McFaul, 1996: 294.
62. Pistor, 1997: 177.
63. Representatives of Ministries had argued for shares to be held 'in holding companies managed in part by ministerial bureaucrats, expand the cross ownership of shares by enterprises and ministries, and keep enterprises under the purview and out of privatization program', but they failed to see their plan implemented (Frye, 1997: 88).
64. Shleifer and Treisman, 1998: 65.
65. Kotz and Weir, 1997: 168, 177.
66. Shleifer and Treisman, 1998: 66.
67. Frye, 1997: 91.
68. Pistor, 1997: 171–2.
69. Frye, 1997: 91.
70. GRF/RECEP (1996: 104) and Pistor (1997: 173). Some businessmen, particularly in the provinces, are involved in a steady trade of faked extracts. 'Unfortunate buyers learn that they have been deceived only when they try to add their names to the official register and discover that their vendor does not appear' (*Financial Times*, 29 Nov. 1994).
71. Åslund, 1999: 72. Transworld, a London-based company which dominates the Russian metal trade, alleges that the share-register at the Krasnoyarsk Aluminium Smelter, one of the world's largest aluminium producers, has been altered in an effort to defraud her. Transworld claims, and the factory confirms, that a 20 per cent stake in the smelter (worth $300 m.) controlled by Transworld proxies, was deleted from the records by factory administrators. Officials at Krasnoyarsk Smelter confirmed that shares held by Transworld had been deleted from the share register, but they contended that the shares had been improperly purchased in the first place (*Financial Times*, 29 Nov. 1994). This shows that factory directors can and unilaterally do alter shareholder registers. Mr David Reuben, president of Transworld, concluded that 'shareholders are completely at the mercy of factory managers' (*Financial Times*, 16 Nov. 1994).
72. A view popular both among academics and protagonists of the transition is that it does not matter the way a new owner comes to possess some wealth. Once private ownership is established, the owner will have an interest in making his wealth productive. Anatolii Chubais is reported to have said in 1995: '[The Russian magnates] steal and steal. They are stealing absolutely everything and it is impossible to stop them. But let them steal and take their property. They will then become owners and decent administrators of their property' (quoted in *Prospect*, Oct. 1998). Propo-

nents of this view often invoke a well-known economic theorem, the Coase Theorem. In fact, the theorem states the opposite: when rights are well defined and the cost of transacting is zero, resource allocation is efficient and independent of the pattern of ownership (see Barzel, 1997: 7; Coase, 1960).

73. Vladimir Potatin also controls the *Izvestiya* and *Russkii Telegraf* newspapers. In 1996 he was appointed first deputy prime minister in charge of finance. Potanin's political patron is the 'reformer' Anatolii Chubais.

74. Åslund, 1999: 69.

75. McFaul, 1996: 305. According to a survey of privatized and state-owned enterprises, 'employees of privatized enterprises were more likely than state enterprise workers to report asset-stripping by managers' and felt 'close' or 'very close' to the Communists than did employees of state enterprises (quoted in Shleifer and Treisman, 1998: 69).

76. Indeed, Western advisers' insistence on the opening of capital accounts facilitated capital flight, as noted by Stiglitz, 1999.

77. In what appears to be a similar instance, Anatolii Sobchak, first democratically elected mayor of St Petersburg, was accused of signing orders that benefited a firm named 'Renaissance' in 1992. This firm was allowed to build an underground garage in the place of a kindergarten. It later surfaced that the firm had 'paid' Sobchak in kind, by giving a fictitious job and two flats to his niece (*Izvestiya*, 15 Dec. 1996). Moreover, some Western advisers had a stake in the emerging Russian markets and, according to an official US document, they 'abused the trust of the United States Government by using personal relationships . . . for private gains' (quoted in Wedel, 1998: 128).

78. It is worth elaborating on this point. Identification is a crucial ingredient of a corrupt exchange. In a world where honesty is the norm, how can the corrupter know who, if offered a bribe, would accept? Corrupters need to identify potential corruptees, persons willing to accept a bribe and not to report them to the authorities. The bribe-taker can engage in activities that signal a willingness to take bribes. For example, joining a political party known for being more corrupt than other parties, could indicate a disposition to accept bribes. Other signals might be used, such as physical and vocal cues. Bribe-givers, however, have to be cautious because they might misinterpret the signal. Bribe-takers must also be cautious since the member of the public can report on the official. By contrast, an overwhelmingly corrupt setting requires much less caution. Identification of a willing bribe-taker is not difficult, for the citizen expects the agent to be one. In other words, once corruption is widespread, the 'identification' problem is more easily solved. The dominant strategy will be always to offer bribes.

79. *ITAR-TASS*, 22 Dec. 1996; *The Economist*, 8 Apr. 1995; *Business Week*, 1 Apr. 1996; *Moscow Times*, 16 June 1998.

80. Treisman, 1996.
81. The bribe must be greater than the reward tax officers gain for good performance.
82. Olson, 1995: 454.
83. According to data released by the Federation Council Chairman Egor Stroev, only 16 per cent of Russian companies honour their tax obligations. Of 2.6 million firms, 436,000 companies pay taxes regularly and in full, whereas at least 882,000 publish no accounts and make no tax payment at all (as of 1 Oct. 1996, tax arrears reached 132 trillion rubles/$US24.4 billion (*ITAR-TASS*, 12 Nov. 1996; *AFP*, 12 Nov. 1996; *OMRI Daily Digest*, 13 Nov. 1996).
84. Earle and Estrin, 1996.
85. McFaul, 1996.

Chapter 2

1. A. Cohen, 1995: 37. See also Handelman, 1994*b*: 89 and 94; Shelley, 1997: 131 and 137 n. 20; Leitzel, Gaddy, and Alekseev, 1995: 28; Leitzel, 1995: 43.
2. Hendley, Murrell and Ryterman, 1999*a*.
3. Ibid. 7.
4. Ibid. 8.
5. Ibid. 39.
6. *Moscow Times*, 25 Jan. 1993; see also Zinoviev, 1976.
7. DiFrancesco and Gitelman, 1984.
8. Miller, Grodeland, and Koshechkina, 1999: 3.
9. The 1994 *NRB* IV, the survey quoted below, was a stratified sample of 1943 Russian adults, representing Asiatic and European Russia, rural and urban areas (see Rose, 1995).
10. Rose, 1995: 38.
11. Almond and Verba—who introduced the concept of 'subjective competence'—defined it as the 'percentage who expect serious consideration both in a government office and from the police'. See Miller *et al.*, 1999: ch. 1, and Almond and Verba, 1963: 171.
12. Miller, Grodeland, and Koshechkina, 1999: ch. 1. When correlating expectations of fair treatment with occupation, farmers and those who lived in villages displayed a higher than average 'trust' than workers, managers, intellectuals, business-people, and those who lived in towns or cities.
13. Boutenko and Razlogov, 1997: 201.
14. *The Independent*, 20 Aug. 1993.
15. In the survey quoted by Hendley *et al.* and dated 1991, 64. 9 per cent do not have 'very much' confidence in the police or have 'none at all'. According to the World Value Survey (1990–3), only 19 per cent of Muscovites have 'a great deal of confidence' in the police. The value for Russia as a whole is 35

per cent, while for Brazil it is 38 per cent. Denmark is at the top of the list with 89, the value for Britain being 77 per cent (Inglehart, Basañez, and Moreno, 1998: table V278).

16. *OMRI*, 7 Sept. 1995.

17. *Izvestiya* 1 Sept. 1995.

18. Abuses of power are not a feature of Perm police only. According to Andrei Babushkin, head of a prison watchdog body, nongovernmental organizations in Moscow alone receive hundreds of complaints every month from people claiming to have been beaten and tortured by the police, yet complaints against the police are almost always dismissed as groundless. One incident highlighted in the press was the killing in police custody of a 19-year-old man in Mordoviya in late July 1995. *OMRI*, 7 Sept. 1995. See also *Newsday*, 27 Oct. 1999; *New Statesman* (21 June 1999).

19. I am especially grateful to Professor Hendley for having read a version of this section and pointed out a number of inaccuracies. She is of course not responsible for any of remaining mistakes.

20. APK, 1992.

21. Autonomous areas and cities with Federal status (Moscow and St Petersburg) also have *Arbitrazh* courts, for a total of eighty-two courts at the first instance. A second, appellate level comprises ten courts, and above them is the Supreme Arbitration Court of the Russian Federation. See VASRF, 1997.

22. See APK, 1995 and Hendley, 1998*b*: 100.

23. APK, 1995: art. 22.

24. The sentences of greater consequences are reported in the *Vestnik Vysshego Arbitrazhnogo Suda*, a specialized journal, which is widely read by Arbitration judges.

25. Litigants have the right to petition to have cases heard collegially (i.e. by the three judges). APK, 1995: art. 14; Hendley, 1998*b*: 100.

26. *Entsiklopedicheskii slovar' v dvukh tomakh*, 1963: 63. The general purpose of the former *Gosarbitrazh* was to deal with disputes between organisations that belonged to different ministries. Settlements of disputes between organs of the same *vedomstvo* (department) were subject to 'departmental' arbitration bodies. Legal controversies have surrounded the nature of *Gosarbitrazh:* was it a court or an administrative organ? The argument in favour of the 'administrative body' was put to me by Judge Tat'yana Aleksandrovna Trapeznikova, of the Perm Arbitration court (for a similar view, see also Pistor, 1995: 15). She pointed out that Soviet Arbitration courts did not operate according to a Code, but rather followed 'rules'. This would mean the *Gosarbitrazh* was not a proper court. This view is echoed in the juridical literature but has been disputed. Settlement of economic disputes is a typical judicial activity, argued Kucherov (1970: 152–3). In this case, the decision of the arbiter was similar to that of a court according to its form and consequences: if not complied with by the losing

party, it could be enforced. According to Kucherov, Soviet *Gosarbitrazh* was a specialized court, similar to military courts in Western countries. As the competence of military courts is limited to soldiers and matters concerning the military, the competence of *Gosarbitrazh* was limited to economic disputes arising from the plan.

27. Berman, 1963: 129.
28. Pistor, 1996: 69.
29. Pistor (1995: 25) noted that the number of civil disputes decided by the Russian *Arbitrazh* in 1993 (264,447 decisions) is quite impressive when compared with other countries. For example, in the US in 1993 a total of 228,568 civil law cases were filed with district courts, with another 218,396 cases pending. Of course, the numbers are not directly comparable, mostly because US data do not discriminate between cases filed by entrepreneurs and ordinary citizens. Moreover, US statistics are based on the number of claims filed or pending, as opposed to decided, and include a larger range of legal issues than the Russian courts. This would suggest a downwards readjustment of US data.
30. To calculate the total of all cases decided by *Arbitrazh* courts, one should also add the cases of bankruptcy (2,269 in 1997 and 2,628 in 1998).
31. Data from Hendley, 1998*a*: 390. Interestingly, few cases involving collateral were heard in the period 1992–7 (Hendley, 1998*a*: 391).
32. The national level of delays at the appellate level is roughly 10 per cent in the period 1996–8. This may be explained by the higher complexity of the cases and the fact that a three judges' panel is required. See Hendley, 1998*a*: 386.
33. APK, 1995: art. 114.
34. See Letter of the Supreme *Arbitrazh* Court of the Russian Federation, 10 Aug. 1994, 'On Means to Help Eliminating the Causes for the Non-Payment Crisis'.
35. A1. Russian Arbitration courts have the power to collect evidence. The arbitrator may order the parties to perform certain acts and to provide documents, information or opinions. A decision of the Arbitration court can be appealed, but only within one month after its publication. According to the present system, the Court of Appeal is made up of the same judges of the lower Arbitration court. A third level also exists: the Supreme Court of Arbitration in Moscow.
36. Hendley 1998*a*: 385.
37. A1.
38. Hendley, 1998*a*: 385.
39. APK, 1992: art. 69.
40. Hendley, 1998*b*: 97.
41. Ibid. 96.
42. Letter of the Supreme *Arbitrazh* Court, 10 Aug. 1994.
43. Usually by submitting an affidavit from its banks confirming the lack of

funds. Sometimes the court will require the petitioner to submit a certificate from the tax inspectorate listing all bank accounts.

44. See Hendley, 1998*a*: 388.
45. A further innovation of the 1995 APK (art. 127) is that judges are required to explain the basis of their decision in greater details than provided by the 1992 APK (see art. 108). For a discussion of this issue see Hendley, 1998*b*: 107–9.
46. See APK, 1995: section 16.
47. The reason for a delay is to allow parties to file an appeal.
48. Banks are threatened with losing their licences if they fail to comply with court orders (Art. 151).
49. Korbatov, Rose, and Karasik, 1994.
50. Hendley, 1998*b*: 111.
51. APK, 1992: arts. 150, 153.
52. Charap and Webster, 1993: 307. Wegren discusses the problems affecting trading at Agricultural Commodity Exchanges. He reports that the process of payment by a purchaser can take 'between several weeks to four months', due to banking system inefficiencies (Wegren, 1994: 219).
53. Boffito, 1995: 135.
54. Johnson, 1994: 981.
55. Ibid.
56. Boffito, 1995: 123.
57. Johnson, 1994: 993.
58. For instance, the Perm-based company AO Dekra had won a suit against Prosveshchenie for a delay in the payment of material duly delivered. The Perm Arbitration Court ordered Prosveshchenie to compensate Dekra for the delayed payment. Two months later the money had not yet entered the bank account of Dekra. Prosveshchenie filed a new suit and a further inquiry discovered that the bank had not yet executed the order (court case 175/1994, Perm *Arbitrazh* Court).
59. Hendley, 1998*b*: 110.
60. Ibid. 113.
61. Ibid. 112.
62. A1.
63. Hendley, 1998*a*: 113–14. The shortcoming of system of implementing decisions has been addressed by two new laws, that will be fully operational by the year 2000. 'According to these new laws, the bailiffs can be armed, and have much more powers than before, they can order people to do things, to check accounts, while before they were old ladies. But the system is still in the stage of formation' (A2).
64. The best English translation of Nashe Delo is probably 'Our Business'. However, especially in the wake of the scam Nashe Delo was involved in, local newspapers have emphasized that the translation into Italian would be 'Cosa Nostra' (lit. 'Our Thing'). 'Cosa Nostra' is the name of the Italian

mafia. Since the applicants were physical people rather than legal entities, the civil court dealt with the case. Since the case involves the same bailiffs' office, it illustrates the limitations on their ability to enforce decisions.

65. See *Mestnoe Vremya*, 6 Jan. 1995; *Molodaya Gvardiya*, 14 Jan. 1995; *Permskie Novosti*, 11 Jan. 1995; *Zvezda*, 4 Feb. 1995.
66. Hendley, 1998*b*: 116.
67. Ibid.
68. *Nezavisimaya Gazeta*, 16 Jan. 1997.
69. Hendley, 1998*b*: 126.
70. Hendley, Murrell, and Ryterrman, 1999*b*: 26.
71. Data on the appelate level, which was introduced in 1996, are not sufficient to identify trends. It appears however that 11–15 per cent of decisions are appellate and that 28–30 per cent of these decisions are reversed.
72. A1.
73. If the applicant loses the case and does not pay, the court will have to enforce payment of the trial's expenditures.
74. Pistor, 1996: 76.
75. 'formal legal institutions and private enforcement can also be complements. Private enforcers often review relevant legal documentation before acting. When a losing defendant fails to pay according to the terms of an *arbitrazh* court decision and the victorious plaintiff seeks the assistance of private enforcement agents, these agents sometimes review the court decision before taking action' (Hendley, Ickes, Murrell, and Ryterman, 1997: 28).
76. The survey was administered in the period Nov.–Dec. 1997. A second questionnaire targeting ninety-six respondents for in-depth interviews was submitted in 1998. See Radaev, 1998: 25.
77. Radaev uses the following factors: I: type and size of the enterprise; II: frequency of breaches of business obligations; III: business position of head/manager as owner and organizer; IV: trust towards regular partners and readiness to render them financial support (1998: 147).
78. Radaev, 1998: 147–54.
79. Hendley (1998*b*: 118) reports that, for banks, 'the Central Bank had issued a regulation requiring a court judgement before a bad debt could be taken off the books'. According to the judges she interviewed, this appears to apply also to other enterprises.
80. This scenario would share some crucial similarities with the medieval *Lex Mercatoria* analysed by Milgrom, North, and Weingast (1990). The extent to which court judgements are enforced in advanced market economies should not be exaggerated. A recent survey of 100 cases in 1997 in the UK found that one-third of creditors, who had won a civil case, did not receive any money, while only one-third were paid in full and in time. Moreover, bailiffs trying to obtain payment or seize debtors' assets have a low successful rate (37.2 per cent in 1998; see data published in *Guardian*, 8 Jan.

2000). Scholars usually explain the continuing use of courts with the high reputational cost for those who do not pay (see e.g. Charny, 1990).

81. Hendley, 1998*b*: 111–12.

82. Incidentally, we can also solve a minor puzzle, related to the results of the survey of 328 Russian enterprise top managers conducted by Hendley *et al.* which led them to conclude that 'the law matters'. They describe their sample as follows: 'The sample included enterprises from six cities (Moscow, Barnaul, Novosibirsk, Ekaterinburg, Voronezh, Saratov), with each city represented roughly equally. The enterprises span ten major *industrial* sectors. Enterprise size ranged from 30 to 17,000 employees, with a median of 300 and a mean of 980. Most of the enterprises were established during the Soviet era, and about three-fourths (77%) are privatized. In virtually all of those privatized, some stock was in the hands of insiders, and nearly a third were entirely owned by insiders. Outsiders held some stock in 60% of the enterprises' (Hendley, Murrell and Ryterman, 1999*a*: 4, emphasis added). Respondents were top managers of recently privatized and still state-owned factories, with a high degree of insider ownership and concentrated in industrial sectors of the economy. They would fall in the first cluster of respondents of the Radaev's survey, rather than represent a wider sector of business-people.

83. Most importantly, new laws have been passed to reform the system of *sudebnye ispolniteli*, although it is still early to assess their impact, as pointed out to me by the Adviser to the President of the Supreme Court of Arbitration: 'Recently, two new laws (*O sudebnykh pristavakh*; *Ob ispolnitel'nom proizvodstve*) have been passed on the execution of decisions. According to these new laws, the bailiffs are now armed, and have greater powers than before, they can order people to do things, to check accounts, while before they were old ladies. But the system is still in the stage of formation' (A2).

Chapter 3

1. Elster, 1982.
2. Gambetta, 1993*a*: 78.
3. Ibid. 40–1.
4. Ibid. 79.
5. In one survey of Muscovites, 26 per cent thought they themselves would become unemployed after the transition to the market (Jones and Moskoff, 1991: 127. See also Peterson, 1990: 4).
6. *Rossiya*, no. 9, 24 Feb. 1992.
7. *Kommersant*, 3 Feb. 1992.
8. *Interfax*, 2 Feb. 1993.
9. *Vladivostok News*, 29 Nov. 1996.

10. In 1990 it was estimated that there was a total of 475,000 personnel in the police as a whole. *TASS*, 27 June 1989 and *Radio Moskva*, 13 Mar. 1990.

11. The MVD troups are largely made of conscripts; Tsypkin, 1989: 16.

12. *Trud*, 24 Aug. 1990.

13. *Izvestiya*, 9 July 1991.

14. *Kommersant-Daily* 16 Feb. 1993.

15. Louis and Louis, 1980: 6.

16. Data from Louis and Louis, 1980: 7–24.

17. *Repubblica*, 11 Sept. 1992. In Vladivostok there is even a gang called the 'sportsmen gang' that controls the traffic of stolen Japanese cars. Reportedly, it is headed by M. G. Mamiashvili and A. V. Slushaev (*Repubblica*, 11 Sept. 1992).

18. *Megalopolis-Express*, 11 Mar. 1991.

19. *The Washington Post National Weekly Edition*, 20–26 Mar. 1995.

20. *Interfax*, 5 Apr. 1995.

21. Ibid.

22. *Moscow Times*, 2 Mar. 1994.

23. Respectively 43, 143, and $US1,400, at the July 1991 exchange rate. *Megalopolis-Express*, 11 Mar. 1991.

24. Committee on Governmental Affairs, 1996: 50.

25. *Komsomol'skaya Pravda*, 27 Dec. 1994.

26. See 'How to protect your business. A "Roof" is needed', by Vladimir Kavichev, *Argumenty i Fakty* no. 16, 1994.

27. In the Soviet period, industrial enterprises, collective farms, and ministries were protected by agencies that were formally part of the MVD apparatus but—as reminded by Galeotti (1998a: 3)—'in practice they reported to local managers and authorities'.

28. See Galeotti, 1995b: 61.

29. Jones and Moskoff, 1991: 92. See also Trehub, 1989: 21.

30. Galeotti, 1998a: 7. See also Volkov, 1999a: 748. See also Volkov, 1999b.

31. *Corriere della Sera*, 14 Apr. 1994.

32. *The Irish Times*, 3 Mar. 1999.

33. *Rossiiskaya gazeta*, 22 June 1996.

34. *Kommersant-Daily*, 13 Mar. 1997. See also *Moscow Times*, 25 Jan. 1997, 14 Mar. 1997 and 9 Apr. 1997; *International Herald Tribune*, 14 May 1997; Maksimov, 1998: 260–6; Galeotti, 1998a: 8; Volkov, 1999: 750.

35. Police officers at various levels consider the provision of private protection services not just a necessity but a positive development. Interpol National Bureau Department head Evgenii Malyshenko (1997) argues that it allows the police to have greater control over the private market for protection, closing down illegal or dubious providers. Also it helps to gather information that might be relevant for investigation, and it gives greater autonomy of police units to run their own superiors in the ministry. Closing down private agencies may however be motivated by a

desire to reduce competition, while 'great autonomy' may lead to a break-down of the chain of command.

36. *Kriminal'naya Khronika*, no. 3, 1999.
37. *Kriminal'naya Khronika*, no. 7, 1995. The 'white cross' is not to be confused with the 'white arrow', reportedly a detachment of policemen who secretly murder criminals (*Sovershenno Sekretno*, no. 7, 1998). There are doubts on the real existence of this 'Dirty Harry' type of organization (see esp. the film *Magnum Force*, 1973). There are of course various parallels in other countries. See for instance, the results of the Lexow Committee's investigation into police corruption in New York at the end of the 19th cent. What the Committee found is that 'in return for pay-offs, they [policemen] protected gambling, prostitution, and other illicit enterprises. Officers extorted peddlers, storekeepers, and other legitimate business-men who were hard pressed to abide by municipal ordinances. Detectives allowed con men, pickpockets, and thieves to go about their business in return for a share of the proceeds' (Fogelson, 1977: 3 quoted in Block, 1983: 19).
38. See Gambetta, 1993*a*: 15–34.
39. Volkov, 2000: 11. See also *Kommersant-daily*, 12 Mar. 1997.
40. See *ITAR-TASS*, 20 May 1997 and *Kommersant-daily*, 12 Mar. 1997.
41. According to Galeotti, total police strength is around 400,000 of the MVD's total of 540,000 police-related personnel. This amounts to a 3:1 ratio of security officers to police officers, which does not differ greatly from the US ratio (see Galeotti, 1998*a*: 1–2, Moran 1995 and *The Economist*, 19 Apr. 1997).
42. Galeotti, 1998*a*: 5.
43. Krishtanovskaya, 1995: 95–96. According to a study of the Moscow-based Institute of Sociology, 80 per cent of the former members of the State Security Apparatus found employment in the private market for protection (*Golos*, no. 42/3, Oct. 1992). See also *Izvestiya*, 26 Jan. 1995; and *Izvestiya*, June 1995.
44. *Kommersant-Daily*, 21 Mar. 1995.
45. They include former KGB deputy Chief Leonid Shebarshin, once head of Soviet foreign intelligence, Mikhail Golovatov, former head of the Al'fa commando unit and founder of Al'fa-A security firm, Colonel A. Markarov, former army intelligence Colonel and founder of Alex, and Aleksandr Gurov, former deputy head of the Ministry of Interior Affairs (MVD) Research Institute and author of scholarly studies on organised crime. See Krishtanovskaya, 1995: 95–6, Galeotti, 1998*a* and Volkov, 1999: 750.
46. *Moscow Times*, 31 Oct. 1995.
47. *InterSec*, 1992: 116.
48. Ibid.
49. Galeotti, 1998*a*: 6.

50. See Alex home page on the internet: http://www.alexsecurity.ru/.
51. Ibid.
52. Galeotti, 1998a: 6. Other well-known companies include Legion and Bastion, based in Moscow. Foreign companies have opened offices in Russia (mainly Moscow and St Petersburg), such as Control Risks based in London, Coral Gables and Ackerman based in the USA, and the Israel-based firm International Security Services (the latter has a training centre in Moscow). Another company, Ranger, specializes in providing female bodyguards protecting women and children. See *Business Week*, 30 Aug. 1993; *Moscow Times*, 9 Apr. 1995; *Komsomol'skaya Pravda*, 5 June 1995; *The European*, 21–27 July 1995, *Moscow Times*, 14 Jan. 1998.
53. *The Washington Post National Weekly Edition*, 20–26 Mar. 1995.
54. Ibid.
55. This is the Foreign Corrupt Practices Act of 1977 (see Noonan, 1984: 680). Sheffet questions the overall efficacy of the FCPA ('It is difficult to determine whether the FCPA has made American corporations more ethical or merely more cautious', Sheffet, 1995: 67). See however the recent FBI investigation into the activities of American businessman James Giffen, who allegedly paid bribes to Kazakh officials or their families, including President Nazarbayev (*Newsweek*, 10 July 2000). In 1997, a wider OECD convention combating bribery of foreign officials was signed (Moran, 1999).
56. *Moscow Times*, 14 Jan. 1998.
57. *Business Week*, 30 Aug. 1993.
58. *Dos'e 02*, 4 Apr. 97.
59. Analiticheskii Tsentr 'Izvestii', 1994b.
60. See *Ugolovnyi Kodeks Rossiiskoi Federatsii*, 1993: 151.
61. 'A large-scale operation recently conducted by the RF Ministry of Internal Affairs showed that, quite often, private bodygurad enterprises and security services are used by criminals as front for the business of armed robbery. Of the more than 5,000 firms checked last year, one-tenth turned out to be criminal.' *Izvestiya*, 12 Mar. 1997.
62. *Kommersant-daily*, 15 Mar. 1997.
63. *Kommersant-daily*, 2 Dec. 1998.
64. *Izvestiya*, 6 Jan. 1995; Martinetti, 1995: 96; Razinkin, 1995: 25.
65. Galeotti, 1998b: 420. 'Vitalii Sidorov, Executive director of the Department of Security of the Association of Russian Banks, formerly Vice-Minister of Internal Affairs; Mikhail Shestopalov, Chief of Security Service of Bank Menatep, formerly Chief of OBASS, Chief of the Dep. for the fight against economic crime in Moscow; Vladimir Zaitsev, Chief of Security Service of Bank Stolichnyi, formerly Chief of Special Detatchment Al'fa in the KGB; Mikhail Gorbunov, Chief of Security Service of InKomBank, formerly Executive of the Intelligence Service' (Krishtanovskaya, 1995: 96).

66. *Kriminal'naya Khronika*, no. 7, 1994.

67. *Izvestiya*, 14 Mar. 1995.

68. See RFE/RL, 5 Dec. 1994, *Moscow Times*, 3 Dec. 1994 and 7 Dec. 1994 and *New Yorker*, 20 Feb. 1995.

69. *Izvestiya*, 14 Apr. 1995. Similarly, M. Leont'ev writes: 'He whose "roof" is higher is right' (in *Segodnya*, 17 Mar. 1995). See also *Moscow Times*, 7 Mar. 1995.

70. On 26 June 1998, Petukhov was assassinated. Yukos denies any involvement in the murder. *Komsomol'skaya Pravda*, 30 June 1998. In a letter dated 16 June 1998 sent to President Boris Yeltsin, then Prime Minister Sergei Kirienko and leaders of the State Duma, Russia's lower house of parliament, Petukhov announced he was undertaking a hunger strike to protest against the 'cynical actions and murderous politics carried out by oligarchs from Rosprom-Yukos and Bank Menatep in the Nefteyugansk region'. The letter calls on the government to bring criminal charges against Rosprom-Yukos for 'concealing taxes in large quantities from 1996 to 1998' (*Moscow Times*, 25 Aug. 1998).

71. Martinetti, 1995: 176.

72. SCO, 1997: i. 75.

73. This in turn leads to an equilibrium where corruption is pervasive and actors themselves simply consider the normal and acceptable method to deal with the state.

74. *UN Crime Prevention and Criminal Justice Newsletter*, nos. 26–7, Nov. 1995. By 1999, the official estimate is 4,600 groups.

75. *Kommersant-Daily* 16 Feb. 1993.

76. Otari Kvantrishvili (1948–94) started his career as a Graeco-Roman wrestler of international class. In the mid-1960s, he was a member of a gang headed by a man nicknamed Mongol and a small-time card sharp. He was arrested for gang rape in 1966 and given a 10-year sentence, but was subsequently released and diagnosed as a schizophrenic. In the early 1980s, Kvantrishvili was a coach at the Dinamo Club. Some of the wrestlers, boxers, and weight lifters that grouped round him in this period later joined criminal gangs such as Lyuberetskaya, Baumanskaya, Domodedovskaya, Balashikhinskaya. He was a close friend of prominent criminals (the so-called *vory-v-zakone*, see Ch. 7) such as Invan'kov (Yaponchik), Kachiloriya (Peso), Bagdasaryan (Rafik-Svo) and others. In 1985, he started his own business, the 21st Century Association, and the Sportsmen's Social Protection Fund. He headed the Sportsmen's Social Protection Fund named after the Russian goalkeeper Lev Yashin and became one of the founders and the director of a Sports Academy, devoted to encouraging sports in Russia. In 1993, he even founded a party supposedly devoted to the interests of sportsmen—Sportsmen of Russia. In August 1993, his brother was killed in a day shoot-out with members of a Chechen

Notes, pp. 68–71

criminal group. On 5 April 1994, he was killed in broad daylight outside a Moscow bathhouse. 'Moscow entertainment and athletic elite' attended his funeral (*Washington Post*, 16 Apr. 1994). Among many possible sources on Kvantrishvili, see *Komsomol'skaya Pravda*, 9 Apr. 1994; Martinetti, 1995: 7–41; Modestov, 1996: 276–89.

77. *Moscow Times*, 16 Apr. 1994. Private protection may also be supplied by gangs of young people who, out of pure pleasure, enjoy patrolling a certain area and exercising their physical strength on innocent victims. A gang of these young people, who make a cult of physical fitness, emerged in Moscow in the 1980s. The *Lyubery*, named after a working class suburb of Moscow, are a party of clean-cut, karate-trained lads who in the early 1990s raided in the capital in order to 'cleanse' it of hippies, heavy-metal rock fans, and other representatives of 'Western decadence', apparently with the tacit support of police (Tsypkin, 1989: 16). According to *Kommersant* (26 Dec. 1990), the gang made use of its skills in the market for protection, co-ordinating a prostitution ring. It is also reported to protect street players of shell games and other confidence games.

78. *La Repubblica*, 30 July 1994.
79. Filippov, 1994: 1.
80. *Kriminal'naya Khronika*, no. 7, 1994. Gambetta documents how the Sicilian mafia intervenes to collect debts or delay repayment. See Gambetta, 1993*a*: 167–71.
81. *Komsomol'skaya Pravda*, 27 Dec. 1994.
82. Ibid.
83. *Literaturnaya Gazeta*, 12 Jan. 1993.
84. *The Irish Times*, 3 Mar. 1999.
85. This story has been reported by Alla Andreeva on the Moscow's weekly *Stolitsa* and recounted in Martinetti, 1995: 119–22.
86. Filippov, 1994: 1. On the Filippov's Report, see Varese (1999).
87. *The St Petersburg Times*, 10–17 Feb. 1997.
88. In the US, the mafia offered its services both to employers in order to control trade unions in the harbour industry and to trade unions in order to scare employers off (Block, 1983; Reuter, 1987, p. vii). In Sicily in 1920 alone the mafia murdered four trade union officials. In the period 1945–65 the same hands killed 41 leaders of the peasant movement (Hess, 1973: 141–2; Lupo, 1996: 199). To the extent that the labour movement provides protection and ensures property rights to the peasants, it is a direct competitor of the mafia. The mafia would have no ideological reasons to refuse supporting workers but objects to others doing it (Gambetta, 1993*a*: 93–4).
89. Not surprisingly, Kuzbass coal costs an average price of $26 to $28 per ton, compared with $12 to $15 a ton for US coal (*Moscow Times*, 4 Feb. 1998).
90. *Moscow Times*, 11 Feb. 1999.

Chapter 4

1. During the 1890s, circles of the Russian Social Democratic Party were active in Perm and the Party Committee was founded in 1902. Motovilikha, the industrial part of Perm (which was not yet within the city limits), was the most revolutionary and controlled by the Bolsheviks during the Revolution. In December 1905, the workers of the Motovilikhinskii Zavod—the oldest plant in the city, opened in 1736 and still operating today—and the railroad workers joined in a political strike. On 12–13 Dec. 1905, a battle erupted in Perm between workers and Tsarist military forces.

2. As I noted above, the area of Motovilikha, the most industrialized part of what is Perm today, did not come under the Perm Soviet, but was governed by a Motovilikha Soviet, controlled by the Bolsheviks.

3. Pipes, 1995: 60–1.

4. Rowland, 1998: 276. Russians make up 90.1 per cent of the population of the city and 83.9 per cent of the Perm region. The Komi-Permyak ethnic group accounts for 4 per cent of the Region's population. This population is concentrated in the north of the region, at the border with the Komi Autonomous Republic. Other ethnic communities in the region are: Tatar (4.9 per cent), Bashkir (1.7 per cent), Ukrainians (1.5 per cent), Udmurt (1.1 per cent) and Others (2.9 per cent) (Administratsiya Permskoi Oblasti, 1993).

5. Despite this, 'improvements in the social infrastructure (health, education facilities) were insignificant during the 1980s, and the natural environment has deteriorated' (McAuley, 1992: 47–8).

6. McAuley, 1992: 51.

7. By mid-1994, the share of state property as a percentage of all property (measured in output production) was 17 per cent, as opposed to a national average of 50.6 per cent. In the region, joint-stock companies and societies employ two-thirds of the working population and produce 88 per cent of the total volume of production. (Data by the Statistical Department of the Regional Administration in *Mestnoe Vremya*, 12 July 1994.)

8. According to the US Department of Commerce (3 Sept. 1999), annual extraction exceeds 9 million metric tons of oil and 500 million cubic meters of gas and 50 per cent of Russia's magnesium, 98 per cent of its potassium and most of its titanium ore come from Perm. See also Sagers, 1996: 570.

9. *Profil'*, 20 June 1999.

10. Clem and Craumer, 1995*b*: 596.

11. Data from Clem and Craumer, 1995*a*.

12. Clem and Craumer, 1996.

13. The number of crimes connected to the illegal sale of drugs increased by 40 per cent when compared with the previous year (N = 280), while the

number of crimes with the use of fire arms dropped by 40 per cent (N = 107). *Dos'e 02*, 20 Jan. 1995.

14. The English word 'hooliganism' should not be confused with the Russian equivalent: the Russian term is defined in article 206 of the Soviet Russian Republic (RSFSR) Criminal Code: 'Intentional actions flagrantly violating public order and expressing a clear disrespect for society.' The Criminal Code distinguishes among petty, ordinary, malicious, and especially malicious hooliganism (see also *Ugolovnyi Kodeks Rossiiskoi Federatsii*, 1993, art. 206).

15. *Zvezda*, 28 Nov. 1995.

16. *Megalopolis-Express*, 6 July 1994.

17. *Dos'e 02*, 20 Jan. 1995. This figure was 58.5 per cent in 1995 and 62.3 per cent in 1996. In that year (1996), the Russian average was 70 per cent.

18. *Dos'e 02*, 20 Jan. 1995.

19. *Zvezda*, 28 Nov. 1995.

20. *Dos'e 02*, 20 Jan. 1995.

21. The selection of one's sample is—as pointed out in *Notes and Queries in Anthropology*—'to some extent determined by circumstances beyond the investigator's control' (1951: 43), and so it was in the case of kiosk owners in this study. I contacted Inna, the first interviewee, through an acquaintance of mine at the local university. She then introduced me to some colleagues of hers who worked in her neighbourhood. At that point, a chain was established and a 'snowball sample' was obtained (on 'snow-ball sampling', see Johnson, Boster, and Holbert, 1989). The selection of interviewees based on 'between-ness' proved important for checking the validity of each response. Equipped with an increasing knowledge of the area and the individuals involved, I was able to improve upon the factual precision of their responses. At the same time, I could draw on Sasha, Lyuba, and Olga for information concerning other parts of the city.

22. In the former Soviet Union, such posts would be filled only by people who had been 'approved' by the officials of a party committee. The sum total of these positions constituted the *nomenklatura*. On the contrary, factory workers, students, shop assistants, and even factory engineers would not need such high-level approval to obtain their position and theirs would not qualify as a *nomenklatura* position. See Rigby, 1990 and below, Appendix B.

23. Bers, 1970: 19.

24. Ibid.

25. Schelling, 1971.

26. In April 1994, Moscow Mayor Yurii Luzhkov declared that the 'age of the kiosk is over' and dedicated himself to ridding city streets of the 16,000 aluminium booths that had sprung up since 1988. The process has been accompanied by charges that kiosks are unsightly and unsanitary. Kiosks have been also accused of being a source of crime (*International Herald Tri-*

bune, 3 Apr. 1995). The Moscow press have hailed Luzhkov's move. *Vechernyaya Moskva* headlined the story: 'The Moscow Government Stops Kidding around with Kiosk Owners' (4 Apr. 1994). *Moskovskii Komsomolets* also carried a similar article (3 Apr. 1994).

27. Inna had been selling fruit and vegetables from a truck for some time when she decided to open her kiosk. After having operated her kiosk for three months, she was, at the time of the interview (June 1994), renting it to somebody else and planning to sell it.

28. Afanas'ev, 1994: 14.

29. He added, rather tellingly, that, by contrast, 'people from the racket never take things from my kiosk: if they want something, they pay for it. This makes sense, because they are protecting me, they do not want to ruin me' (K5).

30. *Zvezda*, 3 Jan. 1993.

31. *Literaturnaya Gazeta*, 1 Dec. 1994.

32. The attitudes towards the state and in particular towards the taxation system revealed a parallel with the respondents of the Charap and Webster study (1993: 305). Twelve out of eighteen interviewees identified erratic and unfair taxation as their largest problem. Other problems included—in this order—inflation, unclear regulations and policies, and ineffective banking.

33. Similar arrangements have also been reported by Ledeneva (1998*b*).

34. 'Once, I was alone and confronted by some Georgians and Armenians who asked me: "who are you working for?" (which meant: "who is protecting you?"). I answered "I work for myself". At this point, they started to scare me and when Sasha arrived, we left' (K1).

35. *Zvezda*, 21 July 1995.

36. As a British journalist put it, '[in Moscow] ironically, the hoods use the very pages of advertising newspapers . . . to find out who is selling what, so that they can tax them appropriately' (*Independent*, 3 Feb. 1994).

37. Serio, 1997: 97. See ibid for another instance of fly-by-night protectors.

38. Committee on Governmental Affairs, 1996: 50. Businessmen also sometimes bluff their connections with high-ranking 'roofs': 'Some businessmen interviewed [by the American Chamber of Commerce] said that there is a strong element of smoke-and-mirrors involved in the *krysha* question. "There is a huge amount of bluffing going on," said one Western business consultant. The bluff may simply be the phone number of a well-connected landlord from your former premises, or the fact that your office is located in a building connected to an influential official' (*Moscow Times*, 31 Oct. 1995). This phenomenon occurs not only when Mafia groups are emerging for the first time. Gambetta was the first to notice it for Sicily: 'A local [Palermo] entrepreneur told me the (to him hilarious) story of a northern firm doing business in Sicily on a large contract. The firm was approached by a man making the vague sorts of threats for which Mafiosi

are renowned. So sure had they been that someone would at some point demand protection money in precisely this way that they took it for granted he was the person. They paid up for about two years before realising they had been conned' (Gambetta, 1993a: 34). Another instance is recalled by Antonio Calderone, a prominent Catania Mafioso turned state witness. An employee of a northern firm operating in Catania started to make extortion calls to the manager, posing as a real Mafioso. It turned out that the same firm employed Calderone himself, precisely in order to be protected. The employee was duly killed (Gambetta, 1993a: 34). Mafia impostors have been reported also in Hong Kong. A senior officer of the Triad Society Bureau recalls: 'Toward the end of 1973, a total of 57 people in good occupations were telephoned by a man who demanded money from them in the name of a triad society . . . all paid except one and as a result of this report to the police, an arrest was made and police learned about the other offences. The person concerned had made a very large sum of money and was never a member of a triad society at all' (*South China Morning Post*, 30 June 1975, quoted in Chu, 1996: 98). For a formal model that addresses this question, see Smith and Varese, 2001.

39. *Zvezda*, 18 Jan. 1995.
40. Posner, 1980 and Landa, 1994.
41. Drawing on economic theory, Landa has argued that such a group is a 'low cost club-like institutional arrangement' (1994: 102). Club-like goods induce consumers to share ownership and limit the number of users. Golf clubs and swimming pools are often quoted examples: even very rich consumers find it senseless to buy an entire golf ground for themselves, but do not want too many players on the green.
42. A respondent in Ledeneva's study (1998a: 173) recalls: 'It was extremely difficult to get recruited into the *nomenklatura*. Marriage could help a lot. I remember one person who was a foreman of a workshop at the plant, and in half a year became a deputy of the Minister of Industry in such a way.'
43. Further evidence is needed to explore a related issue, namely entrance into the network. Can someone who did not belong to the former *nomenklatura* have access to the 'services' it supplies to its members?
44. Gambetta, 1993a: 31–2.

Chapter 5

1. All the names have been changed.
2. Filippov, 1994: 2, emphasis added.
3. Jones and Moskoff, 1991: 85–6, emphasis added.
4. *Novoe russkoe slovo*, 15 Jan. 1990, quoted by Jones and Moskoff, 1991: 85.
5. *Trud*, 19 May 1990, quoted by Jones and Moskoff, 1991: 85.

6. The average daily turn-over of the kiosks in Visim was 220,000–250,000 roubles and was distributed as follows: 30,000–50,000 went to the sellers and garbage collectors; 70,000–80,000 for taxes; 40,000 to night protection (K1–9).

7. Flexibility is reported also in some instances in Moscow. The owner of a dental clinic in Moscow maintains, 'I pay in cash the first of each month— a respectable person with a briefcase arrives in a Volvo 850. This summer we installed new equipment, and I told the *krysha*: "Guys, I've had very big expenses, so I can't pay for three months." They did not bother me for three months, but at the end of the period, exactly on the first of the month, the guy with the briefcase showed up once again.' *Moscow Times*, 31 Oct. 1995. A racketeer interviewed by *Moskovskaya Pravda* (4 Feb. 1992) put it as follows: 'the important thing is not to be too greedy. The "taxpayer" should continue to work, make profit, have an interest in increasing his capital and not go and hang himself out of despair or, worse, report us to the police.' Reportedly, criminal protectors in Moscow allowed their victims to delay payment after the August 1998 crisis. See *Moskovskii Komsomolets*, 22–29 Oct. 1998.

8. *Zvezda*, 22 Mar. 1994.

9. *Zvezda*, 22 Mar. 1994.

10. See the interview with Sorokin in *Zvezda*, 27 May 1995.

11. *Zvezda*, 27 May 1995.

12. *Zvezda*, 11 June 1994; *Zvezda*, 27 May 1995; *Zvezda*, 28 Nov. 1995; J1. The Chief of city UVD, Col. Salakhov, declared in a Nov. 1995 interview: 'Now I have the names of the killers of sergeant Vlasov. These are the hardened criminals Semenov and Popov, with previous convictions. They were arrested and the pistol that killed Vlasov was confiscated. They have been charged with two murders, two cases of causing severe bodily harm with lethal consequences, and of nineteen robberies. I hope that they will not be released on bail' (*Zvezda*, 28 Nov. 1995).

13. *Dos'e 02*, 4 Apr. 1997.

14. See above, p. 90.

15. Anvar's resentment towards Petr (and vice versa) was probably due to the fact that both engage in the informal economy (the informal economy is defined as trading in licit goods obtained eluding established rules. See Castells and Portes, 1989). Petr used to buy his merchandise from a warehouse, which did not issue quality certificates. In this way, he was able to save some money, though not as much as Anvar. This is how Petr put it: 'I could buy my stuff from the warehouse either with quality certificates or without certificates. This certificate is mandatory, but obviously more expensive. So I bought goods without the certificate and got fake certificates' (K2).

16. Along the same lines, Evgeniya asserted: 'The "roof" is able to solve any problem, not only of a professional nature, but also, personal; for instance,

if you need a car, or to get your telephone connected quickly, or if you have problems with your flat' (Y1).

17. See the article by Irina Krasnosel'skikh in *Zvezda* (29 Dec. 1990). This section is based on her reports and the additional information I gathered by interviewing Mrs Krasnosel'skikh (J1).

18. *Argumenty i Fakty-AIF-Prikam'e* (supplement), 28 July 1999.

19. Interview with Boris Sorokin in *Zvezda*, 27 May 1995 and M4.

20. *Obshchaya gazeta*, 17–23 Aug. 1995.

21. Mafia bosses in the movie *The Godfather* (Dir. Francis Ford Coppola, 1972) greet each other in same way.

22. For the concept of 'focal point' see Schelling, 1960.

23. Chu, 1996: 115.

24. See e.g. Olson, 2000.

25. Cf. Gambetta, 1993*a*: 7.

Chapter 6

1. See Terts [Sinyavsky], 1973; Bukovsky, 1978. A museum of the Gulag has now opened at this camp site. See G1; G2; *Permskie Novosti*, 10 July 1998; *Permskie Novosti*, 18 Aug. 1998; *Zvezda*, 25 Aug. 1998; *Moscow Times*, 8 July 2000.

2. Shelley, 1980: 113.

3. Matthews, 1972: 54, quoted by Shelley, 1980: 113–14.

4. Lipson and Chalidze, 1977: 175.

5. Gernet, 1927: 160.

6. Shelley, 1980: 114.

7. Corrective Labour Colony (ITK) no. 6—located near the city of Solikamsk—is also known as Belyi Lebed' (The White Swan). It is famed for its especially harsh living conditions and was visited by several prisoners' rights organizations. See V. Karnaukhov's extensive report on Belyi Lebed' in *Zvezda*, 16 Oct. 1995. It now houses criminals serving life sentences (*Zvezda*, 27 Jan. 2000).

8. *Mestnoe Vremya*, 27 June 1995.

9. *Megalopolis-Express*, 6 July 1994.

10. *Dos'e 02*, 4 Jan. 1993.

11. An interview with Zykov has appeared in *Zvezda* 2 Aug. 1991; see also *Zvezda*, 18 July 1991; *Zvezda* 15 Mar. 1994; *Zvezda* 28 Nov. 1995 and *Zvezda*, 23 June 1998.

12. *Zvezda*, 3 Oct. 1997.

13. *Zvezda*, 3 Oct. 1997. See also *Zvezda*, 6 Sept. 1994.

14. The habit of drinking is strictly forbidden among Sicilian and American mafiosi and it can lead to expulsion from the organization. Buscetta offers an explanation of this ban: 'a drunken person has no secret while a

mafioso must keep self-control and decency in every circumstances. I never met an alcoholic man of honour, neither in Sicily nor anywhere else' (Arlacchi, 1994: 159). The vast majority of the gangs studied by Jankowski strictly prohibited the use of heroin, the rational being that 'the addict has allegiance only to the drug, and undermines the gang's effort to build allegiance to, and trust in, the organization' (1991: 80).

15. The existence of funds to support the families of gang's members while they are in prison or incapacitated is a widespread phenomenon among organized and fairly stable criminal groups. Both the Japanese Yakuza and the Sicilian mafia take care of the member's natural family during incarceration or physical impediment and pay legal fees (Stark 1981: 90; Arlacchi, 1994: 189).

16. Thimblerig is a game where the operator rapidly moves about three inverted thimbles, often with sleight of hand, one of which conceals a token, the other player betting on which thimble the token is under.

17. *Zvezda*, 29 Dec. 1990.

18. On paper, sentencing was harsh: Moroz got seven years, Plotnikov six, Sizov and Ganiev five, Lun'kov and the rest of the gang three years. However, those who were sentenced to three years had their term suspended. Plotnikov, Sizov, and Ganiev were already out by late 1992, while Moroz died in jail the following year. *Zvezda*, 29 Dec. 1990.

19. Permskoe UVD 1995.

20. Ibid.

21. Ibid.

22. Ibid.

23. Ibid.

24. Ibid.

25. *Zvezda*, 13 July 1996.

26. Ibid.

27. Ten out of fifteen defendants were convicted, including Belyaev, for 5 years. See *Zvezda*, 13 July 1996 and M3.

28. Ovchinskii notes that Perm's criminal world 'was also able to forge links with corrupted officials in the City and Regional administration, including law-enforcement and military structures' (1993: 66).

29. *Zvezda*, 11 June 1994; *Megalopolis-Express* 6 July 1994; Boris Sorokin in *Zvezda*, 27 May 1995.

30. *Zvezda*, 5 July 1994. While in Perm, I saw a video of both gatherings, taken by an attendant of the gathering and confiscated by the police (M4).

31. See the interview with Boris Sorokin, head of the Regional Department for Combating Organized Crime, in *Zvezda*, 27 May 1995.

32. Ovchinskii, 1993: 64.

33. Ibid. 65.

34. Ibid.

35. Other victims of the conflict are mentioned by Sorokin in *Zvezda*, 27 May

1995. In 1998, the procurator's office of the Perm Region concluded that Fokin was killed by one of the Mingaleev brothers. Mingaleev accused Fokin of the murder of his brother (*Zvezda*, 6 Jan. 1998).

36. When Yakutenok was freed, a number of welcoming inscriptions on the walls of the main street, Komsomol'skii Prospect, appeared (*Zvezda*, 15 Mar. 1994).

37. *Zvezda*, 3 June 1994; Ovchinskii, 1993: 65.

38. Ovchinskii, 1993: 65; *Zvezda*, 27 May 1995.

39. *Zvezda*, 6 Sept. 1994; *Mestnoe Vremya*, 16 Dec. 1994.

40. Art. 218 and 224 of the Criminal Code (*Zvezda*, 27 May 1995).

41. According to one version, Yakutenok's influence started to decline in conjunction with the decline of the influence of Moscow-based Georgian *vor-v-zakone* Mikho Tsitsadze (*Mestnoye Vremiya*, 7 Feb. 1997).

42. *Dos'e 02*, 13 Oct. 1995; *Zvezda*, 13 Oct. 1995.

43. See the reconstruction of this conflict in *Zvezda*, 23 Dec. 1999.

44. *Zvezda*, 5 July 1997; *Argumenty I Fakty*, 20 Aug. 1997. On 20 June 2000, the body of Krest was found next to the Perm–Lyady highway (*Novyi Kompan'on*, 27 June 2000).

45. See *Permskie Novosti*, 23 June 1998 and 25 June 1998; *Mestnoe Vremya*, 24 June 1998; *Zvezda*, 23 June 1998; *Dos'e 02*, no. 26/1998.

46. *Dos'e 02*, no. 26/1998. A different, rather unconvincing, reason given for the murder of Yakut refers to his part in taking the title of *vor* away from a Chechen criminal who proved unworthy of it.

47. *Zvezda*, 23 June 1998.

48. They carried IZH-71pistols. A security firm with the same name operates in Moscow.

49. *Zvezda*, 30 Oct. 1998.

50. For a review of this debate, see Graebner Anderson (1979: ch. 1), Gambetta (1993*a*: 100–2 and 290–1), Chu (1996: 29–31) and Lupo (1996: 223–4).

51. President Commission, 1967: 6. The 1965 Oyster Bay conferences on organized crime portrayed the mafia as highly organized: 'It is totalitarian in its organisation. A way of life, it imposes rigid discipline on underlings who do the dirty work while the top men of organised crime are generally insulated from the criminal act and the consequent danger of prosecution' (*Combating Organised Crime*, 1966: 19, quoted in Graebner Anderson, 1979: 10).

52. Gambetta, 1993*a*: 111.

53. Ibid. 112.

54. Alternative suppliers exist in Sicily. In Catania, three independent groups—Cargagnusi, Malpassotti, and Cursoti—operate outside the Cosa Nostra. Also, so-called *stidde* (lit. stars) groups compete with Cosa Nostra in Agrigento and Trapani (Gambetta: 1993*a*: 154).

55. Gambetta, 1993*a*: 114.

56. Ibid. 114–16. Arlacchi, having argued against the view of the mafia as an organised entity (see Arlacchi 1983), has later modified his position:

'The testimony of Antonino Calderone forces us to recognise that the mafia *also* is a formal organisation, contrary to what the almost totality of authors, including myself, has maintained so far' (1992: p. vii). Save for the introduction, written by Professor Arlacchi, the book *Gli uomini del disonore* (Arlacchi, 1992) contains the testimony of Antonino Calderone, a mafioso turned state witness, and should be considered as primary source.

57. Bell (1988[1953]), p. 139. The early anti-mafia reports, including the Kefauver's, stressed the Italian origin of the mafia, fuelling an 'Alien conspiracy theory'. According to Lupo (1996: 210), American liberals such as Bell, who opposed ethnic labelling, reacted by interpreting the mafia as an instance of bossism and petty corruption. This however did not stop Ianni (see below) to invoke a purely ethnic interpretation of the mafia and argue *against* it being hierarchically structured.

58. Smith and Alba, 1979.

59. Ianni, 1976: 42; see also Ianni, 1974. Similarly, Albini (1971: 88) argues that 'the Mafia' is a method or a modus operandi, which can exist everywhere.

60. Hess, 1973: p. ix.

61. Hess, 1973: 76; this passage is also quoted by Gambetta, 1993a: 291. In a different part of his book, Hess depicts the mafia as 'small clique-like associations which are independent of each other but maintain relations with one another, which support each other, make arrangements with each other, at times take joint action, but on occasions can be at daggers drawn' (1973: 11). As pointed out by Gambetta (1993a: 291), this passage seems to suggest that some organization and co-ordination exist, and is in contradiction to the one quoted above.

62. Respectively, Chubb, 1982: 140 and Catanzaro, 1985: 34–6. According to Duggan (1989), 'mafia' is a word of abuse that political factions of all sorts level at each other.

63. *South China Morning Post*, 17 Dec. 1975, quoted in Chu, 1996: 78.

64. Gambetta and Reuter, 1995: 119.

65. See Reuter, 1987.

66. He added that often people who work for them are disguised as private security guards. Interview with Aleksandr Markanov (successor of Col. Sorokin) in *Mestnoe Vremya*, 20 May 1998.

67. Igor', Evgeniya's friend, also appears in Ch. 5.

68. J1, *Izvestiya*, 18 Feb. 1995.

69. *Mestnoe Vremya*, 20 May 1998.

70. Gambetta, 1993a: 68.

71. As described by the President Commission, 1967, Arlacchi, 1992, Ch. 2 and Gambetta, 1993a.

72. Jankowski, 1991: 71–2. These are usually divided into various smaller units (called *klikas*), each one fairly independent of the overall gang leader. This gang as a whole is a loose association of *klikas*. Under pressure from outside challenges, one gang agreed to set up a ruling body of about six members, each elected by their respective *klikas*.

73. Gambetta, 1993a: 111.
74. Arlacchi, 1992: 146.
75. Gambetta, 1993a: 66.
76. Arlacchi: 1994: 167.
77. Gambetta, 1993a: 191.
78. Ibid. 30.
79. Ibid. 124.
80. Evidence of the existence of the *commissione* in Sicily emerged roughly fifteen years after its first meeting, see ibid. 112.
81. Schneider, 1994: 111.
82. See ibid.
83. Gambetta, 1993a: 112.

Chapter 7

1. Santerre, 1960: 88. The Soviet government abducted the author in 1945. Because of his unruly behaviour and escape attempts he was put among prisoners (usually criminals), 'refusing labour and discipline' (*otritsalovka*). This gave Santerre an opportunity to mix mainly with criminals (p. 3). On *otritsalovka*, see Rossi, 1989.
2. Santerre, 1960: 92, see also Likhachev, 1935: 62.
3. Santerre, 1960: 63. In some instances, *vory* showed compassion and respect towards men of the church, as they showed high spirituality (Santerre, 1960: 80; See also Glazov, [1976] 1985: 39).
4. Santerre, 1960: 89, Glazov, [1976]1985: 39. Gurov writes of a *vory* tattoo picturing the suits of aces inside a cross and symbolizing membership into the society. In his view, criminals had tattoos 'to prove their strength. The tattoo also had a "communication function". It helped the recidivists to recognize each other'. Accordingly, the *vory* sought to maintain exclusive use of their tattoo designs; non-*vory* found wearing them were punished by death (Gurov, 1990: 111). For a study of prisoners' tattoos see Bronnikov, 1996.
5. This idiom attracted the interest of Dmitrii Likhachev, who stressed the 'magical nature' of the word for these criminals and drew a parallel between primitive people and *vory*. He also noticed that knowledge of the jargon enabled a *vor* to fully assert his position among other criminals (Likhachev, 1935: 63). Chalidze provides a brief discussion of the origin of this language. He maintains that it emerged out of 19th-cent. criminal argot, which in turn was a combination of peddlers' speech, sailors' slang as well as Yiddish and Romany. He concludes that the jargon was greatly influenced by the advent of the Gulag camp system: 'Today . . . there is a great deal of overlapping between prison speech and thieves' slang' (Chalidze, 1977: 57).
6. Santerre, 1960: 63.

7. On this episode of Russian history, see M. Gorky *et al.*, 1935. See also Likhachev's recently published own memoirs (Likhachev, 1995).
8. Likhachev, 1935: 55.
9. Gurov, 1990: 108; see also Gurov, 1995: 104.
10. Quoted in Gurov, 1990: 115.
11. GARF, 9414/4/202/1-40.
12. Monakhov, 1957: 38.
13. GARF, 8131/32/5501/9; GARF, 8131/32/5501/34-5; GARF, 8131/32/4961/14; GARF, 8131/32/6881/26.
14. GARF, 8131/32/4961/63. See also GARF, 8131/32/7037/11 for a report on a *vor* active in Kiev region.
15. Gurov, 1990: 116.
16. Rituals also mark the entry in other organized criminal groups, such as the Japanese Yakuza, the Hong Kong Triads, the Sicilian Mafia, and American Cosa Nostra. The extent to which individual members do actually follow the code of conduct is a different issue.
17. Monakhov, 1957: 9.
18. Ch. was arrested in 1981 and, in the 1980s, was serving his sentence in the Voronezh region. His criminal career includes seven convictions and 25 years behind bars. He agreed to reveal the traditions and rules of the *vory* and completed thirteen notebooks. Gurov collected this evidence and relied on this material for the treatment of the *vory* in his book *Professional'naya prestupnost'* (1990). Later, Gurov and Ryabinin published extracts of the notebooks in Gurov and Ryabinin, 1990; Gurov and Ryabinin, 1991*a*; and Gurov and Ryabinin, 1991*b*.
19. See Falcone and Padovani, 1991: 100. For the meaning of *legavyi*, see Dubyagin and Teplitskii, 1993.
20. Discipline in the Krasnoyarskii krai prisons had been the subject of some concern. According to a report dated 8 Aug. 1939, 'there is practically no cell isolation between prisoners in Krasnoyarskii common prison. By use of threads, cords, ropes, and even planks prisoners systematically pass correspondence, objects, and products from one cell to another. Meetings between prisoners from different cells during transfers became a common practice' (GARF, 9401/1a/0252/10-11). For a similar report for prison no. 1 in the Saratovskii Region see GARF, 9401/1a/0251/6-7.
21. Santerre also refers to *ksivy*. '*Blatnye* refer to their letters as *ksivy* and attach them the importance of a document . . . Such letters are always written by a collectivity and signed *brattsy vory* or *brattsy urki*' (1960: 90).
22. Monakhov, 1957: 7. Monakhov adds that a period of at least three years is necessary to aspire to enter the society: 'In order to become *vor*, one must steal for at least three years, under the guidance of experienced *vory*. The person is called *patsan* and, if he is deemed deserving, he is then allowed to take the oath' (p. 8). No restrictions as far as nationality or religion applied (p. 15).

23. Likhachev, 1935: 61.
24. The way of transmitting coded information was very sophisticated, perfected by many generations of criminals. It consisted of a cryptographic language, which the police claimed to have broken. Every sender had his own code of numbers. Criminals also devised a system to pass information from one camp to another (referred to, in police documents, as 'the postal system'). The spreading of precise information was necessary to inform the prison population about new crownings. It was also crucial for prisoners in one camp to know the destination of a convict who had been transferred. If there were suspicions that he had collaborated with the camp authorities, convicts could organize punishment by fellow criminal bosses in the new camp. A reference to the above is found in Gurov (1993: 38). The study which provides a full description of the code is Bronnikov, 1994.
25. Gurov and Ryabinin, 1990: 82. 'According to the law, there is a complete democracy among *blatnye*, however a scarcely noticeable yet very strong gradation of hierarchy exists. At the top there are the so-called *pakhany* (*pakhan* means father in the *vory* jargon)' (Santerre, 1960: p. 64, see 63). Those who aspired to become *vory*, or, in Sicilian Mafia jargon, to be 'made' members, belonged to the same environment and abided to the same rules of behaviour as the 'made' members.
26. The 'code of conduct' is described in several official documents. In some cases documents reproduce testimonies and declarations of former *vory*, See for instance the notes by *vor* Sherman in a report to the Deputy Procurator General of the USSR, dated 16 June 1956 (GARF, 8131/32/4961/56) and those by *vor* A. M. Bulatov in GARF, 8131/32/4961/12.
27. GARF, 8131/32/4961/27. See also Gurov, 1990: 113. A related rule, reported by Likhachev (1935: 58), is that a *vor* is not supposed to ask a direct question to another *vor*: 'We must note that the rules of proper *vory* behaviour do not allow a thief to ask questions.' Likhachev continues: 'This is not only a precautionary measure in order to keep secrets. This rule lies deep in the language consciousness of thieves and is connected with their subconscious belief in the magic power of the word.' These rules should be evaluated in the context of camp life, where a well-oiled network of informers operated (Graziosi, 1992: 428).
28. Gurov, 1990: 111. The rule prohibiting quarrelling with other members is the fourth rule (out of eight) recited during the Sicilian initiation ritual. See Arlacchi, 1992: 57.
29. Monakhov, 1957: 14; Chalidze, 1977: 54. Shalamov (1994: 413) noticed that newly acquainted *vory* supported each other.
30. Monakhov, 1957: 15.
31. Santerre, 1960: 92.
32. Monakhov, 1957: 14; Santerre, 1960: 62.
33. The rule prohibiting the use of violence between members of the society is

shared by the Japanese Yakuza, the Hong Kong Triads, the Sicilian Mafia, and American Cosa Nostra.

34. GARF, 8131/32/4961/32.

35. GARF, 8131/32/4961/26-7; GARF, 8131/32/4961/62; Monakhov, 1957: 13.

36. See GARF, 8131/32/4961/27; GARF, 8131/32/4961/15 ('we did not plant the forest, so we will not cut it either'); Monakhov, 1957: 11; Santerre, 1960: 51, 64, and 111; and Glazov, [1976]1985: 54 and 239. Monakhov (1957: 28) elaborates fiddling work reports.

37. Santerre, 1960: 63. See also Monakhov, 1957: 14. Refusal to work put the *vory* in the same position as radical Christians, the so-called *Krestiki*, who categorically refused to obey any order coming from the Soviet regime (Santerre, 1960: 53).

38. Official documents refer to hardened criminals who 'systematically refused to work' (GAPO, R-1461/28/2, dated 1940) and went as far as self-mutilating themselves (e.g. GARF, 9401/1a/179/48-49, dated 8 Apr. 1943). Only in the last six months of 1955, 120 letters from ordinary convicts were sent to N. A. Bulganin, then prime minister of the USSR. The letters contain detailed complaints against '*vory-zakonniki*' refuzing to work and victimizing ordinary convicts (see GARF, 8131/32/4961/60).

39. 'It is strange, but the camp administration almost always takes into consideration what the *blatnye* are supposed and not supposed to do, thus avoiding sure troubles' (Santerre, 1960: 63).

40. Monakhov, 1957: 12; Gurov, 1990: 108.

41. Santerre, 1960: 56.

42. Shalamov, [1959] 1992: 5–96.

43. Hereafter, we shall refer in particular to his 'Such'ya voina' and 'Zhenshchina blatnogo mira', both written in 1959 (the latter is translated into English as 'Women of the Criminal World' in Shalamov, 1994: 415–31).

44. Shalamov, 1994: 428–9. Chalidze, on the contrary, takes the cult of motherhood at face value and adds: 'Cases are known in which a thief who is hard pressed by the police risked arrest in order to visit and help his mother' (Chalidze, 1977: 53).

45. Monakhov, 1957: 12. Gurov, 1990: 111 makes the same point.

46. Shalamov, 1994: 419. See also Santerre, 1960: 92.

47. It appears that indifference to the natural family is greater among the traditional *vory* than in other criminal organizations, such as the American Mafia, the Sicilian Mafia, and the Japanese Yakuza. Commitment to the 'family' should be the criminal's primary concern, but attachment to one own natural family is considered acceptable. See Demaris (1981: 4), Arlacchi (1992: 58) and Stark (1981: 89–90).

48. Chalidze, 1977: 52.

49. Ibid.

50. Ibid. 51–2.

51. Shalamov, 1994: 420. Women criminals—their bodies, like the men's, covered with tattoos—existed and were referred to with a variety of words, including *vorovka*, *blatnaya*, *blatnyachka*, and *vorovaika* (Santerre, 1960: 89, 92; Tregubov, 1959: 147). Like the men, they refused to work and occasionally took part in crimes committed by the *vory*. They were not, however, allowed to enter the male fraternity. 'According to the law, a woman cannot enjoy the rights of *blatnye*, even less has she the right to interfere with the affairs of *vory* or discuss their behaviour. There are no *blatnye* women as such. There are the so-called *vorovaiki*. Most often they, even taking part in thefts, are reckoned as transitional wives of *vory*' (Santerre, 1960: 92). It remains unclear whether they formed a separate sorority of their own. This would be the subject of a separate study.

52. Chalidze, 1977: 53.

53. Cosa Nostra in Sicily operates according to a similar logic: 'One becomes a Man of honour mainly as a family inheritance, but not as straightforwardly as in the aristocracy (where the succession is automatic from father to son).' The candidate is under scrutiny for years, before being finally admitted into the organization (Arlacchi, 1992: 7).

54. GARF, 8131/32/6133/18, dated 22–7 Aug. 1958; Vardi, 1971: 31.

55. Glazov, [1976]1985: 44; Solzhenitsyn, 1980: 429.

56. Chalidze, 1977: 47. Soviet citizens were entitled to own items of personal property, as stated by art. 10 of the 1936 Soviet Constitution. See Varese, 1994: 235.

57. Santerre, 1960: 95.

58. Ibid. 62.

59. Both the Yakuza and Cosa Nostra have rules against appealing to the police or law. See Stark, 1981: 240 and Arlacchi, 1992: 57.

60. Shalamov, [1959] 1992: 61.

61. See the statement by prisoner A. M. Bulatov, in GARF, 8131/32/4961/11-13, dated 7 July 1955.

62. A letter published in Perm's weekly magazine devoted to criminal matters *Dos'e 02* (14 Sept. 1994) also testifies to this. The author, a convict, regrets that the criminals of the 1990s who claim to be the heirs of the traditional society have betrayed the old rules. As an indicator of such betrayal is the fact that new *vory* are murderers. 'Thieves-in-Law . . . do not exist any more. If they are thieves, they are not *in-law*, but rather *in-pen*. Thieves in the old times despised murderers, but now every second thief is a murderer. The thieves' law exists no more.' Though a restraint on the use of violence is typical of other organized criminal groups, an explicit rule against murder is peculiar to the *vory*.

63. Santerre, 1960: 56.

64. Ibid.; Glazov, [1976]1985: 45.

65. Monakhov, 1957: 18. See also Chalidze (1977: 52). Glazov ([1976]1985: 43) takes the view that *vory* could leave the fraternity. The procurator of the

Chaun-Chukotskii Corrective Labour camp writes in 1955 that 'It is impossible for *vor* to withdraw from this group in conditions of the camp, as well as in the settlements of the region, because he will be punished with death for that. He can withdraw from the group of *vory* partially in the central regions of the SU, if he wants to have a family' (GARF, 8131/32/3769/184).

66. Gurov and Ryabinin, 1991: 78. *Kalina Krasnaya* (The Red Snowball Tree, USSR, 1974, 100 mins), directed by Vasilii Shukshin, starring V. Shukshin, and Lydia Fedoseeva. After Egor is killed, a woman from the gang regrets his death. The gang's boss says: 'He was just a *muzhik*. There are a lot of them in Russia.'

67. Monakhov, 1957: 9, 14 and 21–4. Both Monakhov and the official documents of the camp administration (see e.g. GARF, 8131/32/4961/66; GARF, 8131/32/4961/58) stress the fascination with the *vory* among the youth and their ability to recruit young people.

68. Monakhov, 1957: 17 and 40. Calderone told Arlacchi: 'You will forgive me if I make this distinction between mafia and common criminals, but it really matters to me. It matters to all mafiosi. It is important: we are mafiosi, the others are ordinary men. We are men of honour. And not so much because we have taken an oath, but because we are the 'elite' of the underworld. We are far superior to common criminals. We are the worst' (Arlacchi, 1992: 5 quoted in Gambetta, 1993a: 46).

69. GARF, 8131/32/4961/34; Monakhov, 1957: 8, 14 and 30. GARF, 8131/32/4961/11.

70. Monakhov (1957: 27) reports that *vory* would extort from other prisoners up to 75 per cent of their earnings and 50 per cent of the value of postal orders. From letters of complaint sent by prisoners to the Soviet PM, the sum appears to be 50 per cent of earnings (GARF, 8131/32/4961/60). See also GARF, 8131/32/4961/10-11 and GARF, 8131/32/5501/38.

71. GARF, 8131/32/4961/64. This fund was also called *vorovskaya kassa* (GARF, 8131/32/4961/21, dated 20 July 1955) and *chernaya kassa* ('the black fund', Gurov, 1990: 231).

72. Monakhov, 1957: 29; GARF, 8131/32/5501/34-5.

73. Gurov, 1990: 115. *Vory* were of course tempted to steal *obshchak* money and, when found out, would be punished by fellow *vory* (see GARF, 8131/32/4961/21; GARF, 8131/32/4961/61).

74. Monakhov, 1957: 13.

75. Shalamov, 1994: 5. See also Shalamov, [1959] 1992: 60.

76. Likhachev, 1935: 56.

77. Likhachev, 1935: 56. On *vory* playing *shtos*, see also Artem'ev, 1956: 96.

78. Likhachev, 1935: 56.

79. Monakhov, 1957: 13; Artem'ev, 1956: 96–7; Glazov, [1976]1985: 44. For instance, *vor* Moshchalgin failed to pay a card debt to Ryabchenkov, also a *vor*, on 26 June 1954. The *vory*'s 'tribunal' sentenced Moshchalgin to

death. He was found dead on 30 July (GARF, 8131/32/4961/30). In another instance, *vor* Karpov lost a considerable sum of money to Mitrakov, another *vor* on 14 Aug. 1948. He was allowed to pay his debt by killing a prisoner named Perchikov, who barely survived the attack (GAPO, R-1366/3/177/14). *Vory* would also kill ordinary prisoners who refused to pay card debts (see e.g. GARF, 8131/32/4961/21).

80. Solzhenitsyn, 1974: 516. See also Solzhenitsyn, 1980: 492 and Santerre, 1960: 68 and 86.
81. Monakhov, 1957: 30.
82. See, for various instances, GARF, 8131/32/4961/63-6 and GARF, 8131/32/3769/185.
83. GARF, 8131/32/3769/185-7.
84. GARF, 8131/32/4961/34. Same point made in GARF, 8131/32/4961/57. See also GARF, 8131/32/6565/232.
85. Santerre, 1960: 55. The word *kodlo* is also used in official reports to refer to the *vory*'s unit in the camps. GARF, 8131/32/4961/56.
86. Monakhov, 1957: 16.
87. Santerre, 1960: 88.
88. Monakhov, 1957: 16–17.
89. Santerre, 1960: 55; Glazov, [1976]1985: 39; and Gurov, 1990: 115. Bukovsky wrote of the *vory* of the 1950s: 'Thieves traditionally lived in "families" and regarded one another as "brothers"' (Bukovsky, 1978: 245).
90. GARF, 8131/32/4961/62.
91. Likhachev, 1935: 55.
92. Shalamov, [1959] 1992: 60.
93. Shalamov, 1994: 420.
94. Monakhov, 1957: 18.
95. Ibid. 'Only in rare cases, when a *tolkovishche* takes place in a prison cell with other convicts, strangers may witness similar meetings' (Santerre, 1960: 57).
96. Santerre, 1960: 58.
97. Monakhov, 1957: 16; Gurov, 1990: 115.
98. See e.g. for a Moscow meeting: GARF, 8131/32/4961/62.
99. Monakhov, 1957: 18.
100. *Vory* were very sensitive to their public performance. Likhachev (1935: 59) notes that a popular motto of the *vory* was: 'In public, even death is beautiful.' By contrast, 'bragging and showing off' are prohibited among members of Cosa Nostra. See Arlacchi, 1992: 57.
101. Likhachev interprets *vory* boasting as shamans' practice. 'Boasting among thieves shares characteristics of the shamans' practice. They are boasting in order to strengthen their own power, self-control, self-confidence and at the same time to consolidate their power over their subordinates. The

majority of thieves' songs also bear an imprint of this boasting. The thieves' song is usually the story of a thief and his heroic deeds, often it is in the first person, singular or plural' (1935: 59–60).

102. Ibid. 59.

103. Ibid.; Gurov, 1990: 113.

104. According to Santerre (1960: 58), this penalty was called 'earthing' (*zemlenie*).

105. Santerre, 1960: 62–3.

106. For such cases, see e.g. Gurov, 1990: 114.

107. Santerre, 1960: 58 and Glazov, [1976]1985: 40. It might have been the case that the meeting decreed that a law-breaker was unworthy of being killed as *vor* and ordered to 'strangle or kill him with logs'. Nevertheless, he would never have been killed while asleep (Santerre, 1960: 58).

108. See the case narrated in 8131/32/3769/189-90.

109. See e.g. GARF, 8131/32/4961/26-30, dated 1 July 1955; GARF, 8131/32/4961/20, dated 20 July 1955; GARF, 8131/32/4961/32, dated 13 June 1956; Monakhov, 1957: 18.

110. GARF, 8131/32/3769/184; Monakhov, 1957: 18–19. In October 1953, *vor* Yurii Sysoev carried out a death sentence against his own brother, also a *vor* (GARF, 8131/32/4961/21).

111. The official report on this case remarks that the *vory* who killed the prisoner knew they were facing almost certain death but did not dare to disregard the decision of the gathering. Monakhov, 1957: pp. 19–20. For another instances, see GARF, 8131/32/4961/60-1 and Artem'ev, 1956: 97.

112. GARF, 8131/32/4961/64. The Siberian *vory* informed their brothers in the Ukraine of a recent decision of the camp administration and urged them to oppose such a decision, simultaneously organizing disturbances that were to take place in January 1955 across the entire Gulag.

113. GARF, 8131/32/4961/32. The same point is repeated in a report to the Deputy Procurator General of the USSR, dated 13 June 1956 (GARF, 8131/32/4961/57).

114. Rossi, 1989: 23.

115. Santerre, 1960: 60–1.

116. Monakhov, 1957: 35, 38.

117. Gurov, 1990: 108.

118. See Trakhtenberg, 1908; Popov, 1912; Potapov, 1927.

119. Likhachev, 1935: 47, 49, 55, 58.

120. GAPO, R-1366/3/177/14, dated 1948.

121. See e.g. GARF, 8131/32/4961/63, dated 27 July 1955.

122. See Shalamov, [1959] 1992: 64, 66, 68, 69, 70.

123. Vorida, 1971: 1, 5.

124. *Zapiski iz mertvogo doma* is based on the author's Siberian notebook, a series of 522 entries that he was able to write down while still in prison. Other sources include Chekhov (1895); Korolenko ([1885] 1966), and ([1886] 1966); Maksimov ([1871] 1891); and Mel'shin (1896).
125. See Dostoyevsky, [1861–2]1985: 41, 32, 84, 87.
126. Ibid. 101.
127. Rossi himself refers to this as a 'legend'. 'Legend has it that, during Tsarist times, the chief of a prison, without vacillating, would release even the most inveterate thief or killer, if the latter gave his word to come back' (Rossi, 1989: 55).
128. Doroshevich, [1903]1935: 37–8.
129. GAPO, 164/1/19/314.
130. See Frierson (1987: 62) and Frank (1999: 129–30). *Arteli* were of course not a feature of the criminal world only. For instance, Russian hunters in eastern Siberia in the 17th cent. organized themselves in *arteli*. See Bychkov (1994).
131. *Nedelya*, 1879 (no. 26): 780–5. See also *Yuridicheskii Zhurnal*, 1860 (no. 3): 189–214.
132. Yakushkin, 1896, quoted by Chalidze, 1977: 40–1.
133. Maksimov, 1869.
134. See Hechter, 1987.
135. Bacon, 1994: 37; see also pp. 27 and 11.
136. Bacon, 1994: 47. To have the full picture of forced labour in the Soviet Union between 1932 to 1947, roughly 2 million forced to reside in labour settlements should be added.
137. Zemskov, 1989: 6–7.
138. Gorbatov, 1964: 141.
139. He had been executed immediately after arrest (Memorial, 2/1/33/1-109).
140. See Monakhov, 1957: 26; Bronnikov, 1994 and Gurov, 1993: 38.
141. The importance of prison as a source of contacts and as a vehicle for the dissemination of information is noted by Reuter, in connection to the American Cosa Nostra. See Reuter (1983: 158). Having been a prisoner provides an inexpensive signal of reliability to other Mafiosi. Once out of prison, interactions are less risky.
142. We might speculate that when unemployment and rising crime rates followed the Russian Revolution, professional criminals faced formidable competition from a new breed of individuals, who had entered the criminal world, such as the *besprizornye* and impoverished middle class. The relative strength of each traditional criminal *artel'* in fencing off penetration from unorganized criminals was surely put to the test and new loyalties forged in hardship. An incentive to distinguish professional criminals and new entrants might have emerged at that point. A national-level organization able to intervene and settle disputes among its members as well as with other organizations and independent criminals operating in

the country might have emerged at this point in history, although further research is necessary to confirm this hypothesis.

143. Gurov, 1990: 119–20.

144. 'In short, there are no thieves 'under the law' nowadays, except perhaps for a few dozen living out their lives in various jails (I managed to meet a few in Vladimir).' Bukovsky (1978: 246).

145. Perushkin, 1995: 5. I plan to undertake a separate study of this episode of Soviet camp history. See however Varese, 1998: 526–31.

Chapter 8

1. '[In the camp] there also existed a mass of unwritten laws, and only the most authoritative thieves were permitted to interpret them and act as judges in disputes. Thieves' courts, or "regulators", were also an ancient and original example of popular law-making. I had many opportunities to observe them in the camps. Since I enjoyed a certain amount of trust, I was even able to be present at them, though not, of course, as a participant. They were based on a sort of processing of claims litigation, if I may put it that way. A thief's trial could not be called by the whole community, there could only be a personal claim by an injured party, or an accusation made in the presence of the most authoritative colleagues—or perhaps of a whole assembly. Grievances were almost never resolved by conciliation— one of the party was adjudicated guilty, and the winning party had to be personally recompensed by the loser (compensation might be exacted in any form, from murder or rape to a simple beating or the acceptance of material payment). And only if the losing party refused to submit to the court's decision did the judge step in and exercise his power to enforce it. Until that had been done, no one could interfere.' (Bukovsky, 1978: 244.)

2. Gurov, 1990: 174.

3. Podlesskikh and Tereshonok, 1994: 239–53.

4. Razinkin (1995: 15) reports that 110 to 200 *vory* were operating in the Moscow Region in 1993. On the data quoted above, see the article by V. Belykh and Col. V. Razinkin in *Izvestiya*, 27 Jan. 1994; *Zvezda*, 3 June 1994; and Handelman, 1994*a*: 18. See also Gurov, 1990: 200; *Moskovskie Novosti* (9 May 1993) and Afanas'ev, 1994: 22.

5. At one criminal 'congress' (*skhodka*) held in Sochi in 1995, 12 new *vory* were supposed to be initiated, but the police intervened and dispersed the meeting. *Izvestiya*, 1 June 1995 and 3 June 1995, and *Kommersant-Daily*, 6 June 1995.

6. In 1995, 25 *vory* were held in pre-trial detention centres in Moscow only, eight of whom were released on bail. *Segodnya*, 21 Dec. 1995 and *Komsomol'skaya Pravda*, 21 Dec. 1995.

7. *Komsomol'skaya Pravda*, 18 Feb. 1999.

8. Razinkin, 1995: 12. In 1994, 85.6 per cent of the *vory* were 30–45 years old. Mishel', a *vor* arrested in February 1994, was 22 years old. Razinkin also reports that Mishel' bought his title.

9. Gurov, 1990: 173, 232.

10. *Kriminal'naya Khronika*, no. 11 (50), 1994.

11. Gurov, 1990: 174.

12. Quoted in Gurov, 1990: 175. The situation described above shares some similarities with the Neapolitan Camorra. The original Camorra was a criminal fraternity allegedly founded in 1820 and dissolved in 1915. In the mid-1970s, a new Camorra, the Nuova Camorra Organizzata (NCO), headed by Raffaele Cutulo, was formed. Disputes emerged among various gangs, claiming to be legitimate heirs of the old Camorra. Naively, an historian also took sides in the debate, declaring the NCO to be just a 'a gangsters' association' which had usurped an old and, to some extent, respectful name (Paliotti, 1993: 15). Even the Sicilian Mafia constantly undergoes a similar process, though not to the same extent as the one described here for the *vory*. Judge Falcone debunked the myth of the 'old mafia': 'We must destroy the myth of the so-called "new mafia", or rather, we must learn that there is *always* a new mafia ready to replace the old. Even at the end of the Fifties, people spoke of a "mafia without principles" which had transformed the old, respectable rural mafia into a criminal organisation which was involved in urban construction projects. At that time they spoke of Tommaso Buscetta as a new-style mafioso, without moral standards or moral values, the same Buscetta who is now described as an old-style "man of honour"!' (Falcone and Padovani, 1991: 104.)

13. *Komsomol'skaya Pravda*, 13 Oct. 94.

14. *Kommersant'-Daily*, 3 May 1995.

15. Razinkin, 1995: 52.

16. *Izvestiya*, 9 Dec. 1994.

17. Some old *vory* (referred to, in the criminal jargon, as 'honest') resent the use of money as a criteria to admit *vory* into the fraternity and refuse to consider the new *vory* as true ones (*Izvestiya*, 1 June 1995; *Delovoi Mir*, 3 June 1995). Old *vor* Ch. concludes: 'what was previously considered a sin is now glorified; what previously was despised, is now allowed' (Gurov, 1990: 173).

18. Razinkin, 1995: 58–9.

19. *Argumenty i Fakty*, no. 6, 1995. Maybe not surprisingly, the Italian police endorse this view. In a report on the 'Russian Mafia', they describe a *brigada* as controlling a given territory and giving its protection to commercial activities in their territory. 'The *brigada* supplies the *krysha* in exchange for a sum of money, solves the disputes with local authorities and supplies protection against criminal bands. In many circumstances, such "protection" leads to the businessman to be dislodged from his own

business.' In some instances, the *brigada* combines a grip over a territory with one over a specific crime sector. SCO, 1997: i. 6–7.

20. Martinetti, 1995: 176.

21. Curiously, we need to turn to Italy to obtain a most unique insight into the activities of the Solntsevskaya. Between 1995 and 1997 the Italian police observed the activities of *vor-v-zakone* Yurii Esin (nicknamed Samosval), who tried to set up a branch of the Solntsevo crime group in Rome. While on a skiing holiday in March 1997, Esin was arrested by Italian police and a three-volume investigation into the activities of his group was produced as evidence for the prosecution. This document, never used by scholars before, is in many ways extraordinary. It contains a general assessment of Russian criminal groups, translation and clarification of jargon words, transcripts of phone conversations between prominent Russian *vory*, records of their financial transactions, and evidence of their criminal activities in Italy and other European countries. It also offers a unique insight into the activities of the Solntsevo in Russia, since many of the conversations recorded and analysed by the Italian police dealt with Russian matters and were between Rome and Moscow. Servizio Centrale Operativo [*Rapporto operativo. Esin et alii*], 3 vols., 1997. Reports of Esin's arrest appeared both in the Italian and Russian press. See *La Stampa*, 19 Mar. 1997; *Repubblica*, 18 Mar. 1997; *Corriere della Sera*, 18 Mar. 1997 and 19 Mar. 1997; and *Izvestiya*, 19 Mar. 1997.

22. SCO, 1997: i. 77. Mikhail Slin'ko, from the Moscow's Procurator's office, maintains that an established group has no less than 300–500 members.

23. Earlier reports indicate that Mikhas' held briefly a Costa Rican diplomatic passport and was appointed an honorary consul in Moscow (*Times*, 18 Nov. 1995).

24. SCO, 1997: i. 7. On Mogilevich, see the BBC *Panorama* programme 'The Billion Dollar Don', 6 Dec. 1999, 'The Magnex Files', http://www.imagenisp.com/howenow/Hrb1v1s5.html, Friedman, 2000 and *New York Review of Books*, 16 Nov. 2000.

25. SCO, 1997: i. 79.

26. This might however prove to be an understatement. In a phone conversation dated 12 July 1996, an accomplice of Esin calls the *vor* and informs him that he has had problems with the gypsies in Prague, who have beaten him. When the gypsies asked him, 'who is your *vor*?', he replied: 'Yuri Ivanovich [Esin]'. The answer of the local gypsies was telling: 'well, then tell your *vor* to come here.' This conversation testifies that Esin has interests in Prague, but distance reduces his ability to be an effective protector. SCO, 1997: i. 188. From a different conversation, we know that Esin is in Prague on the 27 Aug. 1996.

27. See e.g. SCO, 1997: i. 215.

28. SCO, 1997: ii. 134.

29. SCO, 1997: i. 18.

30. SCO, 1997: i. 77.
31. SCO, 1997: i. 18, 77.
32. SCO, 1997: i. 18.
33. This conversation took place in May 1994 and was intercepted by the Austrian police (SCO, 1997: i. 79 and ii. 152).
34. *Komsomol'skaya Pravda*, 15 Dec. 1994. See also Konstantinov, 1997: 206 and 244–9. A recent report on Tambovskaya is in *Versiya*, 25 Apr.–1 May 2000.
35. *Nezavisimaya Gazeta*, 19 May 1993.
36. Martinetti, 1995: 176.
37. SCO, 1997: i. 8, 189.
38. SCO, 1997: i. 240–3.
39. SCO, 1997: ii. 32.
40. SCO, 1997: i. 240–3.
41. SCO, 1997: i. 243. In a telephone conversation (18 Mar. 1996) between Esin and another man, it emerges that the firm Yakutalmazoloto owes protection money to a *brigada* called Orekhovo-Zuevo. Other people, using the Solntsevo name, have been trying to collect these money and are duly punished by the Solntsevo (SCO, 1997: i. 11).
42. SCO, 1997: i. 243.
43. Mikhas' was arrested in Switzerland on 16 Oct. 1996 and was released in 1998. Abramovich testified against Mikhas' and extracts of his testimony were published in *Komsomol'skaya Pravda*, 4 Dec. 1998.
44. Maksimov, 1997: 317.
45. *Nezavisimaya Gazeta*, 19 May 1993. See also an interview with Slin'ko in *Moskovskie Novosti*, 9 Feb. 1996.
46. *Kommersant-Daily*, 13 Jan. 1995.
47. *Kommersant-Daily*, 29 Oct. 1998.
48. SCO, 1997: i. 191, 240.
49. SCO, 1997: i. 30.
50. Ovchinskii, 1993: 75; *ITAR-TASS*, 31 Dec. 1993; *Moskovskii Komsomolets*, 20 Sept. 1994; Razinkin, 1995: 40.
51. *Kommersant-Daily*, 30 July 1997 and Tarabrin, 1999: 453; *Ogonek*, no. 46 (1996).
52. *Izvestiya*, 9 Dec. 1994.
53. Martinetti, 1995: 102–5; Razinkin, 1995: 59; Konstantinov and Dikselius 1997: 320–1; *Komsomol'skaya Pravda*, 11 Sept. 1998; Galeotti, 2000.
54. Razinkin, 1995: 22.
55. *Argumenty i Fakty*, no. 6, 1995.
56. SCO, 1997: i. 10.
57. SCO, 1997: i. 10.See also i. 216.
58. SCO, 1997: i. 192.
59. *Moskovskie Novosti*, 7 May 1993.
60. Ovchinskii, 1993: 70.
61. Ibid. 75.
62. *Izvestiya* 24 Dec. 1994; Modestov 1996: 344–57; Modestov, 1997: 3–38.

Solonik lived for a year in Rome in 1996 and was supposedly killed in Greece on 2 Feb. 1997 (see *Corriere della Sera*, 27 Mar. 1997; *Il Resto del Carlino*, 27 Mar. 1997; *Messaggiero*, 10 Aug. 1998).

63. *ITAR-TASS*, 31 Dec. 1993; Razinkin, 1995: 49.
64. *Moskovskie Novosti*, 7 May 1993; Aleksandr Solonik was charged for the death of Globus as well (see *Izvestiya* 24 Dec. 1994).
65. Handelman, 1994a: 186.
66. Razinkin, 1995: 49; *Kommersant-Daily*, 4 Feb. 1995.
67. Razinkin, 1995: 41.
68. *Argumenty i Fakty*, no. 23, 1994; Razinkin, 1995: 49; *Izvestiya*, 9 Dec. 1994.
69. According to one author, the two groups united in the 1980s (Modestov, 1996: 176), while another (Maksimov, 1997: 301) suggests the early 1990s as a more probable date.
70. *Moskovskii Komsomolets*, 20 Sept. 1994. The death of Sil'vestr features in the Italian report. A number of supporters of Sil'vestr were killed shortly after the summer of 1994. In their telephone conversations some members show fear of being associated with the losing faction and being killed as well. Apparently some individuals killed in the aftermath of Sil'vestr's death did not deserve to die. Slava (Vyacheslav Gavrilov, an associate of Esin in Moscow) tells Esin that, "Drakon had nothing to do with it and it is not known why they killed him." SCO, 1997: i. 7, 204.
71. SCO, 1997: i. 187. See also i. 17.
72. SCO, 1997: i. 7, 204.
73. SCO, 1997: i. 187.
74. SCO, 1997: i. 12.
75. See e.g. Gurov, 1990: 176; Ovchinskii, 1993: 53; *Moskovskie Novosti*, 7 May 1993; Razinkin, 1995: 58–62; Maksimov, 1997: 300.
76. See *Versiya*, 11–17 Apr. 2000.
77. *Argumenty i Fakty*, 30 June 1993.
78. See *Izvestiya*, 27 Jan. 1994.
79. See *Kommersant-Daily*, 4 Feb. 1995.
80. *Kommersant-Daily*, 4 Feb. 1995.
81. Serio, 1992: 6. See also Serio, 1997.
82. For maps for organized crime in Moscow, see Galeotti 1992: 244 and Galeotti, 1995a: 13. For a survey of other ethnic gangs in Moscow, see *Kommersant-Daily*, 18 Aug. 1994; *Kommersant-Daily*, 17 Mar. 1995; *Komsomol'skaya Pravda*, 17 Jan. 1997; *Versiya*, 16–22 May 2000.
83. The explosion left a gaping hole in the back of the 22-floor building. The glass roof of the restaurant was also damaged.
84. This explosion occurred at around 11 a.m. near the entrance to the ministry building on the busy Garden Ring near the Oktyabr'skaya metro station, damaging a fence and several cars parked nearby and shattering windows. No one was injured (*Moscow Times*, 23 June 1999).
85. See also *Argumenty i Fakty*, June 1993 (no. 30) and *Kommersant-Daily*, 4 Feb. 1995.

86. See *Krasnaya Zvezda*, 23 May 1995; *Pravda*, 16 May 1995; *Interfax*, 28 June 1995, *The Times*, 22 Jan. 1996; *Moscow Times*, 28 Oct. 1997.

87. *ITAR-TASS*, 18 Jan. 1997. In July 1997, President Yeltsin formally reinstated Don Cossack regiments in Russia's armed forces (which include border guards). See *Moscow Times*, 28 Oct. 1997. On the Cossack revival, see Grau, 1993.

88. Grau, 1993: 588; *Komsomol'skaya Pravda*, 25 Mar. 1994.

89. *Izvestiya*, 14 Apr. 1995.

90. *Komsomol'skaya Pravda*, 25 Mar. 1994.

91. *Kommersant-Daily*, 5 May 1995. A dozen criminals arrested in Moscow in 1996 belonged to the Union of Cossack Formations (SKF), an organization set up in Nov. 1994 with the aim of uniting all Cossack organizations in the country (*Izvestiya*, 1 Aug. 1996). Its leader, Aleksandr Demin, has been convicted several times (*Kommersant-Daily*, 5 May 1995).

92. See *Komsomol'skaya Pravda*, 18 Feb. 1995; *Izvestiya*, 22 Oct. 1994 and Konstantinov, 1997: 213–4.

93. *Argumenty i Fakty*, no. 24, June 1995. See also *Izvestiya*, 2 June 1995 and 29 June 1995.

94. Konstantinov (1997: 216) describes Kobzon as the mouthpiece (*rupor*) of organized crime. Allegedly, he has been an associate of various shady figures, including Otari Kvantrishvili, the chairperson of the Sportsmen's Social Protection Fund 'Lev Yashin', who was assassinated on 5 April 1994. He has been the subject of many journalistic investigations, especially by Larisa Kislinskaya, who had also written extensively on Kvantrishvili and has been openly threatened, first by Kvantrishvili, and then, Kobzon. Kobzon has responded accusing Kislinskaya of being a woman of dubious morality. She has filed a suit against him for moral damages. See *Zvezda*, 7 Oct. 1994; *Kommersant-Daily*, 26 Oct. 1994; *Komsomol'skaya Pravda*, 5 Jan. 1995. A Moscow court ruled on 6 March 1996 that the newspaper *Sovetskaya Rossiya* and Larisa Kislinskaya should pay damages to Kobzon for claiming that he had ties with organized crime (ITAR-TASS). He has been repeatedly denied visas to enter the United States although recently he attended a seminar at Harvard as member of the Duma (*Boston Globe*, 20 Apr. 2000).

95. He granted a similar interview to *Novoe Russkoe Slovo*, 4-5-6 May 1994. Kobzon was no. 3 on Col. Gen. Boris Gromov's My Fatherland Party list in the Dec. 1995 Duma elections. Only Gen. Gromov was elected. He was elected in the 1999 Duma elections, and is a member of the group 'Regions of Russia' (see http://www.duma.ru/deputats/PERSONS/99102913.HTM).

96. *Izvestiya*, 6 Jan. 1995; Martinetti, 1995: 96; Razinkin, 1995: 25.

97. *Komsomol'skaya Pravda*, 11 Sept. 1998. See also Martinetti, 1995: 102–5; Konstantinov and Dikselius 1997: 320–1.

98. *Argumenty i fakty*, no. 37 (Sept. 1999).

99. The wave of attacks against Italian art treasures included a bomb planted near the Uffizi gallery (via dei Georgofili) on 27 May 1993 (four dead), a bomb at the Modern Art Marquee in Milan (five dead) and a bomb near the Church of San Giorgio in Rome (27 July 1993). Art. 41 *bis* introduced harsher prison conditions for those sentenced for Mafia crimes. See Pezzino, 1999: 79–80.
100. *Moscow Times*, 13 July 1996.
101. *Moscow Times* 11 Jan. 1995. Shchekochikhin's position is reported in *Permskie Novosti*, 22 Dec. 1995.
102. *Moscow Times*, 30 Jan. 1996.
103. *Komsomol'skaya Pravda*, 18 Feb. 1995. See also *Izvestiya*, 22 Oct. 1994.
104. Both quotations are from *Moscow Times*, 14 Sept. 1999.
105. *Dos'e 02*, no. 26/1998. On the murder of Zykov, see also *Permskie Novosti*, 23 June 1998 and 25 June 1998; *Mestnoe Vremya*, 24 June 1998; *Zvezda*, 23 June 1998.
106. *RFE/RL*, 28 Sept. 1998.
107. A list of eighty-seven candidates running for the 1995 Duma elections who were under investigation or had been formerly convicted was released by Central Electoral Commission (TsIK) Chairman Nikolai Ryabov on 23 Oct. 1995. The LDPR led with twelve candidates who had served criminal sentences (*Interfax*, 23 Oct. 995). The list quickly came under severe criticism for its many inaccuracies. Nevertheless, Vladimir Zhirinovsky dropped eleven out of the twelve candidates from his party who appeared on the TsIK's list, according to an AFP report (*OMRI*, 25 Oct. 1995). In the 1995 Duma elections, Zhirinovsky's party was extremely popular among the prison population. According to data released by the Ministry of Internal Affairs, 30–40 per cent of prisoners in pre-trial detention centres voted for Zhirinovsky (Women of Russia, the Beer Lovers' Party, and the Communists all got about 6–10 per cent. *Interfax* 18 Dec. 1995). See also Varese, 1996 and *Moscow Times*, 14 Sept. 1999.
108. *RFE-RL*, 19 Oct. 1999; *St Petersburg Times*, 15 Oct. 1999; *Versiya*, 4–10 Apr. 2000.
109. *Nezavisimaya Gazeta*, 27 Dec. 1997.
110. *Versiya*, 4–10 Apr. 2000.
111. *Komsomol'skaya Pravda*, 23 May 1995.
112. *Versiya*, no. 13, 4–10 Apr. 2000.
113. *Segodnya*, 24 Sept. 1997. Similar investigations are under way in Samara and Ryazan' Provinces.
114. *Nezavisimaya Gazeta*, 28 Dec. 1997.
115. This seems to be the case of ex-convict Gennadii Konyakhin, who was elected mayor of Leninsk-Kuznetskii and later arrested for misappropriation of state property. It appears that he had tried to break up powerful monopolies in the city and had taken on corrupt bureaucrats. A tape incriminating Konyakhin was obtained by *Izvestiya*. After the publication

of the article, President Yeltsin launched a national campaign against Konyakhin. *Izvestiya*, 11 Dec. 1997; 10 Oct. 1997; 3 Oct. 1997; 17 Sept. 1997; 18 Sept. 1997; 19 Sept. 1997; *Zvezda*, 4 Oct. 1997; *Ekspress Gazeta*, no. 40 (146).

116. *Izvestiya*, 14 Apr. 1995.

117. See *Moscow Times*, 28 Dec. 1999.

118. See Martinetti, 1995: 105–10; *RFE/RL Newsline*, 18 Apr. 1997. Ioseliani was sentenced to 11 years in prison in November 1998 (see *Moscow Times*, 17 Dec. 1997 and 12 Nov. 1998). President Shevardnadze announced on 20 Apr. 2000 his intention to free Ioseliani as part of a broader political amnesty (*RFE/RL Newsline*, 21 Apr. 2000).

119. M4.

120. Martinetti, 1995: 100; *Izvestiya*, 6 Jan. 1995.

121. The text of the prayer is in *La Stampa*, 19 Mar. 1997.

122. *Reuters*, 13 Sept. 1999 and *Moscow Times*, 15 Sept. 1999.

123. They include Sergei Dolgushin and Sergei Malafeev (Uralmash gang) and Oleg Vagin (Tsentral'naya gang) and his three body guards. *Daily Telegraph*, 18 Feb. 1997; *Sunday Times Magazine*, 20 Apr. 1997; Zbarsky and Hutchinson, 1997: 197–202.

124. *Sunday Times Magazine*, 20 Apr. 1997; Zbarsky and Hutchinson, 1997: 197–202. Another Russian tradition consists in kissing the cheeks of the deceased, while he is lying in the coffin. Such a tradition survived in Soviet times. A procession of prominent Party leaders would kiss the dead Secretary General. And so do mafiosi. If one fails to kiss, he might signal his involvement in the murder of the deceased. Reportedly, Konstantin Tzyganov, leader of Uralmash, publicly kissed Oleg Vagin, first godfather of the Ekaterinburg's Tsentral'naya criminal group, in order to deny rumours of his involvement in the death of Vagin.

125. *Reuters*, 13 Sept. 1999 and *Moscow Times*, 15 Sept. 1999.

126. M4.

127. Reportedly, he has donated 40,000 pounds to the monastery. *Komsomol'skaya Pravda*, 13 Sept. 1995; *Kommersant-Daily*, 9 Sept. 1995 and *Daily Telegraph*, 18 Feb. 1997.

128. *Kommersant-Daily*, 9 Sept. 1995.

129. *Moskovskie Novosti*, 18–24 May 1999. Following a much-publicized gay scandal, Bishop Nikon was removed from his office, but retained his title (*Moscow Times*, 22 July 1999).

130. Gambetta, 1993*a*: 48.

Conclusion

1. Wedel, 2000.

2. Leitzel, Gaddy, and Alekseev, 1995: 28.

3. Gambetta, 1993*a*: 256.

Appendix A

1. 'The criminal mimicker is an international phenomenon and has been prevalent in Europe since the growth of professional crime during the early fifteenth century' (Maurer and Futrell, 1982: 248, quoted in Gambetta and Pizzini, 1995: 1).
2. The list has been published in Podlesskikh and Tereshonok, 1994: 239–53.
3. Sources include Govorukhin (1994), Handelman (1994a) and articles devoted to organized crime published in *Argumenty i Fakty*, *Izvestiya*, *Kommersant-Daily*, *Komsomol'skaya Pravda*, and Perm's *Zvezda* from 1993 to 1995. Only nicknames of *vory-v-zakone* have been included.
4. Likhachev', 1935: 61.
5. Gambetta and Pizzini, 1995: 2.
6. Ibid. 3.
7. Morgan, O'Neill, and Harré, 1979: 9; similarly Gambetta and Pizzini, 1995: 3, and Rosemberg, 1945: 98.
8. Gambetta and Pizzini, 1995: 3.
9. The parallel phenomenon is that victims of abusive nicknames cannot actively do anything to rid themselves of their nickname. The astute victims will not directly defend themselves, but reply by throwing demeaning nicknames at others.
10. See Massolo, 1990: 284. The various functions identified by authors include social control (Pitt-Rivers, 1954; Kenny, 1966; Cutileiro, 1971), classification (Mook, 1967; Brandes, 1975; Fucilla 1979; Breen, 1982) and boundary-maintaining (Cohen, 1977).
11. Gambetta and Pizzini, 1995: 2.
12. Gilmore, 1982: 687.
13. Morgan, Neill and Harré, 1979: 120.
14. Gambetta and Pizzini, 1995: 3.
15. Gurov and Ryabinin, 1991a: 82. Usually, entry into the brotherhood was also signalled by a tattoo. Until the 1950s, the tattoo depicted a heart, pierced by a dagger. A later version of the 'admittance tattoo' was a picture of the suit of aces inside a cross. Gurov writes that the tattoos 'were done not only in order to prove one's strength. They also had a "communication function". The tattoo helped the persistent offenders to recognize each other'. No other criminal was allowed to bear these tattoos; punishment would be death (Gurov, 1990a: 111).
16. See *Osobennosti povedeniya vorov v zakone* (1994)—a Russian police document on the new *vory*.
17. *Osobennosti povedeniya vorov v zakone* in Podlesskikh-Tereshonok, 1994: 234–5.
18. Likhachev, 1935: 61.
19. Ibid.
20. Morgan, O'Neill, and Harré, 1979: 5.
21. Gambetta and Pizzini, 1995: 14.

22. Gurov, 1990*a*: 108.
23. Handelman, 1994*a*: 23.
24. Gambetta and Pizzini, 1995: 5
25. Gambetta and Pizzini, 1995: 4.
26. *Izvestiya*, 13 Sept. 1994.
27. Stark, 1981: 43.
28. Bykov, 1994: 107–8.

Appendix B

1. The survey was commissioned by Dr Mary McAuley of Oxford University and the data were collected in 1994 by Dr Oleg Podvintsev of Perm University. Dr Oleg Podvintsev has supplied me with the raw, handwritten papers where he recorded the data. I have coded the data (see Table B1), and constructed the mobility table (see Table B2). On mobility tables as a tool for the study of social mobility, see Hout (1983).

2. The *nomenklatura* in the Soviet Union was a detailed list of posts. Such lists defined those Party, Government, and other posts to which individuals may not be appointed without personal interview and prior approval by the offices of a Party committee (Rigby, 1990: 94). Each Communist Party committee had its *nomenklatura* and was responsible for the recruitment of suitable candidates. The *nomenklaturnaya sistema* was institutionalized in the 1920s. In 1922 the first list of positions requiring such approval appeared. Over time, the *nomenklatura* system became more elaborate, with Communist Party committees at all levels—from republican and regional to city and district—being involved in the recruitment of the nomenklatura posts (Hanley, Yershova and Anderson, 1995).

3. Lentini, 1991: 70; see also Hill, 1972.

4. It should be noted that roughly half the university professors in our list were teaching ideologically charged subjects, such as History of the Communist Party of the USSR and Marxism–Lenininsm. Their chairs have been renamed as Chairs of Political Science, International Relations, and Sociology. The other half were Heads of Departments in technological or medical faculties. Humanities and historians of non-Soviet subjects were not represented in the *gorkom* and *obkom*.

5. These findings appear to contradict the 'circulation of elites' thesis advanced by Nee (1989). Nee offered a radical circulation of elite hypothesis in reference to China, arguing that market reform benefits new economic actors and former cadres lose out (1989; see also 1991). He predicted that 'not only are the direct controllers of the redistributive mechanism likely to experience a relative loss, but the value of their political capital

accumulated through prior experience as cadre is likely to diminish as well' (1989: 671). Cadres are relatively disadvantaged, as they have 'little or no net advantage in entering into private entrepreneurship' (ibid.).

6. See e.g. Róna-Tass, 1994, Szelényi and Szelényi, 1995; Hanley, Yershova, and Anderson, 1995.

Bibliography

Archival Sources

Gosudarstvennyi Arkhiv Rossiiskoi Federatsii (GARF)

Fond 9414	Gulag
Fond 9401	MVD
Fond 8131	Fond Prokuratury
OPKh	Osobaya Papka Khrushcheva

Gosudarstvennyi Arkhiv Permskoi Oblasti (GAPO)

Fond 164	Narodnyi sud 12 uchastka Permskogo uezda, zavod Dobryanki, 1911–26
Fond 1365	Prokuratura g. Molotova, 1944–56
Fond 1366	Prokuratura Permskoi oblasti, 1938–73
Fond 1461	Upravlenie ministerstvom yustitsii RSFSR po Molotovskoi oblasti, 1938–58

Arkhiv obshchestvennogo dvizheniya Memorial (Memorial)

Fond 1	K. A. Ivanov
Fond 2	M. T. Adeev; M. L. Antsis; N. G. Bardina; I. N. Bazhanov; L. B. Bernshtein; B. L. Brainin; I. M. Evseev.; L. G. Gavrilov; N. A. Glazov; M. Ts. Kakhana; E. M. L'vov; A. M. Maksimovich; F. Ya. Rabinovich; T. V. Tigonen; Yu. P. Yakimenko; R. L. Volinskaya; Ya. I. Verzhenskaya; A. G. Zaitsev; A. M. Zelenyi

Russian Newspapers and Periodicals

Perm

Dos'e 02
Mestnoe Vremya
Megalopolis-Express
Novyi Kompan'on
Permskie Novosti
Vechernyaya Perm'
Zvezda

Others

Argumenty i Fakty
Izvestiya
Kommersant-Daily
Komsomol'skaya Pravda
Kriminal'naya Khronika
Moskovskie Novosti
Moscow Times
Natsional'naya Sluzhba Novostei (on-line)
Nezavisimaya Gazeta
Ogonek
Segodnya
Vestnik Vysshego Arbitrazhnogo Suda
Versiya

Books and Journal Articles in Russian

Afanas'ev, V. S. (1994) *Organizovannaya prestupnost' v sovremennoi Rossii* (Sankt-Peterburg: Trudy Sankt-Peterburgskogo Filiala Instituta Sotsiologii Rossiiskoi Akademii Nauk).

Analiticheskii Tsentr 'Izvestii' (1994*a*) *Ugolovnaya Rossiya. 1. Bespredel vremen peredela sobstvennosti* (*Izvestiya*, 18 Oct. 1994).

——(1994*b*) *Ugolovnaya Rossiya. 2. vory v zakone zanimayut ofisy* (*Izvestiya*, 19 Oct. 1994).

APK (1992) 'Arbitrazhnyi protsessual'nyi kodeks Rossiiskoi Federatsii', *Vestnik Vysshego Arbitrazhnogo Suda* Rossiiskoi Federatsii, 5: 5–47.

——(1995) 'Arbitrazhnyy protsessual'nyy kodeks Rossiyskoy Federatsii', *Vestnik Vysshego Arbitrazhnogo Suda* Rossiyskoy Federatsii, 6: 25–79.

Artem'ev, V. P. (1956) *Rezhim i okhrana ispravitel'no-trudovykh lagerei MVD* (Munich: Institut po izucheniyu SSSR).

Avilina, I. (1989) 'Arbitrazh ili sud?', *Khozyaistvo i pravo*, 5: 90–8.

Bronnikov, A. G. (1994) *Tainye sposoby svyazi prestupnikov* (Perm': UVD Permskoi Oblasti).

——(1996) *Tatuirovki u prestupnikov v Rossii* (Perm': mimeo).

Bykov, V. (1994) *Russkaya Fenya* (Smolensk: Trast-Imakom).

Chekhov, A. P. (1895) *Ostrov Sakhalin* (Moskva: Tipo-litografiya T-va I. N. Kushnerov I Ko.)

Chernina, N. V. (1994) 'Bednost' kak sotsial'nyi fenomen rossiiskogo obshchestva', *Sotsiologicheskie issledovaniya*, 21/3: 54–61.

Craveri, M. (1995) 'Krizis Gulaga. Kengirskoe vosstanie 1954 goda v dokumentakh MVD', *Cahiers du Monde russe et soviétique*, 36/3: 319–44.

Doroshevich, V. M. ([1903] 1935) *Sakhalin: Katorga* (Parizh: Biblioteka 'Illyustrirovannoi Rossii').

Dubyagin, Yu., and Teplitskii, E. (1993) *Kratkii slovar' ugolovnogo zhargona* (Moskva: Terra).

Entsiklopedicheskii slovar' v dvukh tomakh (1963), vol. 1 (Moskva).

Filippov, P. (1994) *Organizovannaya prestupnost' i perspektivy prikhoda k vlasti v Rossii natsional-sotsialistov*, in *Izvestiya*, 26/1: 1–2.

Gernet, M. N. (1927) *Prestupnost' i samoubiistvo vo vremia voiny i posle nee* (Moskva: Tsentral'noe Statisticheskoe Upravlenie SSSR).

Govorukhin, S. (1994) 'Velikaya Kriminal'naya Revolyutsiya', in id., *Strana Vorov* (Narva: Shans), 167–399.

Gurov, A. I. (1990) *Professional'naya prestupnost'* (Moskva: Yuridicheskaya Literatura).

——(1995) *Krasnaya mafiya* (Moskva: Miko Kommercheskii Vestnik).

——and Ryabinin, V. (1990) 'Ispoved' vora v zakone', *Na Boevom Postu*, 12: 50–62.

————(1991*a*) 'Ispoved' vora v zakone', *Na Boevom Postu*, 1: 75–84.

————(1991*b*) *Ispoved' vora v zakone* (Moskva: Rosagropromizdat).

Kallistratova, R. F. (1961) *Razreshenie sporov v gosudarstvennom arbitrazhe* (Moskva).

Kleimenov, M. P., and Dmitriev, O. V. (1995) 'Reket v Sibiri', *Sotsiologicheskie Issledovaniya*, 22/3: 115–23.

Konstantinov, A. (1997) *Banditskii Peterburg* (Sankt-Peterburg: Folio-Press).

——and Dikselius, M. (1997) *Banditskaya Rossiya* (Sankt-Peterburg: Bibliopolis).

Korolenko, V. G. ([1885] 1966) 'Sokolinets', in id. *Sobranie sochinenii v pyati tomakh*, Leningrad: 'Khudozh. lit-ra', Leningradskoe otd-nie, vol. 1, 262–305.

——([1886] 1966) 'Fyodor Bespriyutnyi', in id. *Sobranie sochinenii v pyati tomakh*, Leningrad: 'Khudozh. lit-rat', Leningradskoe otd-nie, vol. 1, 306–49.

Krishtanovskaya, O. (1995) 'Nelegal'nye struktury v Rossii', *Sotsiologicheskie Issledovaniya*, 22/8: 84–106.

Ladyzhenskii, A. (1994) 'Krysha', *Kriminal'naya Khronika*, 7 July: 4.

Likhachev, D. S. (1935) 'Cherty pervobytnogo primitivizma vorovskoi rechi', *Yazyk i myshlenie*, iii–iv, Moskva-Leningrad, 47–100.

——(1995) *Vospominaniia* (Sankt-Peterburg: Izd-vo 'Logos').

Maksimov, A. (1997) *Rossiiskaya Prestupnost'. Kto est' Kto?* (Moskva: Izdatel'stvo 'Eksmo').

Maksimov, S.V. (1869) 'Narodnye prestupleniya i neschast'ya', *Otechestvennye zapiski*, 182/1: 1–62 and 182/2: 365–403.

——([1871] 1891) *Sibir' i katorga* (St Peterburg: Tipo-litografia N. Stefanova).

Mel'shin L. (1896) *V mire otverzhennykh. Zapiski byvshego katorzhnika* (St Peterburg: Tipo-litografia B. M. Volfa).

Modestov, N. (1996) *Moskva Banditskaya* (Moskva: Tsentrloligrag).

——(1997) *Moskva Bandistskaya—2* (Moskva: Tsentrloligrag).

Monakhov, V. I. (1957) *Gruppirovki vorov-retsidivistov i nekotorye voprosy bor'by s nimi* (Moskva: Izdanie politicheskogo otdela glavnogo upravleniya ispravitel'no-trudovykh kolonii MVD SSSR).

Ovchinskii, V. S. (1993) *Strategiya bor'by s Mafiei* (Moskva: SIMS).

Permskoe UVD (1995) *Doklad o kriminal'noi situatsii v Permi* (Perm': Permskoe UVD).

Perushkin, V. (1995) 'Vory i avtoritety', *Argumenty i Fakty*, 6 (747) February: 5.

Podlesskikh, G., and Tereshonok, A., (1994) *Vory-v-zakone: brosok k vlasti* (Moskva: Khudozhestvennaya Literatura, 1994).

Popov, V. M. (1912) *Slovar' vorovskogo i arestantskogo yazyka* (Kiev).

Potapov, S. M. (1927) *Slovar' zhargona prestupnikov (blatnaya muzyka)* (Moskva).

Radaev, V. V. (1998) *Formirovanie Novykh Rossiiskikh Rynkov: Transaktsionnye Izderzhki, Formy Kontrolya i Delovaya Etika* (Moskva: Tsentr politicheskikh tekhnologii).

Razinkin, V. S. (1995) *'Vory v zakone' i prestupnye klany* (Moskva: Kriminologich-eskaya Assotsiatsiya).

Santerre, Maximilien de (1960), *Sovetskie poslevoennye kontslageri i ikh obitateli* (Munich: Institut po izucheniyu SSSR).

Shalamov, V. ([1959] 1992) *Ocherki prestupnogo mira*, in id., *Kolymskie rasskazy* (Moskva: Sovetskaya Rossiya), ii. 5–96.

Shulus, A. A. (1990) 'Tenevaya ekonomika: realizm otsenok ili predvzyatost'?', *Ekonomicheskie Nauki*, 11: 108–18.

Solzhenitsyn, A. (1980) *Arkhipelag Gulag, 1918–1956*, in id., *Sobranie Sochinenii*, v (Vermont-Paris: YMCA-Press).

Tarabrin, A. (1999) *Vory v zakone i avtoritety* (Moskva: Eksmo-Press).

Trakhtenberg, V. F. (1908) *Blatnaya muzyka (zhargon tyur'my)*, ed. I. A. Boduen-de-Kurtene (St Petersburg).

Tregubov, Yu. A. (1959) *Vosem' let vo vlasti Lubyanki; zapiski chlena* (Frankfurt-on-Main: Possev-Verlag).

Ugolovnyi Kodeks Rossiiskoi Federatsii (1993) (Novosibirsk: YuKEA).

Vardi, A. *Podkonvoinyi mir* (Frankfurt-on-Main: Possev-Verlag, 1971).

Volkov, V. (1998) 'Monopoliya na nasilie i skrytaya fragmentatsiya rossiiskogo gosudarstva. Issledovatel'skaya gipoteza', *Politicheskie issledovaniia*, 5: 39–47.

——(1999b) 'Politekonomiya Nasiliya, Ekonomicheskii Rost i Konsolidatsiya Gosudarstva', *Voprosy Ekonomiki*, 70/10: 44–59.

Vorivoda, I. P. (1971) *Sbornik zhargonnykh slov i vyrazhenii, upotreblyaemykh v ust-noi i pis'mennoi rechi prestupnym elementom* (Alma-Ata: Tip. MVD KazSSR).

Yakushkin, E. (1896) *Obychnoe pravo* (Yaroslavl': Tipo-Litografiya Gubernskoi Zemskoi Upravy).

Zemskov, V. N. (1989) 'Arkhipelag GULAG: glazami pisatelya i statistika', *Argumenty i Fakty*, 45: 6–7.

——(1991) 'Gulag', *Sotsiologicheskie issledovaniya*, 18/6: 10–27.

Books and Journal Articles in Languages other than Russian

Albini, J. L. (1971) *The American Mafia* (New York: Meredith Corporation).

Almond, G. A., and Verba, S. ([1963] 1989) *The Civic Culture: Political Attitudes and Democracy in Five Nations* (Newbury Park: SAGE Publications).

Almakaeva, S. V. (1995) 'Corporate Taxation in the Russian Federation', *Review of Central and East European Law*, 1: 41–64.

Alvazzi del Frate, A., and Goryainov, K. (1994) *Latent Crime in Russia* (Vienna-Rome: UNICRI Issues and Reports, No. 1).

Arlacchi, P. ([1983] 1986) *Mafia Businesses: The Mafia and the Spirit of Capitalism* (London: Verso).

—— (1992) *Gli uomini del disonore. La Mafia siciliana nel racconto del pentito Antonio Calderone* (Milano: Oscar Mondadori).

—— (1994) *Addio Cosa Nostra. La vita di Tommaso Buscetta* (Milano: Rizzoli).

Åslund, A. (1997) 'Economic Causes of Crime in Russia', in J. Sachs and K. Pistor, *The rule of law and economic reform in Russia* (Boulder, Colo.: Westview-Press), 79–94.

—— (1999) 'Russia's Collapse', *Foreign Affairs* 78/5: 64–77.

Augustine (1998) *The City of God against the Pagans*, ed. R. W. Dyson (Cambridge: Cambridge University Press).

Bacon, E. (1994) *The Gulag at War* (London: Macmillan).

Banfield, E. C. (1958) *The Moral Basis of a Backward Society* (New York: The Free Press).

Barzel, Y. (1997) *The Economic Analysis of Property Rights*, 2nd edn. (Cambridge: Cambridge University Press).

—— (1999) *A Theory of the State: Economic Rights, Legal Rights and the Scope of the State* (mimeo).

Bell, D. ([1953] 1988) 'Crime as an American Way of Life: A Queer Ladder of Social Mobility', in id., *The End of Ideology: On the Exhaustion of Political Ideas in the Fifties* (New York: Free Press), 127–50.

Berman, H. J. (1963) *Justice in the USSR* (New York: Vintage Press).

Bers, M. K. (1970) *The Penetration of Legitimate Business by Organised Crime—An Analysis* (Washington: US Department of Justice).

Binmore, K., and Dasgupta, P. (1986) *Economic Organisations as Games* (Oxford: Blackwell).

Blasi J., Kroumova, M., and Kruse, D. (1997) *Kremlin Capitalism: Privatizing the Russian Economy* (Ithaca: ILR/Cornell University Press).

Blok, A. (1974) *The Mafia of a Sicilian Village* (Oxford: Basil Blackwell).

Block, A. A. (1983) *East Side West Side: Organizing Crime in New York 1930–1950* (London: Transaction Publishers).

Boffito, C. (1995) 'The Banking System in Russia', in C. T. Saunders (ed.), *Eastern Europe in Crisis and the Way Out* (London: Macmillan), 123–37.

Boutenko, I. A., and Razlogov, K. (1997) *Recent Social Trends in Russia 1960–1995* (Montreal and Kingston: McGill-Queen's University Press).

Boycko, M., Shleifer, A., and Vishny, R. (1996) *Privatizing Russia* (Cambridge, Mass.: MIT Press).

Brandes, S. H. (1975) 'The Structure and Demographic Implications of Nicknames in Navonagal, Spain', *American Ethnologist*, 2/1: 139–48.

Brannen, J. (1988) 'The Study of Sensitive Subjects', *Sociological Review*, 36/3: 552–63.

Breen, R. (1982) 'Naming Practices in Western Ireland', *Man*, 17/4: 701–13.

Brown, A. (1998) *The Gorbachev Factor* (Oxford: Oxford University Press).

Bukovsky, V. (1978) *To Build a Castle: My Life as a Dissenter*, trans. Michael Scammell (London: Andre Deutsch).

Bychkov, O. V. (1994) 'Russian Hunters in Eastern Siberia in the 17th-Century—Life-Style and Economy', *Arctic Anthropology*, 31/1: 72–85.

Castells, M., and Portes, A. (1989) 'World Underneath: The Origins, Dynamics and Effects of the Informal Economy', in A. Portes, M. Castells, and L. A. Benton (eds.), *The Informal Economy: Studies in Advanced and Less Developed Countries* (Baltimore: The John Hopkins University Press), 11–37.

Catanzaro, R. (1985) 'Enforcers, Entrepreneurs and Survivors: How the Mafia has Adapted to Change', *British Journal of Sociology*, 35/1: 34–55.

——(1988) *Il Delitto come impresa. Storia sociale della mafia* (Padova: Liviana Editrice).

Chalidze, V. (1977) *Criminal Russia: Essays on Crime in the Soviet Union* (New York: Random House) (orig. edn. *Ugolovnaya Rossiya*, New York: Khronika Press, 1975)

Charap, J., and Webster, L. (1993) 'Constraints on the Development of Private Manufacturing in St. Petersburg', *Economics of Transition*, 1/3: 299–316.

Charny, D. (1990) 'Nonlegal Sanctions in Commercial Relationships', *Harvard Law Review*, 104/2: 373–467.

Chu, Y. K. (1996) *Hong Kong Triads: The Core Business of Organized Crime* (Ph.D., University of Exeter).

——(2000) *The Triads as Business* (London and New York: Routledge).

Chubb, J. (1982) *Patronage, Power, and Poverty in Southern Italy: A Tale of Two Cities* (Cambridge: Cambridge University Press).

Clem, R. S., and Craumer, P. R. (1995a) 'The Politics of Russia's Regions: A Geographical Analysis of the Russian Election and Constitutional Plebiscite of December 1993', *Post-Soviet Geography*, 36/2: 67–86.

————(1995b) 'The Geography of Russian 1995 Parliamentary Election: Continuity, Change and Correlates', *Post-Soviet Geography*, 36/10: 587–616.

————(1996) 'Roadmap to Victory: Boris Yel'tsin and the Russian Presidential Elections of 1996', *Post-Soviet Geography and Economics*, 37/6: 335–54.

Coase, R. (1960) 'The Problem of Social Cost', *The Journal of Law and Economics*, 3: 1–44.

Cohen, A. (1995) 'Crime without Punishment', *Journal of Democracy*, 6/2: 34–45.

Cohen, E. N. (1977) 'Nicknames, Social Boundaries and Community in an Italian Village', *International Journal of Contemporary Sociology*, 14/1–2: 102–13.

Combating Organised Crime. A Report of the 1965 Oyster Bay, New York Conferences, 1966 (Albany: State Capital).

Committee on Governmental Affairs (1996) *Russian Organized Crime in the United States. Hearing before the Permanent sub-Commitee on investigation* (Collingdale, Pennsylvania: Diane Publishing Company).

Conquest, R. (1978) *Kolyma: The Arctic Death Camps* (London: Macmillan, 1978).

CSIS (Center for Strategic and International Studies) (1997) *Russian Organized Crime: Global Organized Crime Project* (Washington, DC: Center for Strategic and International Studies).

Cunningham-Burley, S. (1985) 'Rules, Roles and Communicative Performance in Qualitative Research Interviews', *International Journal of Sociology and Social Policy*, 5: 67–77.

Cutileiro, J. (1970) *A Portuguese Rural Society* (Oxford: Clarendon Press).

Davis, J. (1975) *Law and Family in Pisticci* (London: London University Press).

Davis, J. A. (1988) *Control and Conflict: Law and Order in Nineteenth-Century Italy* (London: Macmillan).

Demaris, O. (1981) *The Last Mafioso: The Treacherous World of Jimmy Fratianno* (New York: Times Books).

DiFrancesco, W., and Gitelman, Z. (1984) 'Soviet Political Culture and Covert Participation in Policy Implementation', *American Political Science Review*, 78/3: 603–21.

Dornbusch, R. (1991) *Priorities of Economic Reform in Eastern Europe and the Soviet Union*, Centre for Economic Policy Research Occasional Paper no. 5 (London).

Dostoyevsky, F. M. ([1861–2] 1985) *House of the Dead* (London: Penguin Books. Orig. title: *Zapiski iz mertvogo doma*).

Duggan, C. (1989) *Fascism and the Mafia* (New Haven and London: Yale University Press).

Earle, J. S., and Estrin, S. (1996) 'Employee Ownership in Transitional Economies', in R. Frydman, C. Gray and A. Rapaczynski (eds.), *Corporate Governance in Central Europe and Russia*, vol. 2 (Budapest, London, and New York: Central European University Press), 1–61.

Elster, J. (1982) 'Marxism, Functionalism and Game Theory', *Theory and Society*, 11/4: 453–82.

Falcone, G., and Padovani, M. (1991) *Cose di Cosa Nostra* (Milano: Rizzoli).

———— (1993) *Men of Honour*, trans. E. Farrelly (London: Warner Books).

Fogelson, R. M. (1977) *Big-City Police* (Cambridge, Mass.: Harvard University Press).

Frank, S. P. (1999) *Crime, Cultural Conflict and Justice in Rural Russia, 1856–1914* (Berkeley, Los Angeles, and London: University of California Press).

Frierson, C. (1987) 'Crime and Punishment in the Russian Village: Rural Concepts of Criminality at the End of the Nineteenth Century', *Slavic Review*, 46/1: 55–69.

Frye, T. (1997) 'Russian Privatisation and the Limits of Credible Commitment', in D. L. Weimer (ed.), *The Political Economy of Property Rights* (New York: Cambridge University Press), 84–108.

Frydman, R., Rapaczynski, A., and Earle, J. (1993) *The Privatization Process in Russia, Ukraine and the Baltics* (Budapest: Central European University Press).

Fucilla, J. G. (1979) 'Portuguese Nicknames as Surnames', *Names*, 27/2: 73–105.

Galeotti, M. (1992) 'Organised Crime in Moscow and Russian National Security', *Low Intensity Conflict and Law Enforcement*, 1/3: 237–52.

——(1995a) *Mafiya: Organised Crime in Russia* (*Jane's Intelligence Review*, Special report no. 10).

——(1995b) *Afghanistan: The Soviet Union's Last War* (London: Frank Cass).

——(1998a) 'Private Security and Public Insecurity: The Rise and Implications of the Russian Security Industry' (mimeo).

——(1998b) 'The Mafiya and the New Russia', *Australian Journal of Politics & History*, 44/3: 415–29.

——(2000) 'What Is the Russian Mafiya?' *Jane's Intelligence Review*, 12/3 [http://jir.janes.com/].

Gambetta D. (1988a) (ed.), *Trust: Making and Breaking Co-operative Relations* (Oxford: Basil Blackwell).

——(1988b) 'Anatomia della tangente,' *Meridiana*, 4: 237–47.

——(1993a) *The Sicilian Mafia* (London: Harvard University Press).

——(1993b) 'Trust and Co-operation', *The Blackwell Dictionary of Twentieth-Century Social Thought* (Oxford: Blackwell), 678–80.

——(1999) 'Corruption: A Conceptual Map' (Mimeo: University of Oxford).

——and Pizzini, V. (1995) 'The Nicknames of Sicilian Mafiosi' (Mimeo: University of Oxford).

——and Reuter, P. (1995) 'Conspiracy among the Many: The Mafia in Legitimate Industries', in G. Fiorentini and S. Peltzman (eds.), *The Economics of Organised Crime* (Cambridge: Cambridge University Press), 116–36.

Getzler, J. (1996) 'Theories of Property and Economic Development', *Journal of Interdisciplinary History*, 26/4: 639–69.

Gilmore, D. D. (1982) 'Some Notes on Community Nicknaming in Northern Spain', *Man*, 17/4: 686–700.

Glazov, Y. ([1976] 1985) ' "Thieves" in the USSR as a Social Phenomenon', in id., *The Russian Mind since Stalin's Death* (Dordrecht, Boston, and Lancaster: D. Reidel Publishing Co.), 36–50 and 337–40.

Gorbatov, A. V. (1964) *Years Off my Life*, trans. G. Clough and A. Cash (London: Constable).

Gorky, M., Averbakh, L., Firin, S. G., and Williams-Ellis, A. (1935) *The White Sea Canal: Being an Account of the Construction of the New Canal Between the White Sea and the Baltic Sea*, trans. A. Williams-Ellis (London: John Lane).

Graebner, Anderson A. (1979) *The Business of Organised Crime* (Stanford: Hoover Institution Press).

——(1995) 'The Red Mafia: A Legacy of Communism', in E. P. Lazear (ed.), *Economic Transition in Eastern Europe and Russia* (Stanford, Calif.: Hoover Institution Press), 340–66.

Grau, L. W. (1993) 'The Cossack Brotherhood Reborn: A Political/Military force in a Realm of Chaos', *Low Intensity Conflict and Law Enforcement*, 2/3: 578–612.

Graziosi, A. (1992) 'The Great Strikes of 1953 in Soviet Labor Camps in the Accounts of their Participants. A Review', *Cahiers du Monde russe et soviétique*, 33/4: 419–46.

GRF/RECEP (Government of The Russian Federation/Russian–European Centre for Economic Policy) (1995) *Russian Economic Trends 1994*, 3/4 (London: Whurr Publishers).

—— (1996) *Russian Economic Trends 1995*, 4/4 (London: Whurr Publishers).

—— (1999) *Russian Economic Trends*, 8/3 (London: Blackwell Publishers).

Gurov, A. (1993) 'Tradizioni e tipologie della criminalità russa', *Modernizzazione e Sviluppo*, 4/1–2: 34–40.

Handelman, S. (1994a) *Comrade Criminal* (London: Michael Joseph).

—— (1994b) The Russian 'Mafiya', *Foreign Affairs*, 73/2: 83–96.

Hanley, E., Yershova, N., and Anderson, R. (1995), 'Russia—Old wine in New Bottle? The Circulation and Reproduction of Russian Elites, 1983–1993', *Theory and Society*, 24/5: 639–68.

Hay, J. R., Shleifer, A., and Vishny, R. W. (1996) 'Toward a Theory of Legal Reform', *European Economic Review*, 40/3–5: 559–67.

Hechter, M. (1987) *Principles of Group Solidarity* (Berkeley, Los Angeles, and London: University of California Press).

Hellman, J. S. (1998) 'Winners Take All: The Politics of Partial Reform in Post-communist Transitions', *World Politics*, 50/2: 203–34.

Hendley, K. (1998a) 'Temporal and Regional Patterns of Commercial Litigation in Post-Soviet Russia', *Post-Soviet Geography and Economics*, 39/7: 379–98.

—— (1998b) 'Remaking an Institution: The Transition in Russia from State Arbitrazh to Arbitrazh Courts', *American Journal of Comparative Law*, 46/1: 93–127.

—— Ickes, B., Murrell, P., and Ryterman, R. (1997) 'Observations on the Use of Law by Russian Enterprises', *Post-Soviet Affairs*, 13/1: 19–41.

—— Murrell, P., and Ryterman, R. (1999a) 'Law Works in Russia: The Role of Legal Institutions in the Transactions of Russian Enterprises' (Mimeo).

——————— (1999b) 'Law, Relationships and Private Enforcement: Transactional Strategies of Russian Enterprises', *Euro-Asia Studies*, 52/4: 627–56.

——————— (1999c) 'A regional analysis of transactional strategies of Russian enterprises' (Mimeo).

——————— (1999d) 'Do "Repeat Play" Behave Differently in Russia? An Evaluation of Contractual and Litigation Behaviour of Russian Enterprises' (Mimeo).

Hess, H. ([1970]1973) *Mafia and Mafiosi: The Structure of Power*, trans. E. Oser (Lexington, Mass.: Lexington Books).

Hill, P. (2000) *Botaiho: Japanese Organized Crime Under the Boyokudan Counter-Measures Law* (Ph.D., University of Stirling).

Hill, R. J. (1972) 'Continuity and Change in USSR Supreme Soviet Elections', *British Journal of Political Science*, 2/1: 47–58.

Hood, R., and Sparks, R. (1970) *Key Issues in Criminology* (London: Weidenfeld and Nicolson).

Hout, M. (1983) *Mobility Tables* (London, Beverly Hills, and New Delhi: Sage Publications).

Hunt, C. (1936) *The Development of Business Corporation in England, 1700–1867* (Cambridge, Mass.: Harvard University Press).

Ianni, F. A. J. (1974) *The Black Mafia: Ethnic Succession in Organised Crime* (New York: Simon and Schuster).

——(1976) 'The Mafia and the Web of Kinship', in F. A. J. Ianni and E. Reuss-Ianni (eds.), *The Crime Society: Organised Crime and Corruption in America* (New York: New American Library).

Inglehart, R., Basañez, M., and Moreno, A. (1998) *Human Values and Beliefs: A Cross-Cultural Sourcebook* (Ann Arbor: The University of Michigan Press).

InterSec (1992) 'The Eastern Mafia', *InterSec*, 2/4: 115–19.

Jacquemet, M. (1992) 'Namechasers', *American Ethnologist*, 19/4: 733–49.

Jankowski, M. S. (1991) *Islands in the Street: Gangs and American Urban Society* (Berkeley: University of California Press).

Johnson, B. T., Holmes, K. R., and Kirkpatrick, M. (1999) *The 1999 Index of Economic Freedom* (Washington: The Heritage Foundation and The Wall Street Journal).

Johnson, J. C., Boster, J. S., and Holbert, D. (1989) 'Estimating Relational Attributes from Snowball Samples through Simulation', *Social Networks*, 11/2: 135–59.

Johnson, J. E. (1994) 'The Russian Banking System: Institutional Responses to the Market Transition', *Europe–Asia Studies*, 46/6: 971–95.

Jones, A., and Moskoff, W. (1991) *Ko-ops: The Rebirth of Entrepreneurship in the Soviet Union* (Bloomington and Indianapolis: Indiana University Press).

Kenny, M. (1961) *A Spanish Tapestry: Town and Country in Castile* (London: Cohen & West).

Kiser E., and Barzel, Y. (1991) 'The Origins of Democracy in England', *Rationality and Society*, 3/4: 396–422.

Korbatov, I., Rose, G., and Karasik, O. (1994) 'Commercial Arbitration for Companies in Russia', *The Moscow Letter*, 3: 66–7, 76–9, 88–90.

Kotz, D., and Weir, F. (1997) *Revolution from Above: The Demise of the Soviet Union* (London: Routledge).

Kucherov, S. (1970) *The Organs of Soviet Administration of Justice: Their History and Operation* (Leiden: E. J. Brill).

Landa, J. T. (1994), *Trust, Ethnicity and Identity* (Ann Arbor: The University of Michigan Press).

Lazarevskii, A. (1994) 'It Is Nice to be an Owner, but too Tedious', *Novoe Vremya*, Feb.: 20–1.

Ledeneva, A. L. (1998a) *Russia's Economy of Favours. Blat, Networking and Informal Exchange* (Cambridge: Cambridge University Press).

——(1998b) 'Shadow Barter: Economic Necessity or Economic Crime?' (paper prepared for the Conference on Barter in Post-socialist Societies, Cambridge, Dec. 13–14.)

Leitzel, J. (1995) *Russian Economic Reform* (London: Routledge).

Leitzel, J., Gaddy, C., and Alekseev, M. (1995), 'Mafiosi and Matrioshki', *The Brookings Review*, Winter: 26–9.

Lentini, P. (1991) 'Reforming the Electoral System: The 1989 Elections to the USSR Congress of People's Deputies', *Journal of Communist Studies*, 7/1: 69–74.

Levi, M. (1998) 'Perspectives on "Organised Crime": An Overview', *The Howard Journal*, 37/4: 335–45.

Lipson, L., and Chalidze, V. (1977) (eds.), *Papers on Soviet Law* (New York: Institute on Socialist Law), vol. 1.

Louis, V. E., and Louis, J. M. (1980) *Sport in the Soviet Union* (New York: Pergamon Press).

Lupo, S. (1984) *Agricoltura ricca e sottosviluppo. Storia e mito della Sicilia agrumaia (1060–1950)* (Catania: Idoneo Giovanni).

——(1996) *Storia della mafia dalle origini ai giorni nostri. Nuova edizione* (Rome: Donzelli).

Luttwak, E. (1995) 'Does the Russian Mafia Deserve the Nobel Prize for Economics?', *London Review of Books*, 3 Aug.: 7.

McAuley, M. (1992) 'Politics, Economics, and Elite Realignment in Russia: A Regional Perspective', *Soviet Economy*, 8/1: 46–88.

——(1997) *Russia's Politics of Uncertainty* (Cambridge: Cambridge University Press).

McCracken, G. (1988) *The Long Interview* (London: Sage).

McFaul, M. (1996) 'The Allocation of Property Rights in Russia: The First Round', *Communist and Post-Communist Studies*, 29/3: 287–308.

Mak, L. F. (1981) *The Sociology of Secret Societies: A Study of Chinese Secret Societies in Singapore and Peninsular Malaysia* (Kuala Lumpur: Oxford University Press).

Malyshenko, E. (1997) 'Interaction of the Police and Private Security Services in Combating Terrorism: The Experience of Other Countries', *Low Intensity Conflict and Law Enforcement*, 6/2: 141–4.

Martinetti, C. (1995) *Il padrino di Mosca* (Milano: Feltrinelli).

Massolo, M. (1990) 'Teenage Grauny: Portrayals of Women in Falkland Islands Nicknames', *Names*, 38/4: 283–94.

Matthews, M. (1972) *Class and Society in Soviet Russia* (New York: Walker).

Maurer, D. W., and Futrell, A. W. (1982) 'Criminal Monickers', *American Speech*, 57/4: 243–55.

Milgrom, P. R., North, D. C., and Weingast, B. W. (1990) 'The Role of Institutions in the Revival of Trade: The Law Merchant, Private Judges and the Champagne fairs', *Economics and Politics*, 2: 1–23.

Miller, W. L., Grodeland, Å., and Koshechkina, T., (1999) *A Culture of Corruption: Bureaucratic Encounters in Postcommunist Europe* (mimeo; Forthcoming: Budapest: Central European University Press).

Mook, M. A. (1967) 'Nicknames among the Amish', *Names*, 15/2: 111–18.

Moran, J. (1995), 'Privatizing Criminal Justice', *Crime and Justice: The Americas*, June–July: 10–15.

——(1999), 'Bribery and Corruption: The OECD Convention on Combating the Bribery of Foreign Public Officials in International Business Transactions', *Business Ethics: A European Review*, 8/3: 141–50.

Morgan, J., O'Neill, C., and Harré, R. (1979), *Nicknames: Their Origins and Social Consequences* (London: Routledge & Kegan Paul).

Morozov, A. (1996), 'Tax Administration in Russia', *East European Constitutional Review*, 5/2–3: 43–7.

Naishul', V. (1993) 'Liberalism, Customary Rights and Economic Reforms', *Communist Economies and Economic Transformation*, 5/1: 29–44.

Nee, V. (1989), 'A Theory of Market Transition', *American Sociological Review*, 54/5: 663–81.

——(1991), 'Social Inequality in Reforming State Socialism', *American Sociological Review*, 56/3: 267–82.

Noonan, J. T., Jr. (1984) *Bribes* (New York: Macmillian).

North, D. C., and Thomas, P. (1973) *The Rise of the Western World* (Cambridge University Press).

Notes and Queries in Anthropology (1951) (London: Routledge & Kegan Paul).

Nove, A. (1977) *The Soviet Economic System* (London: G. Allen & Unwin)

Oakley, A. (1981) 'Interviewing Women: A Contradiction in Terms', in H. Roberts (ed.), *Doing Feminist Research* (London: Routledge & Kegan Paul), 30–61.

OCTF (Organized Crime Task Force) (1988) *Corruption and Racketeering in the New York Construction Industry* (New York: ILR Press).

Olson, M. (1965) *The Logic of Collective Action* (Cambridge, Mass.: Harvard University Press).

——(1982) *The Rise and Decline of Nations* (New Haven: Yale University Press).

——(1995) 'Why the Transition from Communism is so Difficult', *Eastern Economic Journal*, 21/4: 437–61.

——(2000) *Power and Prosperity* (New York: Basic Books).

Paliotti, V. (1993) *Storia della Camorra* (Roma: Newton Compton Editori).

Pejovich, S. (1997) 'The Transition Process in an Arbitrary State: The Case for the Mafia', *IB Review*, 1/1: 18–23.

Peterson D. J. (1990) 'New Data Published on Employment and Unemployment in the USSR', *Report on the USSR*, 2/1 (Jan. 5): 3–4.

Petrova D. (1996), 'Post-Communist Obstacles to the Effective Protection of Basic Rights', *East European Constitutional Review*, 5/4: 62–72.

Pezzino, P. (1999), *Le Mafie* (Firenze: Giunti).

Pipes, R. (1995) *Russia under the Bolshevik Regime, 1919–1924* (London: Fontana Press).

Pistor, K. (1995) 'Courts, Arbitration, and Private Enforcement in Russia'. Mimeo.

——(1996) 'Supply and Demand for Contract Enforcement in Russia: Courts, Arbitration and Private Enforcement', *Review of Central and Eastern European Law*, 1: 55–87.

——(1997) 'Company Law and Corporate Government in Russia', in J. Sachs and K. Pistor, *The Rule of Law and Economic Reform in Russia* (Boulder, Colo.: Westview Press), 165–88.

Pitt-Rivers, J. (1954), *The People of the Sierra* (London: Weidenfeld and Nicolson).

Ponomarev, P. G. (1996) 'Legal Measures against Legalization of Criminal Assets as Means of Combating Organized Crime in Russia', *Academy of Criminal Justice Sciences*, 14/4 (Jan./Feb.): 1–3.

Posner, R. (1980), 'The Theory of Primitive Society, with Special Reference to Law', *Journal of Law and Economics*, 23 (April): 1–53.

——(1992) *Economic Analysis of Law*, 4th edn. (Boston: Little, Brown and Co.).

——(1995) 'The Cost of Enforcing Legal Rights', *East European Constitutional Review*, 4/3: 71–83.

Presidential Commission on Law Enforcement and Administration of Justice (1967), *The Challenge of Crime in a Free Society* (Washington, DC).

Putnam, R. (1993) with R. Leonardi and R. Nanetti, *Making Democracy Work* (Princeton: Princeton University Press).

Raeff, M. (1983), *The Well-Ordered Police State: Social and Institutional change through Law in Germanies and Russia, 1600–1800* (New Haven: Yale University Press).

Rawlinson, P. (1997) 'Russian Organized Crime: A Brief History', in P. Williams (ed.), *Russian Organized Crime* (London: Frank Cass), 28–52.

Reuter, P. (1983) *Disorganised Crime: The Economics of the Visible Hand* (Cambridge, Mass., and London: MIT Press).

——(1987) *Racketeering in Legitimate Industries: A Study in the Economics of Intimidation* (Santa Monica: The RAND Corporation).

Rigby, T. H. (1990) *Political Elites in the USSR* (Aldershot: Edward Elgar).

Róna-Tass, A. (1994) 'The First Shall be Last? Entrepreneurship and Communist Cadres in the Transition to Socialism', *American Journal of Sociology*, 100/1: 40–69.

Rose, R. (1995) 'Russia as an Hour-Glass Society: A Constitution without Citizens', *East European Constitutional Review*, 4/3: 34–42.

Rosemberg, B. (1945) 'Meet the Gang', *Journal of Criminal Law, Criminology and Police Science*, 36: 90–102.

Rossi, J. (1989) *The Gulag Handbook* (New York: Paragon House).

Rowland, R. (1998) 'Metropolitan Population Change in Russia and the Former Soviet Union, 1897–1997', *Post-Soviet Geography and Economics*, 39/5 (May): 271–96.

Rutland, P., and Kogan, N. (1998) 'The Russian Mafia: Between Hype and Reality', *Transitions*, March: 24–34.

Ryan, A. (1987) 'Property', in J. Eatwell, M. Milgate, and P. Newman (eds.), *New Palgrave Dictionary of Economics*, iv (London: Macmillan Press), 1029–31.

Sabetti, F. (1984) *Political Authority in a Sicilian Village* (New Brunswick, NJ: Rutgers University Press).

Sagers, M. J. (1996) 'Russian Crude Oil Production in 1996: Conditions and Prospects', *Post-Soviet Geography and Economics*, 37/9: 523–87.

Sartori, G. (1971), 'La politica comparata: premesse e problemi', *Rivista Italiana di Scienza Politica*, 1: 7–66.

——(1991) 'Comparazione e metodo comparato', in L. Morlino and G. Sartori (eds.), *La comparazione nelle scienze sociali* (Bologna: Il Mulino), 25–45.

Schelling, T. C. (1960) *The Strategy of Conflict* (Cambridge, Mass.: Harvard University Press).

——([1971] 1984) 'What is the Business of Organized Crime?', in id., *Choice and Consequence* (Cambridge, Mass., and London: Harvard University Press, 1984), 179–94.

Schneider, A. (1994), *Mafia for Beginners*, illustrations by O. Zarante, (Cambridge: Icon Books).

SCO (Servizio Centrale Operativo) (1997) *Rapporto operativo. Esin et alii*, 3 vols. (Rome: Polizia di Stato).

Sereni, E. (1971) *Il capitalismo nelle campagne* (Torino: Einaudi).

Serio, J. (1992) 'Shunning Tradition: Ethnic Organised Crime in the Former Soviet Union', *CJ International*, 8/6: 5–6.

——(1997) 'Threats to the Foreign Business Community in Moscow', in P. Williams (ed.), *Russian Organized Crime* (London: Frank Cass), 88–108.

Shalamov, V. (1994) *Kolyma Tales*, combined 2-vol. edn. (London: Penguin Books).

Sheffet, M. J. (1995) 'The Foreign Corrupt Practices Act and the Omnibus Trade and Competitiveness Act of 1988—Did they Change Corporate Behavior?' *Journal of Public Policy & Marketing*, 14/2: 290–300.

Shelley, L. (1980) 'The Geography of Soviet Criminality', *American Sociological Review*, 45/1: 111–22.

——(1984) *Lawyers in Soviet Work Life* (New Brunswick, New Jersey: Rutgers University Press).

——(1995) 'Post-Soviet Organised Crime and the Rule of Law', *John Marshall Law Review*, 28/4: 827–47.

——(1997), 'Post-Soviet Organised Crime: A New Form of Authoritarianism', in P. Williams (ed.), *Russian Organised Crime: The New Threat?* (London: Frank Cass), 122–38.

Shlapentokh, V. (1996) 'Early Feudalism—The Best Parallel for Contemporary Russia', *Europe-Asia Studies*, 48/3: 396–411.

Shleifer, A., and Treisman, D. (1998) *The Economics and Politics of Transition to an open market economy. Russia* (Paris: OECD).

——and R. Vishny (1998) *The Grabbing Hand: Government pathologies and their Cures* (Cambridge: Harvard University Press).

Smith, Adam ([1776] 1986), *The Wealth of nations* (London: Penguin Books).

Smith, Alastair and Varese, F. (2001) 'Phony Mobsters: Policing Reputation in the Underworld', *Rationality and Society*, 13/3.

Smith, D. C., and Alba, R. D. (1979) 'Organised Crime and American Life', *Society* Mar.–Apr.: 32–8.

Solzhenitsyn, A. (1974) *The Gulag Archipelago 1918–1956* (trans. T. P. Whitney) (Glasgow: Collins/Fontana).

Stark, D. H. (1981) *The Yakuza: Japanese Crime Incorporated*, Ph.D. Thesis (Ann Arbor: University of Michigan).

Stiglitz, J. E. (1998). 'More Instruments and Broader Goals: Moving Toward the Post-Washington Consensus', Wider Annual Lectures, 2 Jan. 1998.

——(1999) 'Whither Reform? Ten Years of the Transition', Annual Bank Conference on Development Economics, Keynote Address, 28–30 Apr. 1999, repr. in Johnson's Russia List, #3317, 1 June 1999.

Struyk, R. J., and Daniell, J. (1995) 'Housing Privatisation in Urban Russia', *Economics of Transition*, 3/2: 197–214.

Szelényi, I., and Szelényi, S. (1995) 'Circulation or Reproduction of Elites during the post-Communist Transformation of Eastern Europe', *Theory and Society*, 24/5: 615–38.

Tentler, T. N. (1977) *Sin and Confession on the Eve of Reformation* (Princeton: Princeton University Press).

Terts, A. (A. Sinyavsky) (1973) *A Voice from the Chorus* (London: Collins & Harvill Press, [1973] 1976).

Torstensson, J. (1994) 'Property Rights and Economic Growth: An Empirical Study', *Kyklos*, 47/2: 231–47.

Transparency International (1996), 'The Index of Corruption', http://www.GWDG.DE/~uwvw/icr.htm

Trehub, A. (1989) 'Hard Time for Soviet Policemen', *Report on the USSR*, 1/23, June 9.

Treisman, D. (1996) 'The Politics of Inter-Regional Transfers in Post-Soviet Russia', *British Journal of Political Science*, 26/3: 299–335.

Treml, V. G. (1991), 'Drinking and Alcohol Abuse in the USSR in the 1980s', in A. J. Jones, W. D. Connor, and D. E. Powell (eds.), *Soviet Social Problems* (Oxford and San Francisco: Westview Press), 119–36.

Tsypkin, M. (1989) 'Workers' Militia: Order instead of Law?', *Report on the USSR*, 1/46: Nov. 17: 14–17.

United Nations (1995) *Demographic Yearbook 1993* (New York).

——(1996) *Demographic Yearbook 1994* (New York).

——(1998) *Demographic Yearbook 1996* (New York)

——(1999) *Demographic Yearbook 1997* (New York).

UN/ECE (United Nations/Economic Commission for Europe) (1994) *Economic Survey of Europe in 1993–94* (New York and Geneva).

——(1995) *Economic Survey of Europe in 1994–95* (New York and Geneva).

——(1996) *Economic Survey of Europe in 1995–96* (New York and Geneva).

——(1997) *Economic Survey of Europe in 1996–97* (New York and Geneva).

——(1998) *Economic Survey of Europe 1998 No. 2* (New York and Geneva).

——(1999) *Economic Survey of Europe 1999 No. 3* (New York and Geneva).

Varese, F. (1994) 'Is Sicily the Future of Russia? Private Protection and the Rise of the Russian Mafia', *Archives Européennes de Sociologie*, 35/2: 224–58.

——(1996) 'What is the Russian Mafia?', *Low Intensity Conflict and Law Enforcement*, 5/2: 129–38.

——(1997) 'The Transition to the Market and Corruption in Post-socialist Russia', *Political Studies*, 47/3: 579–96.

——(1998) 'The Society of the *Vory-v-Zakone*, 1930s–1950s', *Cahiers du Monde Russe*, 39/4: 515–38.

——(1999) 'The Russian Mafia' and 'The Filippov Report', in *The Mafia. 150 Years of Facts, Figures and Faces*, CD-Rom (Cliomedia Publisher).

——(2000), 'Pervasive Corruption', in A. Ledeneva and M. Kurkchiyan (eds.), *Economic Crime in Russia* (London: Kluwer Law International), 99–111.

Volkov, V. (1999*a*) 'Violent Entrepreneurship in Post-Communist Russia', *Europe–Asia Studies*, 51/5: 741–54.

——(2000) Between Economy and the State: Private Security and Rule Enforcement in Russia (Forthcoming, *Politics and Society*).

Wallich, C. I. (ed.) (1994) *Russia and the Challenge of Fiscal Federalism* (Washington: World Bank).

Wedel, J. R. (1998) *Collision and Collusion: The Strange Case of Western aid to Eastern Europe 1989–1998* (New York: St Martin's Press).

——(2000) 'Tainted Transactions: Harvard, the Chubais Clan and Russia's Ruin', *The National Interest*, 59: 23–34.

Wegren, S. K. (1993) 'Trends in Russian Agrarian Reform', *RFE/RL*, 2/13, 26 Mar.: 46–57.

——(1994) 'Building Market Institutions', *Communist and Post-Communist Studies*, 27/3: 195–224.

Weimer, D. L. (1997),'The Political Economy of Property Rights', in id. (ed.), *The Political Economy of Property Rights* (New York: Cambridge University Press), 1–19.

Werth, N. (1999) 'A State against its People: Violence, Repression and Terror in the Soviet Union', in S. Courtois (ed.), *The Black Book of Communism* (Cambridge, Mass.: Harvard University Press. Orig. edn. *Le Livre noir du communisme*, Paris: Robert Laffont, 1997), 33–268.

Williams, B. (1988) 'Formal Structures and Social Realities', in D. Gambetta (ed.), *Trust: Making and Breaking Cooperative Relations* (Oxford: Basil Blackwell), 3–13.

Williams, P. (1997), 'Introduction', in id. (ed.), *Russian Organised Crime: The New Threat?* (London: Frank Cass), 1–27.

World Bank (1998) *World Development Indicators* (Washington: The World Bank).

Zablotskis, N., and Zvekic, U. (1994), *Crime and Crime Prevention in Moscow* (Rome/Moscow: UNICRI and Ministry of Internal Affairs, Russian Federation).

Zbarsky, I., and Hutchinson, S. (1997) *Lenin's Embalmers* (London: The Harvill Press).

Names and Subjects Index*

Index

Index

279